D0759346

RETHINKING THE
LATIN AMERICAN CITY

DISCARD

RETHINKING THE LATIN AMERICAN CITY

Edited by
Richard M. Morse and Jorge E. Hardoy

The Woodrow Wilson Center Press
Washington, D.C.

The Johns Hopkins University Press
Baltimore and London

307.76
R 438

Editorial Offices
The Woodrow Wilson Center Press
370 L'Enfant Promenade, S.W.
Suite 704
Washington, D.C. 20024-2518 U.S.A.

Order from
The Johns Hopkins University Press
2715 North Charles Street
Baltimore, Maryland 21218-4319
Telephone 1-800-537-5487

Originally published as *Repensando la ciudad de América Latina*
© 1988 Grupo Editor Latinoamericano S.R.L.

© 1992 by the Woodrow Wilson International Center for Scholars

Printed in the United States of America
⊗ Printed on acid-free paper

9 8 7 6 5 4 3 2 1

Library of Congress Cataloging-in-Publication Data

Repensando la ciudad de América Latina. English
    Rethinking the Latin American city / edited by Richard M. Morse
and Jorge E. Hardoy.
        p.   cm.
    Includes bibliographical references and index.
    ISBN 0-943875-43-9 (alk. paper)
    1. Urban policy—Latin America. 2. City planning—Latin America.
3. Urbanization—Latin America. 4. Cities and towns—Latin America.
I. Morse, Richard M. (Richard McGee), 1922–   . II. Hardoy, Jorge
Enrique. III. Title.
HT127.5.R4713   1993
307.76'098—dc20   92-37307
                                                                CIP

WOODROW WILSON INTERNATIONAL CENTER FOR SCHOLARS
BOARD OF TRUSTEES
William J. Baroody, Jr., Chairman; Dwayne O. Andreas, Vice Chairman; Robert
McC. Adams; Lamar Alexander; J. Burchenal Ault; James A. Baker III; James
H. Billington; Henry E. Catto; Lynne V. Cheney; Gertrude Himmelfarb; Carol
Iannone; Eli Jacobs; John S. Reed; S. Dillon Ripley; William L. Saltonstall;
Samuel K. Skinner; Louis W. Sullivan; Robert H. Tuttle; Don W. Wilson

The Center is the "living memorial" of the United States of America to the
nation's twenty-eighth president, Woodrow Wilson. The U.S. Congress
established the Woodrow Wilson Center in 1968 as an international institute
for advanced study, "symbolizing and strengthening the fruitful relationship
between the world of learning and the world of public affairs." The Center
opened in 1970 under its own presidentially appointed board of directors.

In all its activities the Woodrow Wilson Center is a nonprofit, nonpartisan
organization, supported financially by annual appropriations from the U.S.
Congress, and by the contributions of foundations, corporations, and
individuals. Conclusions or opinions expressed in Center publications and
programs are those of the authors and speakers and do not necessarily reflect
the views of the Center staff, fellows, trustees, advisory groups, or any
individuals or organizations that provide financial support to the Center.

Woodrow Wilson International Center for Scholars
Smithsonian Institution Building
1000 Jefferson Drive, S.W.
Washington, D.C. 20560
(202) 357-2429

CONTENTS

PREFACE

Richard M. Morse

In June 1986 the Latin American Program of the Woodrow Wilson International Center for Scholars sponsored a conference in Washington, D.C., on "Rethinking the Latin American City." The meeting formed part of a series planned under the general rubric "Toward Ideological Reconstruction in Latin America." These colloquia aimed to examine the conceptual categories currently used in explaining the society, culture, and institutions of Latin America and to explore fresh paths for adjusting scholarly discourse to contemporary phenomena as we are now beginning to discern them. The field of urban studies offered an obvious handle on this challenging assignment, for by the 1980s the cities seemed to have escaped the strategies of analysis that were imposed on them during the first phase of post-World War II cityward migrations, from the 1959 United Nations meeting on "Urbanization in Latin America" in Santiago de Chile into the decade of the 1970s.

In organizing this symposium we selected a varied group of social scientists, humanists (including writers), and persons having professional experience with cities such as architects, planners, and administrators. They were asked to discuss the constraints and possibilities of Latin American urban societies and to describe what the future may hold, as that might be determined by historical forces and by the imagination of those professionals, practitioners, and ordinary citizens who are recreating urban societies. What distinguishes the papers published here, and the lively discussions they elicited at our meeting, from comparable symposia held fifteen years ago is the concern with "cities as people." Until recently urban studies have featured the application of academic disciplines and administrative devices to the solution of urban "problems." By dint of such strategies, which included programs of guided self-help for the disadvantaged, the "people" were to be absorbed or incorporated into urban societies that were projected to become integrated and systemic.

Since the 1970s, and under further pressure from economic crises of the early 1980s, this evolutionary vision has faded. In some cities there has been an overflow of population into the central city (Lima), in others an overflow of poverty upward across class lines (Montevideo). Only where iron political controls have managed to corral the poor into invisible ghettoes around cosmetic city centers (Chile), or where cityward migrations have been halted or redirected and minimal social security provided, are there variants of the new urban condition. From the viewpoint of managerial cadres, cities are "out of control": socially, economically, politically, administratively, culturally. If this be so, the future lies not primarily with the managers but with the people themselves. Their intentions, voices, and traditional or spontaneous forms of association and endeavor must be heeded. The urban design must arise from them and not from ministries, agencies, and universities nor from consecrated urban ideals of the bourgeois, industrial West. This, for me at least, was the theme that underlay the papers and discussions of our meeting.

Among the colleagues in many countries who gave moral and intellectual support for this symposium on "Rethinking the Latin American City," I want to extend special appreciation to two long-time friends and collaborators: Guillermo Geisse of the Center for Environmental Research and Planning (CIPMA) in Santiago de Chile, who spent three months at the Wilson Center as a guest scholar in 1985, and Jorge Enrique Hardoy, of the International Institute for Environment and Development–Latin America in Buenos Aires, who has assumed a commanding role in organizing international urban symposia since the 1960s.

I also wish to thank the staff of The Woodrow Wilson Center and of its Latin American Program for their support and the Pew Trusts for the grant that made the conference financially possible. Joseph Tulchin, my successor as director of the Latin American Program, provided institutional support for publishing this book and reviewed the manuscript in its last stages. Leah Florence helped pull the manuscript together. Translations from the Spanish were done by Norman Thomas di Giovanni.

INTRODUCTION

Jorge E. Hardoy

Between 1966 and 1979, sometimes with Richard Schaedel, sometimes with Schaedel and Woodrow Borah, Richard Morse and I organized seven symposia on Latin American urbanization from its origins to our time, under the auspices of the World Conferences of the International Congress of Americanists.[1] Morse and I organized two additional symposia, held at Stanford in 1982 and Port-au-Prince in 1986; these concentrated primarily on urbanization after 1850.[2] The nine symposia include around 175 papers, looking at urban issues from pre-Columbian times to the present. Most of the participants came from the Latin American nations and the United States, but Europeans and Canadians were well represented.

In 1984 Morse left Stanford University and became director of the Latin American Program at The Woodrow Wilson Center. Soon we began discussing the possibilities of organizing a more focused symposium, one that could attract not only the contributions of academics from different disciplines but also novelists, politicians, poets, and public administrators. The idea was to obtain a vision of the modern Latin American city more comprehensive and rounded than a sheerly academic one. The result is the papers that form this volume on Rethinking the Latin American City.[3]

The symposium, held in June 1986, revealed a widespread interest in the complex problems Latin American cities face. Latin America was experiencing political and economic transition that was clearly reflected in its urban structures and social situation. Called the lost decade by many, the 1980s also brought substantial changes of perspective. In 1986 Argentina and Peru were attempting to revive their democratic institutions. Brazil and Uruguay soon followed and then Chile. In 1990 all South American nations had elected governments for the first time in almost three decades. Never a tradition in Latin America, local democracy was now seen as a way to counteract the negative influence of political and administrative centralization and to reinforce participatory forms of democracy. "In Latin America," Jordi Borja writes, "the low level and fragmented nature of socioeconomic development and the shallow penetration of the state into society are at one and the same time the cause and consequence of the weakness of local governments." These governments have never before acted as agents of development and, in Borja's view, "are in no position to control the phenomenon of rapidly growing cities nor to make an even minimal response to the demands of the people."

By the time of the conference in 1986, some major trends affecting Latin American cities were clear. First, the annual rate of population growth of the largest agglomerations in each country—most of them national capitals—had begun to decline. Second, the growth of the central district in each of the largest agglomerations was slower than that of the municipalities in the first ring around the central city, and the rate of growth in this first ring was much lower than that of the municipalities of the second or third rings, when these existed. Third, the highest annual rates of population growth occurred in the mid-sized agglomerations and also in some small-size urban centers. Fourth, urbanization in the 1980s was spreading to regions that were unsettled or sparsely settled during the 1940s and 1950s and even during the 1960s. Finally, if these trends continued, Latin America and the Caribbean were likely to lose rural populations in absolute numbers during the 1990s. Such loss had already begun in some of the most populated and urbanized countries of the region. Future urban growth, therefore, was likely to be largely the result of natural increases rather than a result of rural migration to the cities.

Even though the rate of growth was slowing, the annual increase as in Mexico City, São Paulo, Rio de Janeiro, Lima-Callao, and Buenos Aires could be counted by the hundreds of thousands. In Bogotá, Caracas, and many other cities the annual increase numbered in the tens of thousands. Goiânia, with 131,000 inhabitants in 1960, grew to 1,300,000 in 1985; Curitiba jumped from 141,000 in 1950 to 2.8 million in 1985. Cities that had scarcely more than 100,000 residents in 1950 had seven to ten times that many by 1985. As Jorge Wilheim notes, many new cities are emerging in the Amazon region and elsewhere. Latin Americans move easily throughout their countries. Bolivians began to populate their eastern region after the 1950s; Mexicans have made their northern frontier one of the mushrooming urban systems of the continent, while the Patagonia region of Argentina and Chile is the fastest growing region in both countries, although it is still a thinly settled area. The urban centers on the coast of Ecuador are growing much faster than those in the highlands, which has been the main population center since before the Spanish conquest. Similar changes in the spatial distribution of population are taking place in every country.

Poverty and despair are behind many of these massive displacements of people. Contemporary migrations to large cities, writes Bryan Roberts, are "the exodus of whole households as rural areas cease to meet the subsistence needs of family members." "The basis of household subsistence," he adds, "is now more easily found in the city." The 1950s, 1960s, and 1970s witnessed the creation of many new urban settlements, some officially founded, many spontaneously created. It was a new stage in the long history of Latin Americans who opened new frontiers in search of new sources of livelihood. The settlement of these new urban areas followed processes similar to those that had occurred a century earlier.

Many troubling trends in Latin American cities were apparent when the symposium was convened in Washington. The quality of the living and working environments of the poor remains the most overwhelming problem in urban areas. Basic needs, such as sanitation, garbage removal, and adequate supplies of clean water, go unmet in the squatter settlements of most Latin American cities. Millions of low-income families have built their makeshift housing on unsuitable public and private land, subject to periodic floods, landslides, earthquakes, and other natural and man-made disasters. Foresight, land-use planning, and a more humane attitude toward the poor might have kept the poor from settling in these dangerous areas, which have caused so much death and destruction.

Perhaps the key issue discussed during the seminar was how to build, maintain, and manage cities of the poor, who live in crowded rooms and shelters surrounded by disease and lacking basic infrastructure and services. We recognized that there could be no development without health, but how could health be improved when tens of millions of undernourished people, especially children and adolescents, live in such poor-quality shelters and settlements?

In many cases, people from the countryside "slipped into the city . . . through the back door, uninvited and without manners, and made the city their own, seizing, invading, and carving out a territory for themselves, modifying it, making it grow to be what it is today." Abelardo Sánchez León was describing Lima, but he could have been speaking of Caracas, Curitiba, Goiânia, Santa Cruz de la Sierra, Guayaquil, Ciudad Juárez, or Santiago de los Caballeros. In the span of one generation, some of the largest agglomerations changed so rapidly— physically, economically, socially, and visually—that we could call them new cities. Little is left of Lima's historical center to remind one of the proud capital of the viceroys of Peru, a cultural and commercial center with few rivals in the American continent during the seventeenth and eighteenth centuries. Earthquakes have partially destroyed many beautiful buildings of Cusco, Popayán, León, Quito, and other urban centers that displayed distinguished religious and civil architecture until a few decades ago. But poverty has been one of the principal reasons for this decay, a poverty so widespread and intense that many colonial and nineteenth-century dwellings that constitute the cities' cultural legacy have eroded because their owners or their tenants or the governments cannot afford the cost of maintenance or because the poor have invaded them in the ceaseless search for shelter.

Most Latin American cities, including most national capitals, are not industrial cities. Unemployment is rampant and thousands work in the "informal sector" without rights or protection. "While political structures and formal economies of a society organize the daily life of all its members delimiting their possible fields of action and administering relationships between individuals," write Larissa Lomnitz and Rodrigo Díaz, "not all social activity that develops in a city is wholly a consequence of the rules of [formal] political and economic structures." The urban economies are based on a great number and variety of small-scale enterprises that provide little social security, do not guarantee jobs, and have few or no promotion prospects. "Shanty-town dwellers and others who knowingly work without a contract and on the periphery of the law," writes Rogelio Pérez Perdomo, "compromise their ability to claim their work rights within the formal system."

The problems of Latin American cities, clear enough two or three decades ago, were exacerbated by the economic crisis that hit Latin America in the 1970s and remains today. Yet there has been a notable lack of concrete strategies to meet these challenges. Very few have reflected on what the future city will look like or on the significant areas of knowledge that need to be developed. The city is not now a subject of discussion as it was among some of the great thinkers in certain periods of the past, as Manfred Max-Neff remarks.

Thus, it became urgent to rethink the ways in which Latin American governments could intervene in the process of urbanization so that limited resources are put to maximum effect, so that conditions for lower-income groups are improved at a cost the nation can afford. With such rethinking, it was clear that governments must address several interlinked aspects: housing conditions and basic services must be improved; real incomes for lower-income groups must be increased; and the infrastructure and services that support economic expansion must be made more efficient.

Every new crisis imposes growing pressures on already scant resources and delays the incorporation of new resources. This situation affects the poor in many ways. They are so concerned with surviving that they hardly have the time or the inclination to think of anything else. Circumstances force them to build or improve their own shelters, to improve the areas immediately surrounding their shelters, and to divide their time among seeking jobs, taking care of their children, carrying water, and searching for low-priced essential foodstuffs. As the populations and physical size of Latin American cities expand, human communication deteriorates and human contacts weaken or change, as Max-Neff points out. "The less the citizens know each other," he writes, "the more they are 'known' by the police. . . . When everyone is under surveillance by the authorities, human beings have less eye contact with each other."

Despite growing knowledge about how Latin American cities are built and managed, little has been done to solve these problems. Governments and public agencies claim they can improve the earning potential and the living conditions of low-income groups. But that has not happened and cannot happen until a more equitable distribution of incomes and opportunities is achieved. In every city there is a growing competition among low-income groups, who usually make up half or more of the population, for one of the relatively few stable jobs, for space to build a house or a shack, for a seat on a bus, for a corner of a sidewalk or in a square to set up a market stall. Every day people must compete for a place in a school or a bed in a hospital or a container of potable water. Governments have had little impact on urban problems, and poverty will not be eradicated by international aid or by poorly funded and poorly coordinated national welfare programs.

The symposium participants were acutely aware of the problems. All traveled frequently in their countries and throughout Latin America. They were students of cities and knew their cities as well as anybody else. Henry Pease García was in 1986 deputy mayor of Lima. Jorge Wilheim had been São Paulo's secretary of planning. Jordi Borja held a senior position in the municipality of Barcelona, Spain. Shortly after the seminar, Mariano Arana became a national senator in Uruguay. Matthew Edel, John Friedmann, Richard Morse, and Bryan Roberts were teachers and researchers in universities of the United States; Arana, Enrique Browne, Pease García, Guillermo Geisse, Hardoy, Larissa Lomnitz, Manfred Max-Neef, Rogelio Pérez Perdomo, and Abelardo Sánchez León were all associated with universities in their respective countries.

In rethinking the Latin American city symposium participants sought answers to questions such as: What makes cities grow in ways which increasingly show that social and economic inequalities have become a block to efficient democratic institutions? What can realistically be done given that economic resources will be scarce for the foreseeable future? Why do governments give city problems such a low priority? Why are urban problems so seldom discussed in the mass media?

Even if the worst visible effects of the economic crisis end and the slowdown in the growth rate of urban populations is confirmed, a continuation of current trends spells a bleak future. By the year 2000, Latin America can expect:

- More shantytowns and overcrowded and deteriorating tenement districts
- Increasing competition among low-income people to find cheap or vacant public and private lands to occupy
- Poorer services and a rise in the number and incidence of diseases related to a deteriorating environment
- Persistent unemployment, more illegal workers, and more households with unstable incomes
- More people, especially children, sleeping on the streets
- Urban agglomerations spreading endlessly outward, which will increase costs for building and maintaining infrastructure and make commutes longer and more expensive
- Environmental problems of unprecedented nature in some metropolitan areas, resulting largely from industrial and car emissions

Almost half a century ago those symptoms became increasingly serious. While the central city in practically all metropolitan areas stagnated, the peripheries have grown demographically and extended physically to dimensions that challenge the combined capacities of central, state, and local governments to provide solutions to the most pressing needs of the population. Neither politicians nor technocrats have found ways to overcome, for instance, the effects of growing poverty and the proliferation of squatter settlements and sites of illegal urbanization, where around 40 percent of the population in metropolitan areas and large cities lives in degraded environments.

Urban planning has proved fruitless when faced with agglomerations adding 100,000, 200,000, 300,000, or even more new inhabitants per year, especially when most social policies are discontinued because of the pressures of economic readjustment programs. Latin American cities are now built—as in the past—by countless individual and community initiatives outside the norms and regulations of local authorities. This is not new, but never in the history of Latin American cities have the numbers been so large nor have the gaps been so wide between the basic needs of so many and investments made to relieve them from the worst effects of poverty and destitution.

NOTES

1. The papers were collected in the following volumes: Jorge E. Hardoy and Richard P. Schaedel, eds., *El proceso de urbanización en América desde sus orígenes hasta nuestros días* (Buenos Aires: Editorial del Instituto Di Tella, 1969); J. E. Hardoy, E. Palm, and R. P. Schaedel, eds., "The Process of Urbanization in America since Its Origins to the Present Time," *Verhandlungen des XXXVIII Internationalen Amerikanistenkongresses,* Vol. 4 (1972): 9–318; R. P. Schaedel, J. E. Hardoy, and D. Bonavia, eds., "Urbanización y proceso social," *Actas del XXXIX Congreso Internacional de Americanistas,* Vol. 2 (Lima, 1972): 7–404; J. E. Hardoy and R. P. Schaedel, eds.; *Las ciudades de America Latina y sus áreas de influencia a través de la historia* (Buenos Aires: Ediciones SIAP, 1975); J. E. Hardoy and R. P. Schaedel, eds., *Asentamientos urbanos y organización socioproductiva de América Latina* (Buenos Aires: Ediciones SIAP, 1977); J. E. Hardoy, R. Morse, and R. P. Schaedel, eds., *Ensayos histórico-sociales sobre la urbanización en América Latina* (Buenos Aires: Ediciones SIAP-CLACSO, 1978); and J. E. Hardoy, and G. Stelter, eds., *Urbanización en las Américas* (Buenos Aires: Ediciones SIAP, 1980)—this last volume was also published in English by the History Division of the National Museum of Man, Ottawa, in 1980.
2. Jorge E. Hardoy and Richard M. Morse, eds., *Cultura urbana latinoamericana* (Buenos Aires: Ediciones CLACSO, 1985); and Jorge E. Hardoy and Richard M. Morse, eds., *Nuevas perspectivas en los estudios sobre historia urbana latinoamericana* (Buenos Aires: GEL/IIED-América Latina, 1989).
3. The papers were published in Spanish under the title *Repensando la ciudad de América Latina,* edited by Jorge E. Hardoy and Richard M. Morse (Buenos Aires: GEL/IIED-América Latina, 1988).

I

Historical Themes and Vistas

1

Cities as People

Richard M. Morse

In the Western world the inherited ways of classifying cities tend to fall into taxonomies determined by those who design them (classical and baroque cities), by functions that cities perform (for administration, religion, defense, maritime and internal trade, agrarian-based activities, industry, leisure), by modes of transportation that condition their growth (animal haulage, canals, railways, automobiles, airplanes), by sociological paradigms (orthogenetic-heterogenetic), and so forth. When cities are identified with social actors (José Luis Romero's aristocratic, creole, patrician, bourgeois, and massified cities, for example), the actors in question may be treated more as representing than as creating a social order, or as being exemplars rather than agents of urban change. In setting the stage for the chapters that follow this one, and in providing historical context for their central theme of "cities as people," I will draw on a number of my previous essays, adapting them for the present occasion. Along the way I will sketch contrasts between the cities of Latin and North America. I do so because the U.S. city (and by extension the city of the industrial West), which was once a model for emulation in Latin America, serves today an equally important function as an antimodel.

To establish an urban matrix, let me identify the two grand families of New World cities by examining two sets of urban experience and aspiration that the European colonizers carried with them. In the Ibero-American tradition one can identify four ideal types: (1) the Greek notion of *polis,* an agro-urban community based not on a covenant among consenting individuals but on a "political" entity of functionally integrated groups; (2) the Roman notion of the municipality (*civitas*) as an instrument for "civilizing" rural peoples; *civitates* in turn were the constituent parts of empire and even of a universal City of Mankind; (3) the Augustinian notion of a City of God, or City of the Beyond, which opposed Christian ideals to the sordid strivings and sins of the earthly city; (4) the redemptive vision of either a presumably extant City of Gold or terrestrial paradise or a prospective city of poverty and piety to be founded under ecclesiastical guidance.

Alongside these urban ideals, reinterpreted from classical sources, are three sets of understandings of less ancient vintage that crossed the Atlantic with those who settled New England. The first two I present as urban ideal types that were elaborated *ex post facto* by Pirenne and Weber. The third derives from socioreligious beliefs entertained by the Puritans.

The centripetal city. Henri Pirenne was largely responsible for the idea that the northwest European city was a flash point for economic change, that it grew by absorbing commercial energies from a surrounding countryside. Although his thesis is subject to qualifications, the full statement in his two-volume *Les villes et les institutions urbaines* (6th ed., 1939) contains abundant caveats and exceptions. The point here is that the dynamic of the European bourgeois city, implanted in northern Spain after the eleventh century along the pilgrimage route from the Pyrenees to Santiago de Compostela, did not take full hold in the peninsula. What prevailed was the use of cities as instruments of *repoblación concejil* in central and southern Spain—that is, urban nuclei embedded in the politico-administrative structure of the state. In Spain, as later in Ibero-America, the city became an instrument for appropriating land and for "incorporating" and "civilizing" people, while economic forces were subordinated to the policies of a patrimonial center. In America imperial, mercantilist decisions accounted for the eminence of Havana and Lima, while commercial imperatives accounted for that of Boston, New York, and Baltimore. When Buenos Aires achieved wide commercial hegemony in the eighteenth century, its reward was promotion to viceregal, patrimonial status. In this same tradition, Sarmiento's visionary Argirópolis, Kubitschek's Brasília, and President Alfonsín's proposal to make Viedma the capital of Argentina perpetuate the belief that frontier expansion and economic development require direct linkage to a patrimonial urban center—and, by the same token, that long-established centers tend to become monopolistic and atrophied.

The city as commune. For Pirenne and Max Weber, the medieval European city grew under a fortified shelter; it lived by commerce and manufacture, enjoying exceptional law, administration, and jurisdiction that made it a privileged body. The city dweller, whatever his economic hardships, was free of the ascriptive relationships of the manorial countryside. Municipal communal organization created a legal order that assured commercial and contractual freedom. When transplanted to North America, the urban communal spirit was unleashed across the countryside. On his visit to the United States in 1847, Sarmiento found the small town a far cry from the stationary municipal control center that was its counterpart in South America. Wherever ten ragged and illiterate Yankees assembled to form a township, he observed, they had to agree on rules of association before felling the first tree.

The "city upon a hill." In the "city upon a hill" of Puritan New England, the religious ethic reinforced the commercial one. All relations save those between parents and children were presumed to be voluntary and to depend on a covenant between contracting parties. The Puritan township possessed no corporate identity in the sense that it, as a social body, was antecedent or superior to the contractual arrangements of its members. Urban society was not "organic." Moreover, so long as its members remained sinless, their community was thought an embodiment, not an imperfect replica, of the divine order. In contrast, the Ibero-American city was a microcosm of the imperial and ecclesiastical order wherein it was embedded. The ideal of the "sinless," or paradigmatic, community was relegated to specialized religious communities.

Juxtaposing the Ibero- and Anglo-American urban traditions brings to light two sets of premises about the political community that again have become visible in this era of urban "crisis." These political traditions are not historical straitjackets but flexible antinomies, not molds but patterns of dialectic. Thus for Ibero-American society there arises a central political tension between the ideal of social incorporation—or integration of an organic body social of interfunctional parts—and the politics of pragmatic or amoral statecraft aimed toward enhancing the power and efficacy of political control. The positions were staked out in the sixteenth century in polemics over the ideas of St. Thomas and those of Machiavelli. Today's social scientists prefer to designate them clinically as the politics of inclusion and of exclusion.

In the "individualist" society of Anglo-America, the central tension, inherited from political debates in seventeenth-century England, revolved around the binomial liberty-versus-order. Society was seen as an aggregate of individuals, and the dominant political issue was where to draw the line between their innate right to freedom and the requirement of society for a minimum of order. From this presumption, the term *state* could not enter the northern political vocabulary as referring to a central political apparatus. What in the south was the "state" became in the north "government" or "administration." The state-versus-society dichotomy could not catch hold as it has so prominently in the south.

Vicenta Cortés Alonso illustrates how the municipal unit mediated between the imperial system and grass-roots productive forces in seventeenth-century Ibero-America in her analysis of the city of Tunja in New Granada. In the 1620s Tunja had 3,300 adult Spanish males and, in the city center, at least 70 families of *encomenderos* inhabiting two-story tile-roofed domiciles with interior patios. Beyond were the humbler houses of merchants and artisans and beyond them, beyond the city's *traza*, the *bohíos* of non-Europeans and half-castes. Of the city's 476 recognized structures, 20 were churches and only 7 were public buildings and "industries." This hierarchical, concentric arrangement echoed the external involvements of the city. In the political sphere Tunja was a point of shifting equilibrium for the claims and favors of a transatlantic church and state vis-à-vis the separatism of the *encomenderos;* the administrative base for *pueblos de españoles* that it had colonized within a 100-mile perimeter; and the control center for 161 *encomiendas* representing villages of 80 to 2,000 Indians. Commercially, leading merchants imported fine cloth and luxuries from Spain; others conducted trade by mule teams with much of New Granada; and locally, the Indian *tianguis* handled domestic commodities.

This schematic picture of Tunja exemplifies the ideal types just discussed. In fact, of course, the grand urban design for Spanish America (and the more informal one for Brazil) suffered early erosion. One cause was the growth of regional trade circuits and the gradual intrusion of the cash nexus into social relations. Another cause was the large-scale demographic, social, and economic change and displacement, such as high Indian mortality rates, European immigration, and importation of African slaves; rapid miscegenation and multiplication of *castas;* regimentation and relocation of workers for coerced labor in mines, *obrajes*, and on farms. For example, the division between *pueblos de españoles* and *pueblos de indios* became blurred by the differential incidence of economic opportunity. The carefully delimited residence zones for Indian workers within larger cities were slowly effaced. In 1692 the savant Carlos Sigüenza y Góngora complained that the Indians of Mexico City, protected by Spanish householders, were moving to the city center, impeding tax collection, and filling it with "lazy, vagabond, useless, and indolent people" given to crime and cloaked in anonymity. By the same token the Indian barrios were infiltrated by predatory blacks, mulattoes, and mestizos.

To offer more immediate historical context for contemporary cities, let me now sketch some trends that appeared in the period from about 1750 to the early twentieth century to affect the functions, interrelationships, and internal composition of cities. Demography yields a starting point. From 1570 to 1750 the population of Ibero-America hovered at 10 or 11 million people (less than the population of modern São Paulo city). This total conceals abrupt shifts in ethnic composition, but the global figure remained steady. After about 1750 the population began rising owing to the demographic recovery of the Indian peoples and higher levels of European and forced African immigration. By 1800 the population reached 19 million, and by 1825, 23 million. This global increase, however, was accompanied by an urban "primacy dip" that lasted until the second half of the nineteenth century. That is, large cities tended to lose population relative to rural and frontier zones. Various factors help explain the trend: First, large urban concentrations were more vulnerable to epidemics than scattered rural populations. Second, African slaves, imported in increasing numbers, usually went to rural destinations. Third, this period saw a "second conquest" of America marked by the creation of hundreds of new towns, agrarian centers, missions, and forts in frontier areas from California to Chile and Argentina that served to nucleate spatially expanded agropastoral production, modernized mining activity, and tropical forest extraction with simultaneous enlargement of military perimeters and relocation of Indians. This array of activity responded to the growing demand of overseas markets, now reached by swifter maritime shipping; the spread of a market economy; and diversification of economic production.

The eighteenth-century phase of the "primacy dip" was therefore not a period of urban "decadence." Indeed, measured by indices of *urbanism* (elegant public buildings and improved public services, street-paving, flood control, cultural and educational centers, and so forth) rather than *urbanization* (relative population growth), these decades saw qualitative enhancement of large urban centers. At the regional level, moreover, there sometimes appeared mixed economies based on domestic industry and diversified agriculture, whereby smaller towns were linked in complementary production and trade that diminished their reliance on primate centers. Such were the cases of the Bajío in Mexico, the Socorro region of New Granada, the internal towns of the Plata viceroyalty, and the towns of Minas Gerais in Brazil where the economy diversified after the collapse of the mining boom. In other words, just as new political arrangements with the mother countries were contemplated in the late eighteenth century to favor decentralization and local autonomy, so in the economic sphere was there evidence to suggest development as well as mere growth.

Other features, however, were less promising from the developmental point of view. For example, late-colonial port cities such as

Havana, Guayaquil, and Buenos Aires that tapped newly opened hinterlands offered nothing so elaborate as the commercial and financial institutions of Boston, New York, and Philadelphia. Moreover, administrative capitals such as Mexico City, Rio de Janeiro, and Buenos Aires tended to centralize commercial functions rather than diffuse them across their tributary regions, as the French traveler Saint-Hilaire discovered in preindependence Brazil when he looked for wholesale houses in urban centers outside Rio. In Guadalajara credit was in the hands of the church and private persons; capital circulated within a small elite of businessmen, clergy, and landowners, and the volume of loans dropped in the late eighteenth century. Finally, just when elaborate schemes for classifying the mixed-race *castas* were multiplying, socioethnic features were losing significance in urban society. Large cities were crucibles for ethnic mixing—as Sigüenza y Góngora had reported for Mexico City in 1692—and had produced societies split into *gente decente* and the *plebe*. In Mexico City the latter formed an urban culture of *leperismo*, named for the racially indistinct *lépero*, seen by observers as insolent, vagrant, and given to vice and thievery. This homogenization of the dispossessed marked the collapse of the old ecclesiastical and juridical ideal of social "incorporation." In Lima, Salvador, and Rio—as in Mexico City—the resentment and occasional group protests of the *plebe* represented not so much the recognition of common cause (or "class consciousness") as a common sense of disinheritance. On the eve of independence large cities were arenas for modernization without development and for a dichotomization of complex societies that would, in the long run, have momentous political consequences.

The "primacy dip" lasted until the mid-nineteenth century and in some countries well beyond it. The wars and aftermath of independence, however, introduced a new mix of factors that explain its continuance. At the very time that western Europe and the northeastern United States were undergoing rapid urbanization and industrialization, Latin America experienced a period of decentralization, or even ruralization, of society. Not only had some of the larger cities suffered damage or disruption during the wars, but they were badly prepared to assume the political, administrative, and economic functions to be expected of new national capitals. National treasuries were exhausted, and urban elites—commercial, bureaucratic, ecclesiastical—who had enjoyed favor under the Bourbons were harassed or expelled. The beneficiaries of independence were landowners who well knew that the colonial cities had been control centers, not sources of economic energy, and that wealth would now be more easily reconstituted in rural areas. There ensued a half century of political disintegration and *caudillismo* that was a golden age for rural elites, including new groups on the rise, who often opposed modernization (telegraphy, railroads, electric power, rural police, schools), fearing that such improvements would deliver local control to urban outsiders and cause emigration of rural workers. Without protection at the local or national level, and confronted by liberalization of external trade and improvements in overseas transportation that benefited foreign suppliers, the incipient development based on constellations of secondary urban centers now collapsed. As for large cities, the case might be made that the diversity of specialized urban employment opportunities was scarcely greater at the end of the nineteenth century than it had been at the start.

In the United States, in contrast, the urban population (in towns over 8,000 population) fluctuated between 4.6 percent (1730) and 2.7 percent (1780) of the total, superficially accompanying the "de-urbanization" of Latin America. After 1780, however, the urban fraction in the United States rose to 4.9 percent in 1810, held steady during the decade of the War of 1812, then climbed continuously to 8.5 percent (1840), 16 percent (1860), and 33 percent (1900). The "Great Turnabout" was precisely the decade of 1810–20, when U.S. dependency on foreign commerce fell sharply and just when Latin America was about to incur heavier reliance on foreign suppliers. Yet even before 1780, the apparent ruralization of North American society had represented an extension of urban commercial energies to the countryside. It was a time of coiling the economic mainspring. The vital indicator was not movement of products but migration of people, people accustomed to a relatively high standard of living and who carried in their heads the commercial imperative. This urban exodus has been called the financial equivalent of the modern mass tourist industry.

In Latin America commercial activity continued into the nineteenth century within a framework of mercantilist design, patrician status objectives, and prebendary administration. Urban merchants were adept at keeping open alternatives for social advancement and for enhancing the career orientation of their sons. They failed, that is, to create an enduring mercantile class. In short, if North American cities developed and decentralized their commercial functions, Latin American cities did little to generate them and less to disperse them.

A corollary to these trends is the fact that between, roughly, 1800 and 1850 per capita income in the United States rose from $165 to $274 (in 1950 dollars) while that of Brazil dropped from 38 percent to 26 percent of the U.S. figures and that of Mexico declined in absolute value from 44 percent to 20 percent. If these statistics reflect broad economic movements and do not directly document the stagnation of urban energies in Latin America, they do however place that region in dramatic contrast with the United States and northwest Europe, demonstrating a productive lag, or economic asymmetry, that has conditioned international relations and domestic development until the present.

The second half of the nineteenth century finally brought a turnaround in the growth rates of large Latin American cities as export earnings soared; national markets were expanded; steam navigation funneled trade through principal seaports; railroads and telegraphy helped to unify nations; and political control was centralized. Primate cities now reasserted their prominence as loci where political patronage and economic concessions were dispensed, financial intermediaries thrived, national elites and foreigners tasted urban pleasures, and basic industries appeared. Havana led the parade in the 1840s with its early railroads, tobacco factories, and sugar exports; Rio followed during the Brazilian political "conciliation" of the 1850s; and these were followed by Lima and Buenos Aires in the 1860s, Bogotá in the 1870s, and Caracas and Santiago de Chile in the 1880s. Mexico City, after a preliminary spurt in the 1880s, resumed its advance after 1900.

The significance of urban growth in both Latin America and the United States in the nineteenth century can more easily be seen in the context of agrarian change. For the United States, economic historians have contrasted the "homestead" form of production in the Northeast and Midwest with the "plantation" form of the South. Homestead agriculture brought with it a wide diffusion of land ownership, a need for nearby intermediary services that created trading and processing towns, and replacement of a dependent labor force by application of technology. In other words, it was an agrarian system that required diffusion of the commercial, processing, and financial functions of large cities. In the plantation economy of the antebellum South, planters acquired goods and services directly from seaboard factors who, from a few cities, united functions that in the North were spatially diffused. Profits from the export of cotton tended to be channeled to the purchase of land, slaves, and consumption goods rather than toward diversification and production technology. Large cities were therefore relatively few; urban systems were weak. Clearly, the tension between the homestead and plantation economies was deeply entwined with the causes for the U.S. Civil War.

From the North American viewpoint, the plantation-homestead polarity is construed as one between a "traditional" system based on dependent labor and a "modernizing" one associated with free labor and competitive entrepreneurship. This dualism is often projected on nineteenth-century Latin America in a wishful effort to detect a comparable, if more embryonic and slothful, pattern of development. It is true, of course, that Latin America did host some homesteading experiments, often carried out by immigrant groups as in northeast Argentina, southern Brazil, and Cuba. In fact the lively classic by Fernando Ortiz, *Cuban Counterpoint, Tobacco and Sugar* (1940, trans. 1947), adopts precisely this antinomy and traces, inter alia, the implications for urban development (although by endorsing the "homestead" alternative of Cuban tobacco farmers, he incurs the Marxist accusation of having petty-bourgeois sympathies).

More central to the agrarian experience of nineteenth-century Latin America, however, is the split between "hacienda" and plantation agriculture. On one hand is what can generically be called the hacienda system: labor intensive, requiring little capital or machinery, dependent on the church and merchants for loans, managing with modest accumulations of capital, serving local markets, needing little infrastructure (roads, transportation, energy), monopolizing a land area, and binding its workers by a noncash nexus. On the other hand is the plantation system: dependent on foreign capital, profit-oriented, employing rational cost-accounting, needing modern financial intermediaries, requiring transport to points of export, forcing proprietors into political participation at the national level, and establishing a cash nexus with the work force along with seasonal unemployment and elimination of marginal subsistence agriculture. Thus plantation agriculture, which in the United States was the trailing edge or "traditional" sector of the economy became in Latin America the leading edge or "modernizing" sector. As early as 1883, the Brazilian historian-statesman Joaquim Nabuco recognized the common misunderstanding that São Paulo was a node of "development." São Paulo province, he wrote in *O abolicionismo* (1883), was not the Massachusetts of Brazil but its Louisiana, and São Paulo not its Boston but its New Orleans.

One may therefore summarize positive and negative urban implications of the transition from hacienda to plantation. Among "positive" effects were: the growth of strategic seaports that channeled import-export flows, the introduction of complex financial institutions and practices, remodeling and modernization of capital cities financed by export earnings, and adoption of urban residence by rural elites. "Negative" or inconclusive effects included new infrastructure for rural production that was often installed on plantations rather than in small towns, regional urban networks that remained weak, disruption of traditional villages that was not accompanied by the growth of small commercial towns, and a labor force that was no longer tied to rural areas but that often migrated to large cities where social mobility was uncertain.

Returning to the case of large cities, let me now as a shorthand device draw on a previous essay that compares some commentators on Latin and Anglo-American cities who will serve as a link to the contemporary scene. I start with two social pathologists of Bogotá and Lima. In *La miseria de Bogotá* (1867) and *Retrospecto* (1896), Miguel Samper portrayed the Colombian capital as a parasitic city, the seat of ruling groups and nonproductive consumers, an asylum for functionaries, aspirants, pensioners, lawyers, and adventurers. As it had acquired political supremacy, so it later monopolized trade and distribution, squandering its wealth to subsidize an army of beggars, pickpockets, drunks, lepers, and lunatics that was swelled by displaced clergy, bureaucrats, and military. The city's moral, social, and political illness required, in Samper's view, class harmony and proper personal habits. Despite his liberalism, he felt that the state might intervene to restore social equilibrium. Joaquín Capelo's four-volume *Sociología de Lima* (1895–1902) presented a similar analysis. He too posed as a physician confronting a sick organism, a society unclearly demarcated whose extended families traversed all social levels. Lima was composed of petrified institutions; it lacked voluntary associations or even sustenance for scientific and intellectual life; it was plagued by an unholy trinity of monopoly, usury, and confiscatory fiscal policies; most of its population was unproductive and lived off the rest.

In *The Intellectual versus the City,* Morton White and Lucia White (1962) summarized urban attitudes in the United States, offering a handy benchmark for comparison. They detected two stages for nineteenth-century cities. First was the period before the Civil War of 1861–65, the early phase of industrialization, when North American writers, alarmed by the European example, were apprehensive of the urban potential for crime, immorality, depravity, and mob violence. Second were the four post–Civil War decades, when the urban population quadrupled. The nightmare seemed to have become reality as city populations passed the one-million mark and as their industrial and commercial energy appeared to cause moral degradation along with severe deterioration of the quality of life. Cities came to be seen as arenas of corruption and pollution in contrast to the image of small towns where life seemed neighborly and free of original sin. If the Latin American master image was the city-as-parasite, the North

American one was the city-as-cancer. The parasite fed on the body social of the whole nation; the cancer poisoned the conditions for amiable, petit-bourgeois urban life.

Perhaps the most innovative proposals for urban therapy in the United States came from practitioners who looked for inspiration to an idealized tradition of small-town, rural life. Such were Charles Loring Brace, whose programs for social welfare accommodated the precepts of encroaching bureaucracy and rationality to spontaneous village-type organization, and Frederick L. Olmsted, whose plans for city parks advocated a landscape art that would cultivate natural social relations and a sense of freedom in an urban setting now threatened by massification, pollution, and routinization. By the end of the century, however, such attempts to recover earlier precedents that might deflect the forces of a Darwinian world gave way to activist prescriptions. Political reformers took the lead with their instrumental remedies for the urban crisis, such as making municipal elections nonpartisan, granting local rule to cities, and giving mayors the functions of business executives. By and large, urban diagnosticians no longer labored under the incubus of history. One searches in vain for a U.S. counterpart to the sociological probing of the Latin Americans. From North Americans now came exposés, not sociology. The exposé assumes that it will appeal to common decency and that the exposer need supply only technical formulae for reform. Latin Americans, in contrast, felt themselves confronting deep and perennial moral issues. Their experience led them to expect little from the morality of any man, common or uncommon. How could they offer easy remedies if the need was for moral regeneration, not institutional tinkering? Time and again they identified the causes of urban stasis and dysfunction as being the ancient theological evils of avarice, pride, envy, shamelessness, ostentation, and usury.

After 1920 Latin American intellectuals broke the positivist mold of their predecessors to devise more private and imaginative ways of viewing the urban phenomenon. In *Sobrados e mucambos* (1936) Gilberto Freyre examined the reconstitution of rural, patriarchal life within the nineteenth-century urban domain. In so doing he broke with the century-long denunciation of the Iberian heritage to establish a relativist position that yielded richer explanations for the logic of urban institutions. He showed special sensitivity to correspondences between the physical form of the Brazilian city—its private architecture and public spaces—and its changing social organization.

For Freyre the heart of urban society was the "urban patriarchy," whose decay he chronicled in rich detail and with nostalgic condescension. He dealt with "citification" (social, cultural, attitudinal), not urbanization (sociological, political, economic). The city was a vehicle, not an engine, for change, while his human beings were actors, not agents. Yet if Freyre failed to convey a sense of the relentless dialectic of history in the capitalist age, his patience with the minutiae of human experience rendered urban society visible, gave intellect fresh anchorage in perception after the positivist interregnum. In highly personal fashion, he domesticated the Western city to processes of the Iberian world.

The analysis of Buenos Aires by Ezequiel Martínez Estrada in *X-ray of the Pampa* (1933, trans. 1971) and *La cabeza de Goliat* (1940) drew, as did Freyre, upon psychoanalysis. Here, however, this meant retreating from the history of the external world to show how it was telescoped as images and obsessions in the private psyche. Rather than projecting his *own* obsessions on the nation in Freyre's self-indulgent manner, he undertook to psychoanalyze the mind of the collectivity.

Martínez Estrada plunged the reader into a setting where not only the colonial past was still present, but a prehistoric world—decked with fantasies and resisting orderly processes of evolution—undergirded the gratuitously imposed nation. Here human settlements were recidivous; they renounced civilization and returned to sheer animal existence. Buenos Aires, the oneiric delusion of Argentina, was a severed Goliath's head, capital not of a nation but only of itself, a teratological creature condemned to live alone and not for the species. The chapters on Buenos Aires in *X-ray* each took the title of a famous book and inverted the message. One chapter was named for Sarmiento's *Argirópolis*, which advocates a new city to invigorate internal trade and create a network of prosperous inland centers. Martínez Estrada described a metropolis whose inhabitants lived on the periphery of Europe; to look "inland" was for them to look abroad. In "La gran aldea," named for Lucio V. López's novel of 1884 about the sociable *haute monde* of the young metropolis, the city was bathed in melancholy, its Calle Florida a fetish for consumers, its cabaret life smothered in the immense night of the pampas, its notorious tango a soulless dance of possession without pleasure.

For both Freyre and Martínez Estrada, coming to terms with the modern city meant coming to terms with its history rather than proposing an agenda of practical "reform." For Freyre that history was relatively benign and offered cultural guidelines for adapting urban life and institutions to the contemporary world. These suggestions later became explicit in his studies on "Luso-tropicology." For Martínez Estrada the history of Argentina was oppressive because it had been suppressed. Modern urban society was without shape, structure, or spiritual binding force. Only by bringing to consciousness the ghosts of the past, he insisted, could they be exorcised so that Argentines might live together in health.

Another benchmark for urban studies was *La multitud, la ciudad y el campo en la historia del Perú* (1929) by the Peruvian historian Jorge Basadre. Although Basadre drew on the "crowd" theories of Tarde and Le Bon, his analysis was less psychologistic than those of Freyre and Martínez Estrada. In fact, his book forecast many central themes of Latin American urban historiography as it has been practiced until now. These include: a caution against easy analogies between Incaic and European urban institutions, a functional contrast between European and Spanish colonial cities, a functional taxonomy of colonial Andean cities, the distinction between "natural" and "political" causes of urban origin, the blend of "feudal" and "bourgeois" influences on Andean cities, the disruptions wrought by the Spanish on the Incaic symbiosis of town and country, and the failure of the nineteenth-century "liberal" state to create regionalist strategies to counteract the heritage of *gamonalismo.*

The guiding motif of the book, however, is Basadre's characterization of successive types of crowd (*multitud, muchedumbre*) that gave their stamp to urban evolution. Here he anticipated the theme of "populism," giving it historical specificity that is lacking in most treatments of the contemporary phenomenon. It is precisely this theme that most adequately allows the insertion of the urban phenomenon of the 1980s into long-term historical context. Basadre characterized five types of historical urban "crowd" from the Incaic period to the 1870s. After summarizing his taxonomy, I will adduce four subsequent types that lead to the urban *problemática,* addressed by the papers of this volume, which require a "rethinking" of the Latin American city.

Basadre's five sequential types are : (1) the Incaic crowd, which, although submissive and dominated, shared with its masters a matrix of tradition, belief, and institutions; (2) the religious, aulic crowd of the early colonial period, convoked on occasions of public pageantry; (3) the heterogeneous "creole" crowd of the Bourbon century, whose protests foreshadowed the split between creoles and peninsulars; (4) the more openly political crowd of the 1820s and 1830s, not given to Jacobin extremism, serving more as seismograph than as instigator, protesting vaguely against oligarchy and militarism without religious mysticism or socioeconomic agenda; (5) the "patriotic" crowd of the 1860s and 1870s with its firmer collective conscience, defined political goals, and menacing homicidal disposition.

To reformulate these categories for subsequent periods—and with reference now to Latin America as a whole rather than the Andean region—one might propose the following four stages:

(1) The first period of import substitution from the 1890s to the 1920s, when a vision of modernization inspired creation of basic industries and attracted European immigration. The unionization of workers and their adoption of strike tactics seemed to herald the era of a proletarianized city, with industrial workers asserting intermittent control over urban public spaces. Yet from the start it was apparent that the new proletariat would be split between those whose privileged organizations made them susceptible to co-optation by industry and government and those who fell into the unprotected ranks of a "reserve army."

(2) The populist era of the 1920s to the 1950s. In this period large cities became increasingly an arena for mass meetings and for the emergence of an urban populace as a political constituency without regard to status as defined by syndical organization. Electoral politics came to focus increasingly on an undifferentiated urban electorate. National leaders attempted to create a direct, indiscriminate bond with the urban proletariat and the lumpen. National governments were especially generous in dispensing economic favors to large urban populations, as was notoriously the case for Mexico City.

(3) The period of so-called marginalization of the 1950s to the 1970s. The cityward migrations following World War II overflowed existing facilities for the poor and created self-built barrios on the periphery and in interstices of the inner city. As these settlements became "visible" to authorities and elites, and as their inhabitants— disenchanted with the populist politics of the preceding period— presented more sharply focused demands to municipal and state governments, the conviction arose that they should be incorporated into a "systemic" central city. Reassurance for such a policy arose from the example of urban "squatters" who, in ten to twenty years, managed by their own efforts to convert their original shanties into two-story stuccoed domiciles enjoying basic urban services. Policies of incorporation sponsored by public and private agencies included, on the physical side, provision of sites, services, low-cost housing, and guided self-help, and on the political side, formal or informal measures for accommodating local patronage structures to central power that would parallel archaic administrative structures. The assumption behind such measures was that a manageable reallocation of resources and modification of the political process would redirect cities to a more acceptable version of the Western urban model.

(4) The era of the "permanent" informal sector. By the late 1970s, and with the economic setbacks of the early 1980s, it became clear that marginal sectors—whether defined spatially, economically, politically, or socially—were not about to disappear. The controversial definition of "marginal" sectors gave way to a sharper definition of an "informal" sector characterized, as Alejandro Portes and Michael Jones formulated it, by relations that *fail* to demonstrate either a clear separation or contractual relationship between capital and labor or a wage-labor force whose conditions of work and pay are legally regulated. From 1950 to 1980 the informal sector held steady at 30 percent of the urban labor force, and the self-employed at slightly over 20 percent of employment in manufacturing. If one defines the informal sector by exclusion from social security coverage, it leaps to over one half of the *economically active* urban population.

In short, a new urban civilization has arisen where the political claims of the disinherited have assumed more militant, more diffuse, more culturally rooted expression. In some ways one is reminded of the culture of *leperismo* of Mexico City in the era of independence reflected in Latin America's first novel, *El periquillo sarniento*, by Fernández de Lizardi. That was a period when the social dispositions of Spanish rule broke down. Neither could disadvantaged groups be kept "in their place," socially or spatially, nor could those in power keep up with social change and the economic needs of the society. It might also appear that the formal and informal sectors are a reprise of the late-colonial split between *gente decente* and the *plebe*.

While such historical analogies may inspire creative understandings of the present situation, they do not signify that history has "repeated itself." The contemporary period culminates a century or more of change characterized by the industrialization first of agriculture, then of manufactures, and utilizing a subproletariat that provided a highly restricted market for the commodities it produced. Under these conditions the customary linkage process of economic development was short-circuited. The subproletariat was recruited first from abroad and then from national populations inflated by demographic pressures. Yet accelerated population growth was not the root cause of what in the 1950s and 1960s was called "marginalization." The informal sector does not constitute a "reserve army" but, as it has assumed permanent features, an alternative rather than a subordinate realm of urban society. People in both the formal and informal realms make strategic and voluntary crossovers, and both realms are linked by a range of social and economic activities. Because the informal side has a significant component of entrepreneurs and professionals, average income is comparable to that of the formal. This symbiosis derives from the fact that, given the nature of the economy, its markets, and its calculations of cost, modern enterprise profits by reducing the maintenance expenses of its work force to a minimum and "subproletarianizing" the proletariat itself.

The point is, therefore, that not only resources, management, and political institutions but also the incentives are lacking for what was recently called the incorporation of the marginals. As migrants continue to pour into cities, as the best economic strategies imposed from above go awry, as middle classes collapse into a "lumpen-bourgeoisie," and as even "democratized" regimes squabble over what democracy is and how it can be achieved—one understands why the heart of the urban question has been misconstrued. One may continue to speak of incorporating the marginals but only by redefining marginals. For impoverished migrants are not marginals; they are the *people*. The marginals are the elites, technicians, bureaucrats, and academicians. It is *they* who require incorporation.

The studies on urban carnival by the Brazilian anthropologist Roberto Da Matta provide an emblematic caricature of the social inversion that is occurring. During carnival the people occupy the central urban spaces and parade in the finery of bygone aristocratic classes. Elite groups retreat to private clubs and take off their elegant clothes to dance virtually naked. In the absence of a consensual ranking and functional institutions, the outcome can only be the inversion of hierarchy, which must be anarchy. Anarchy is quite different from the "liberty" of the industrial West, as defined by the binomial "liberty versus order." Order means control, while hierarchy means a "natural" arrangement of the social universe. Once this arrangement collapses, the *people* must invent a new one, doing so without norms or chaperones.

What then—the urbanist or urbanologist must ask—are the implications of this urban social inversion for reconceiving the city? Clearly we must set aside the guidelines inherited from the classic tradition of city planning that extends from the Renaissance to Geddes, Mumford, and Le Corbusier—an ultimately bourgeois tradition that promises comfort, services, green spaces, and defense of the resident as masterminded by planners, technicians, and politicians. Now, however, the people are taking over. This is no longer the process of "contamination" that was identified by the "Chicago school" of sociologists whereby bourgeois entrepreneurs continued to make their profits. It is rather a people's invasion that appropriates the city center, creates its own space for commercial activity, causes deterioration of tourist hotels and promenades, and in seaboard locations appropriates the beaches. For the first time since the European conquest, the city is not an intrusive bastion against and control center for the rural domain. The nation has invaded the city. Urban physical and social space now reflects national society as a whole.

This urban transformation requires sweeping redefinition of the urban *problemática* and full recognition that rehabilitation of the new city cannot rely on the limited resources, institutions, and traditional policies of the public sector. The city as a whole must increasingly depend on popular initiative for reworking institutions, for providing security and dispensing justice, for reconceiving the physical city, for developing alternative services (transport, health, education, religion, leisure), and for creating fresh norms for language and the literary and expressive arts. What the common folk have accomplished in the peripheral or interstitial residential areas during the past forty years now offers guidelines for what must happen to the city as a whole. Cities are now nodal points for the nation and not its citadels of control.

2

Theory and Practice of Urban Planning in Europe, 1850–1930: Its Transfer to Latin America

Jorge E. Hardoy

In 1972 I wrote a paper on the theory and practice of urban planning in Europe from the fifteenth to the seventeenth centuries and its transplantation to the countries of Latin America (Hardoy 1972). In that essay I tried to analyze the way in which urban planning practices in the European countries that colonized America—Spain, Portugal, Holland, France, England, and Denmark—resulted in cities sited for purely functional needs, with planning and architecture responsive to utilitarian criteria. The European colonial city in Latin America was thought of not as a work of art but as a center from which administrative, trading, and production functions spread out over the territory and where they linked up with European markets. Factors external to the occupied territories and decisions made in the imperial capitals of Europe resulted over a few years in a series of centers whose size and function differed according to the region. This hierarchy of cities, set during the colonial period, continues today in many parts of Latin America. In its layout and architecture, the Spanish American city introduced and retained features that clearly distinguish it from those cities founded by the Portuguese in Brazil, by the French, English, and Danes in the Caribbean, and by the Dutch in northeastern Brazil and the Caribbean.

In this essay I intend to explain how urban theory and practice, developed in Europe from about 1850 to 1930 as a reaction to the impact of the Industrial Revolution and the development of capitalism, were transplanted—but only partly applied—to Latin America. Scientific and technological developments and certain urban planning theories favored in Europe from 1870 to 1880 immediately dominated Latin American urban practice, determining many of the features of the cities during the critical period of rapid demographic and physical growth that many of them experienced during the final decades of the last century. Up to the Second World War and, in many countries, for some years thereafter, these theories and practices also dominated the teaching of architecture and urban planning.

These influences were not imposed involuntarily. Although applied piecemeal, they reflected a clear cultural and technological dependence that was linked to the entry of Latin American countries into world trade. The best examples of these influences are almost always found in national capitals and in cities whose population and economy were booming and that served as links between the primary, exporting economies of Latin America and European industrialized markets and exporters of capital and technology. In the face of massive immigration and, in the first phase of industrialization, as a substitute for importing, the towns of the Atlantic coast were the first to try to modernize their administrative structures and to seek solutions to the problems that they considered most pressing—sanitation; wholesale markets; road surfacing, traffic, and street layout; the creation of squares and parks; public transport; public buildings, hospitals, and schools; housing; and, in some cases, the modernization of ports. These efforts were followed, many years later, by those of towns in the Pacific countries, Mexico, and Cuba, then by those in the countries of northern South America and Central America. The urban problems that Latin American countries faced were conditioned by the size and growth rate of each city, by the potential of each national economy, by the interest of these economies to the industrialized countries, and by their social and political structure. But in almost all the capitals and other large cities, solutions based on European theory and practice were adopted to some extent, even in dealing with minor problems.

There is an explanation for this. The opening up of Latin American countries to world trade had profound effects on their cities. With certain exceptions, until the 1850s or 1860s, and possibly to 1870, change had been hardly noticeable. The laying out and zoning of the colonial cities took in an area that was sufficient for all or most of the population that made up these cities until relatively recent times. There was little if any settlement outside the original colonial ground plan. A few neighboring villages—which years later were incorporated within the new city limits—retained a certain economic and social autonomy. The most significant changes were in architecture and land use in the old cities and in some cities of the interior.

Around 1850, in the coastal cities of Argentina, Uruguay, and southeastern Brazil the population growth rate began to accelerate (Hardoy and Langdon 1978, 115-73). Between 1852 and 1910, Uruguay's population increased ninefold, Argentina's increased sevenfold between 1850 and 1914, and Brazil's almost tripled between 1856 and 1913. In 1850 all the Latin American countries were predominantly rural, consisting of vast unoccupied or very sparsely populated regions. Then, in the following decades, a process of rapid concentration of the population at certain points in each territory began to take place. After the 1890s the modern Latin American city emerged. These were industrial conurbations that, in the most developed countries of the region, presented all the salient features of urbanization in terms of space, demography, and economics.

No city in Latin America had a million inhabitants in 1900. Only Buenos Aires with 806,000 and Rio de Janeiro with 692,000 had more than half a million. Another twelve—Mexico City, Santiago, Havana, Montevideo, São Paulo, San Salvador, Valparaiso, Lima, Recife, Rosario, Guadalajara, and Bogotá—had more than 100,000 inhabitants. The great majority of the cities were much smaller. Their rates of demographic increase were slow and almost wholly the result of natural growth.

Through the second half of the nineteenth century and the first years of the twentieth century, there was intense pioneer work in the interior of various Latin American countries, with the result that new political and administrative needs, the incorporation of farming and mining areas, the extension of the railroad, and settlement of frontier and previously unexplored territories required the founding of thousands of villages all over Latin America. It was a period of great activity for surveyors in the laying out and recording of new and already existing settlements, in the establishment of international and provincial boundaries, and in the designing of new public works. The demand for more functional and complex public and private works required more highly skilled professionals. From 1860 or 1870 on, there was a great influx and influence of engineers, many of them foreigners. Technical departments were created at national and provincial levels, many of them with a direct role in the construction and administration of cities.

Around 1880 or 1890, a growing number of architects and engineers were appointed to positions in the public and private sectors. Many of them were foreigners; among the native-born, most were trained abroad. Only toward the end of the nineteenth century did architects begin to graduate from the recently established Latin American schools of architecture, which had started out in university engineering departments. The first city planners, who were also trained in Europe, made their appearance in the 1920s and 1930s.

I know of no general history of urban planning in Latin America nor of any urban history of any individual country during the decades of the great transformation of the cities. Only recently has solid research begun into working-class housing and the evolution of the urban infrastructure. Historians of architecture, who have usually concerned themselves with describing the most representative buildings of any given period, have now begun to branch out into wider themes with a broader viewpoint, but few have an adequate grounding in history. The history of the building and administration of cities during these years has yet to be undertaken.

The present essay includes a selection of the main European urban theories and practices evolved between 1850 and 1950 and explores how they were used in Latin America. Despite its incompleteness, the essay shows a changing attitude of governments and wealthy classes toward the city and its needs. This attitude arises from needs that cannot be put off and from cultural aspirations as well as from a marketplace that favors laissez-faire practices, which have been only partially successful in solving the most pressing urban problems.

URBAN PLANNING IN EUROPE

The ideas of the principal European urban theorist in the middle of the nineteenth century, the Catalan engineer Ildefonso Cerdá (1816–76), had no influence on the thinking of the mayors of Latin American cities or their experts. Cerdá, like his contemporary Haussmann, saw the city as a whole and proposed to decentralize the old heart of Barcelona by distributing urban services and functions evenly throughout the city in such a way that would make them accessible to the entire population. This concept of an open city without distinctions, which Cerdá put forward for the expansion of Barcelona, was drafted in 1859 and consisted of a huge grid twenty-two blocks from east to west and fifty-five from north to south, paralleling the Mediterranean coast and intersected by diagonals and avenues, with two great parks on the north and south edges of the city. One of the most serious problems was the integration of the old city into this new expansion. Traffic movement between the two areas was resolved by the creation of the Rondas forming Cataluña Square, sited as a link at the edge of the old city.

Cerdá's ideas (1867) found no echo in western Europe or North America. His democratic, socialistic ideas, included in his vision of an integral plan that would combine the basic needs of the population with greater economic efficiency, clashed with the predominant thought of the period, especially in Prussia, which emphasized a policy of adopting a radial system of neighborhoods according to class as a way of broadening out and decongesting the old centers of cities, thus avoiding a slump in ground-floor property values. According to these proposals, a city should be constructed by private building on a layout of streets whose width and direction were complemented by planned rows of houses. As a result, square blocks closed around their perimeters arose, as, inevitably, did unequal land values, which reflected the different earning power of the residents.

The most typical example of the period was the plan for Berlin by the engineer James Hobrecht (1825–1903), officially commissioned and published in 1862. Hobrecht's plan was implemented, with minor alterations, up to 1919 and influenced subsequent building regulations approved for Berlin until the end of the century (Sutcliffe 1981, 20). The plan, however, resulted in a proliferation of neighborhoods of tenements of high density, built in huge blocks two to three hundred meters square, bounded by wide streets but crisscrossed by alleyways and little courtyards.

In the years that followed, several plans for city expansion were prepared in Germany for whole cities, replacing earlier plans that had concentrated only on peripheral districts. In them, the defects of Hobrecht's plan were repeated as were the uniformity and width of the streets and the lack of open spaces (Sutcliffe 1981, 22). This situation led to criticism in Germany and in other European countries, especially in architects' and engineers' associations and among independent professionals concerned about the environmental problems of cities in rapid growth. German industrial development from 1890 on resulted in a high concentration of the population in certain cities, a process begun some decades before and prompted by internal migrations. Between 1858 and 1890, the population of Berlin went from 458,637 to 1,578,794; that of the twenty-five next most important cities together, including outlying areas rose from 2,295,800 to 7,077,476 (Weber 1963, table XLIV).

Demographic pressure and the incorporation of electric tramlines led to the creation of suburbs in all the cities of more than 100,000 inhabitants, which by 1910 contained 21 percent of the population of Germany, compared with only 4 percent in 1871 (Sutcliffe 1981, 17). To deal with the manifold city problems, competitions were held for plans for expansion, which became the basis of future plans for whole cities; municipalities were given wide powers to carry them out. Alongside these, the sanitation movement developed, with the aim of curbing, through building codes and other regulations, the worst effects of speculation and the construction of totally inadequate housing. Although the results were still incomplete by the beginning of the First World War, there was now broad support for the control of city growth.

The English contribution was important in various ways. Economic pressures brought English and Scottish workers and Irish immigrants into the industrial cities of the United Kingdom, and the resulting housing emergency led philanthropic societies to build houses without paying much attention to their quality. During this period all housing was built by individual owners or by private firms; initiatives by central and local government had not yet begun. Philanthropic societies started to operate during the 1840s and 1850s, but only after the 1870s did their activities have an impact, concentrating on buildings of up to five stories. Without doubt this British initiative, like others in France, Germany, and Belgium, was studied in some Latin American countries and also copied, though—as shall be seen—on a much smaller scale. But as Tarn (1980) clearly points out, the activities of philanthropic societies had no influence on urban planning theory of the period. Rather, in different neighborhoods of the city, partial and temporary solutions led to the sanction of basic norms for the construction of workers' housing in subsequent decades.

Much more important was the movement by English sanitation engineers, who prompted the passing of the public health laws of 1848 and 1875. The 1875 law was the basis of urban regulations passed in the following decades and, in general, of all urban legislation approved before the end of the nineteenth century. These laws, like the laws of 1868 and 1875 on the demolition of tenements, and the principles of the sanitation movement, were studied in Latin America, where they inspired Rawson and Gache in Argentina and others in different countries.

The main English contribution to planning theory was the residential garden suburb. The first steps in this field were made by entrepreneurs with advanced social consciences for the period. Initially the idea took the form of a small town or garden village, such as the factory and dwellings for 800 workers that the industrialist Sir Titus Salt built on some 20 hectares in 1851. Port Sunlight, planned in 1888 and backed by the firm W. H. Lever; Bournville, on the outskirts of Birmingham, founded by George Cadbury in 1895; and Earswick are a few of the most outstanding examples. In the United States garden neighborhoods had been constructed for factory workers, in Lowell, Massachusetts, in 1822, and Pullman, Illinois, in 1880; the Pullman factory was one of the first to use mass production techniques.

The idea of rural cities for England had been put forward by the architect J. B. Papworth. In the United States a city to be called Hygeia was planned in Kentucky but was never built. Its center was to contain public buildings; large garden zones, with strict regulations for their subdivision into lots, completed the general design. The construction of the railroads led to the development of numerous residential suburbs. Some, such as Lake Forest, built in 1856, and Riverside, in 1869, both near Chicago, and Rochelle Park, in 1885, in New Rochelle, New York, were for the wealthier classes. Others, such as Garden City, Long Island, built in 1869, were for white-collar workers.

In 1898, in his book *Tomorrow: A Peaceful Path to Real Reform*, Ebenezer Howard (1850–1928) brought together the ideas of his period and incorporated others of a practical nature, based in part on previous experiments. Howard put his ideas into practice in the construction, in 1903, some fifty kilometers north of London, of the first garden city, Letchworth. Perhaps Howard's most important contributions were to limit the population to 32,000, of which 30,000 were to live in the city and 2,000 in the neighboring farmland; to set aside an area of 2,400 hectares, 400 of which were for the city; and to channel the excess population to new centers, thus forming a nucleus with a number of satellites. Other proposals were the municipal ownership of urban land, the principles of zoning, the grouping of public buildings in a civic center, and the forward planning of streets. Howard's garden city was to take the form of concentric rings with the center occupied by public buildings. Industry was to occupy a planned area on the outskirts. Howard tried to avoid speculation on land and services in a self-sufficient community, but in practice Letchworth functioned almost from the start as a residential suburb of London. Years later in England the idea of residential suburbs was planned around existing small towns. Hampstead Garden Suburb, founded by a private firm, is one of the best examples.

Howard's idea of a garden city with a high degree of self-sufficiency in production and culture, yet linked to other similar garden cities, had a great influence in England, Holland, the United States, and the Scandinavian countries, but the concept was never transported to Latin America. Latin America, however, was attracted to the idea of the garden suburb, a piecemeal concept of residential developments for the middle classes, which have long since become bedroom suburbs a long way from the workplace and reliant on only the most basic services. The bedroom garden suburb idea was also tried in some neighborhoods of low-cost housing, although prices were too high for the great majority of the working class. In 1933 two housing projects were built in Mexico City (Colonia Balbuena). In 1947 in Panama City, Vista Hermosa was built containing semidetached houses and apartments, two schools, and a business and civic center, but at a cost that was too high for working-class people. In 1942 in Rio de Janeiro, the neighborhood of Realengo was constructed for 10,000 factory workers, with a combination of four-story apartment houses and rows of single-family dwellings. And in Buenos Aires, during the 1940s, the garden city of El Palomar was built, together with two other garden cities to the south. All these were conceived as bedroom suburbs convenient to public transportation routes.

HAUSSMANN'S CONTRIBUTIONS

When in 1853 Georges-Eugène Haussmann (1809–91) was appointed prefect of the Department of Seine by Napoleon III, the population of Paris had passed well over the million mark (Weber 1963, table XXXVI). Between 1801 and 1856, Paris doubled its population, and its area was increased by 50 percent by a decree of June 16, 1859, through which a number of nearby villages were annexed and converted into nuclei of suburban neighborhoods. The area of Paris went from 3,437 to 7,802 hectares, incorporating the present-day thirteenth to twentieth *arrondissements.*

The city had very serious crowding and traffic problems, a chaotic urban structure, and poor amenities, which included deficiencies in the supply of drinking water, sewage, lighting, and cemeteries. Napoleon III and Haussmann's grand plans for the transformation of Paris have been discussed and analyzed by a number of writers (Poëte 1924; Lavedan 1952; Saalman 1971; Pinkney 1958; Giedion 1955; Choay 1969). In the main these were for the improvement of public health by the eradication of sources of infection; the speeding up of city traffic by linking the railroad stations—Saint-Lazare, built in 1842; du Nord, in 1843; de Lyon, in 1847–52; de l'Est, d'Austerlitz, de Sceaux, and de Versailles—with the business and recreational centers; the facilitating of the means of crowd control in the event of riots; and the improvement of the appearance of the city by creating principal public buildings. To achieve these objectives, Paris was to be adapted to the needs of a big city with problems arising from industrialization while retaining examples of its ancient architectural tradition. In his seventeen years as prefect, Haussmann endowed Paris with its great parks—the Bois de Boulogne to the west, the Bois de Vincennes to the east, Parc de Montsouris to the south, Parc de Monceau to the northwest, and Parc des Buttes Chaumont to the northeast—and many of its great squares. He set out a network of tree-lined boulevards and avenues that eased north-south and east-west movement; developed new neighborhoods; encouraged a homogeneous architectural style along the new avenues and around certain squares; and, among other improvements, set up markets and built an administrative center on the Île de la Cité. Many of Haussmann's projects took several years to complete; the Avenue de l'Opéra was finished by 1878, Boulevard Raspail by 1907, and Boulevard Haussmann by 1925 (Lavedan 1952, 3:242).

An administrator loyal to his patron, from whom he received the political support to undertake the redesigning of a great city on a scale hitherto unknown, Haussmann emerged as a formidable figure and the prototype public servant of a monarchic government. The funding of his Paris projects deserves to be better understood, because for the first time he integrated new and old ideas in a plan for a rapidly expanding city (Haussmann 1890). Haussmann sold municipal bonds both to the public and to private banks. He created a fund to finance public works and drew up contracts with private development and construction firms, making them responsible for paying compensation for expropriated land even though these firms were only paid in municipal bonds guaranteed by a government land bank. He also used the surplus from recent municipal income and gave great freedom of operation to private developers, who benefited from credit and tax exemptions. Haussmann's basic idea was to take advantage of the larger sources of taxes that would arise from the economic growth of a city in rapid expansion. His plan for the transformation of Paris aimed, above all, at solving the emerging problems of the Parisian middle class, which had grown rich from commerce, finance, and building speculation.

Paris was one of the first European cities to incorporate simultaneously solutions to the problems of both traffic and green areas within a huge conurbation. Haussmann's concern to create an urban aesthetic is still reflected in the uniform facades in the neoclassic style along his new avenues and transverses. These were laid out to cut through districts that had acquired their shape as neighborhoods and their urban appearance down through the centuries. This aesthetic emphasis had a great influence on Europe and was imitated in the cities of Germany as well as in Rome in the 1870s, when it became the capital of a unified kingdom (Lavedan 1952, 3:243–44).

The Latin American municipalities incorporated some of Haussmann's ideas, such as baroque lines against an architectural background formed by an already existing building or monument, as in the

Parisian avenues that radiate out from the Arc de Triomphe, or deliberately created, as in the Opéra de Garnier, which is set off by the Avenue de l'Opéra. They also adopted the inevitable surgery through lower-class and sometimes middle-class neighborhoods. Using some of Haussmann's planners, they went in for tree-lined avenues and extensive public parks, with layouts reminiscent of the English landscape designers. But none of these ideas was ever incorporated on the scale adopted by Haussmann and they were far less comprehensive than in the Paris of the second half of the nineteenth century.

THE VIENNESE INFLUENCE

During the last four decades of the nineteenth century, Vienna was the undisputed capital of music, theater, architecture, and city planning. Its moment coincided with the consolidation of the middle class and the rise and eclipse of the Liberal party, which, having failed in its attempt to attract workers and peasants, shared political power with the aristocracy and imperial bureaucracy (Schorske 1981). As with the transformation that was taking place in Paris at that time, the Liberals, in control of the Vienna city administration, rapidly and efficiently developed an excellent system of drinking water, a public health program that included the opening of the first municipal hospital, and a series of parks. In 1859, the Liberals adopted a plan for redeveloping the space left free where the fortifications surrounding the old city had been pulled down and separating the city from the new suburbs, which reached as far as a second line of fortifications, which had been designed without heed to the needs of the growing conurbation.

An international competition had been announced in 1858 to redesign the area covered by the inner fortifications and by the intervening space that had been kept clear of building for security reasons (Breitling 1980). But, in the end, once the prizes were awarded, the development of the area—the Ringstrasse—was handed over to a commission for the expansion of the city under the control of the national government. The hopes of Vienna's Liberal administration were thus frustrated.

Although development of the Ringstrasse was acclaimed as comparable with the redesigning of Paris in the Second Empire, in practice the Ringstrasse brought about the social isolation of the inhabitants of the old city (Schorske 1981, 24–115). The design was centered on the layout of a tree-lined avenue, which was bordered by the facades of the newly commissioned buildings, some of which had won prizes in the

1858 competition. The different styles adopted by the planners—
baroque for the Burgtheater, Renaissance for the university buildings,
Greek classical for the Parliament—underscored the separateness of
each of these imposing piles set in too large a space. "In combination,"
Schorske (1981, 45) pointed out, "the monumental buildings of the
Ringstrasse were true expressions of the values of the ruling liberal
culture." The contrast with the dense layout of the old city is
noteworthy.

The development of the Ringstrasse was, to a great extent, financed
by the sale of lots built with apartment buildings of four to six stories,
constructed by private firms for the new elite middle classes who
sought to separate their place of residence from their place of work.
These buildings featured imposing Renaissance facades, grand stair-
cases with wide hallways, and the sacrifice of inner space to allow a
greater number of apartments to front on the street.

At this time, some architects working in Vienna had a strong influence on the theory of urban planning. This influence was broad in
Europe, and years later their work also came to be known in Latin
America. Camillo Sitte (1849–1903) put his ideas in the book *Der
Städtebau,* published in 1889 (Collins and Collins 1965). Sitte defended
the spatial relationships found in Greek and Roman cities and the
closed nature of medieval and Renaissance squares that formed a unit
with their surrounding buildings. His energetic defense of irregularity
and asymmetry, his rediscovery of the experience of the past, and his
criticism of isolated and visually unconnected buildings, straight lines
and regularity, and abstraction in city design as it had begun to be
conceived made him a critic of the proposal for the Ringstrasse development, although not of the architectural styles used. Sitte's idea was
to incorporate squares into the Ringstrasse, which would answer the
needs of the community and its culture.

A new competition for a basic plan for metropolitan Vienna was
announced by the municipality at the end of 1892. This competition
emphasized social and sanitation problems, traffic movement, and a
rationalization of land use. The proposal by Otto Wagner (1841–1918)
was diametrically opposed to Sitte's ideas. Wagner's chief concern was
transport, which would allow the city unlimited physical growth. He
was interested not in the aesthetic adornment of Vienna but in its
economy and efficiency. "Necessity is the only master of art," he said.
To Wagner, the key to the planning of Vienna lay in an efficient transport system that would allow satellite districts to be built around civic
centers with gardens, according to how necessary they were. He rejected the development of a greenbelt around the city, which he felt

would cut off the city (Schorske 1981, 98). The architecture of the apartment buildings designed by Wagner and his prototypes for urban districts, included in 1911 in his proposal for a modular plan for an expandable city, were forerunners of the theories of Le Corbusier and of the use of new materials and techniques (Wagner 1895, 1911).

EUROPEAN INFLUENCES IN LATIN AMERICA

Between 1870 and 1880 rapid transformation began of the main cities of the Atlantic coast of Latin America, particularly the capital cities of Argentina, Brazil, and Uruguay. These cities had been the first to receive overseas immigrants and foreign investment and to set up factories as a first step toward stemming imports. From 1900 on, the changes were more evident in the architecture of individual mansions designed by European architects and engineers or by local professionals trained in Europe than in public buildings. The old colonial centers were modernized, incorporating amenities such as drinking water, road surfacing, sidewalks, sewers, and tramlines (Álvarez Lenzi, Arana, and Bocchiardo 1986). Railroad stations and a few factories were built on the outskirts of the old centers. In the port cities, docks, breakwaters, and warehouses were constructed on an unprecedented scale. But the real transformation of this period came about outside the built-up areas of the colonial cities. The old family estates and open lots were rapidly transformed into residential areas for the various income levels.

The first building and environmental ordinances and the beginnings of municipal regulation were an attempt to respond to ideas on public health that had developed in Europe; these regulations called for community services such as drinking water, green areas, and fresh air in cities that were beginning to become congested. Even at best, provision of these services was a slow process. Lacking human and financial resources, the municipalities had to resort to borrowing abroad or granting concessions to private firms to surface the roads and build drinking water and sewage systems, public baths, new hospitals, and cemeteries.

Perhaps Haussmann's most lasting influence lay in the idea of creating parks. In Buenos Aires existing parks and green areas were expanded, and during the 1880s these parks were embellished with imported trees and plants, artificial lakes, and sculptural elements arranged according to a design that combined pedestrian paths and roads for vehicular traffic. Palermo Park is one of the earliest examples, and it was imitated in subsequent years in the smaller Argentine cities of Rosario, Mendoza, Córdoba, Paraná, and Tucumán. Completely different in aim, size, and layout is Buenos Aires' splendid Botanic Garden. In Mexico City, the Paseo de la Reforma, built during the government of Porfirio Díaz, was modeled on the principles of the Bois de Boulogne—as were Santa Lucía hill and its adjoining park, laid out in 1872–75 on the initiative of Mayor Benjamín Vicuña Mackenna, the Parque Forestal, the Quinta Normal de Agricultura, and forestation of the Alameda all in Santiago de Chile. In Montevideo the Prado was destined to become the future Bois de Boulogne, according to the French diplomat Count de Saint-Foix.

In some cities certain streets in the old centers were widened to form avenues, such as Corrientes, Córdoba, and Belgrano in Buenos Aires and a number of streets in the old city of Rio de Janeiro. Perhaps the best example of an avenue built on the expropriation system was the Avenida de Mayo in Buenos Aires, which was begun in 1894 and completed a few years later. Less successful and slower to be completed were the north and south diagonals (the latter only four blocks long), which converge with the Avenida de Mayo in the old colonial Plaza de Armas, now the Plaza de Mayo, which still retains its function as the civic center. Another example is the extended perspective of the Avenida Agraciada in Montevideo, cut off at its far end by the Congress building. The plan for the street's surroundings was never completed, because private investors turned their real estate interests to more dynamic neighborhoods than those bisected by the new avenue.

Haussmann's ideas, in general, were used selectively and were limited to solutions and specific projects in cities that at the turn of the century were subject to a strong French cultural influence. Haussmann's ideas perhaps may be seen most fully in the alterations undertaken by the engineer Francisco Pereira Passos, prefect of Rio de Janeiro from 1903 to 1906, during the administration of Rodrigues Alves. From 1857 to 1860 Pereira Passos lived and studied in Paris, a city that he visited many times during subsequent decades, and he was well acquainted with Haussmann's work, for which he had great admiration (Needell 1985). Pereira Passos put together a highly professional team that was very knowledgeable about the modifications that had taken place in other European cities and in Buenos Aires, and he managed to coordinate federal and municipal support for independent projects, such as the construction of the port and Leme tunnel. The demolition of unsanitary areas, the introduction of carrefours and widening of avenues to speed up the traffic flow, the renewal of Campo de Santana Park, a concern with the aesthetic appearance of the city, and the system of broad streets all followed principles of urban planning initiated by Haussmann in Paris.

Between 1883 and 1886, the mayor of Buenos Aires was Torcuato de Alvear, an enterprising man who had close ties with those in power in Argentina. His work is comparable to that of Pereira Passos. He widened, straightened, lined with trees, and surfaced almost all the main avenues in the city, which today are still the principal traffic routes around the center. He made parks of many squares, which had been unused empty spaces, and he planned the Paseo de la Recoleta. He created public welfare, enlarged the hospitals, and made smallpox vaccination compulsory. It was during his administration that the Avenida de Mayo was planned. On his death, the *Revue Illustrée du Rio de la Plata* of December 8, 1890, described him as the Argentine Haussmann, a sobriquet given years later to Pereira Passos.

Two other aspects of Haussmann's influence were lasting. One of them was the teaching of architecture in the universities. Until the mid-1940s, Latin American architecture schools were under the sway of the École des Beaux Arts in Paris. This influence was visible in the kind of projects and designs that the students had to carry out—drawing an Ionian column or designing for a park a small temple in the Corinthian style—and in the architectural works awarded prizes each year by municipal commissions. The courses in city planning and even postgraduate teaching in the first institutes of city planning consisted of a selective review of certain theories in vogue in Europe and North America before the Second World War, complemented by a few principles of urban analysis.

In many ways this approach clashed with the supposedly more advanced concepts of the CIAM groups (Congrès International d'Architecture Moderne), which were trying to apply these concepts both in the teaching of architecture and urban planning and in the execution of outline plans.

A good example of the concept of outline plans of the 1920s is the "Organic Project for the Urbanization of the Municipality" of Buenos Aires, drawn up by the city hall's commission on urban aesthetics and published in 1925. In putting together their building program, the commissioners called for reclaiming the riverfront; the completion of the north and south diagonals and of Santa Fe Avenue; the construction of several public buildings such as the city hall and the ministry of trade and industry; the refurbishment of the old South district; the redesigning of the Plaza de Mayo; the layout of the Plaza del Congreso, the Paseo Colón, and certain squares; the construction of working-class neighborhoods, gardens, and sport stadia; the embellishment of the suburbs; the relocation of the poorhouse; and the decoration of railroad bridges, which spoiled the look of Alvear Avenue, the city's so-called grand entrance from the north.

The plan drawn up by the commission, made up of three architects and an engineer with conflicting artistic tastes, replaced the plan proposed by the French urban planner Bouvard, public works chief of Paris, who had been contracted in 1906. Bouvard spent some weeks in Buenos Aires and Rosario and projected a layout of diagonal avenues, with squares at the intersections, and a widening of other avenues, which was approved in 1911. Work on the Diagonal Norte began the following year; what may have been Bouvard's best idea, the construction of a bathing facility, the Balneario Sur, began in 1917. Bouvard tried to apply certain concepts appropriate to the French Academy in a city that reflected the technological and aesthetic aspirations of a culturally undefined society. Praised by some and criticized by others, the Bouvard plan was pretentious and could not be executed on the scale proposed. Fortunately, it was quickly forgotten.

While Benjamín Vicuña Mackenna was mayor of Santiago, that city's first "Transformation Plan" was drawn up and partially implemented. Among other works, the plan called for a ring road that surrounded the city, dividing the center and its residents from the outlying areas. Twenty years later, in 1892, Santiago's Transformation Plan was approved. It proposed new avenues, radial traffic systems, and new streets in different planning areas. These projects, without doubt inspired by the redesigning of Paris begun by Haussmann, never came to fruition.

It is interesting to see the importance attached to the maintenance and landscaping of public gardens. The French landscape architect Jean C. N. Forestier (1861–1930), who also spent some weeks in Buenos Aires as consultant to the municipality, praised the care given the gardens, as well as their design. The muncipality maintained nurseries and greenhouses at each park and employed numerous caretakers and groundsmen for the parks and squares. In his report, Forestier pointed out the difficulty, owing to administrative fragmentation, of carrying out plans for embellishing the municipalities near Buenos Aires, adding that "in a few years, if events are not anticipated, Buenos Aires will find itself imprisoned by hastily and chaotically built suburbs" (Forestier 1925). If these problems were not solved, the city's principal accesses, its buildings, railroad stations, cemeteries, hospitals, and other public services, would not be able to be conveniently located, he warned. Forestier recommended setting aside land for suburban parks and rural reserves, following the examples of Vienna and

Cologne and Haussmann's proposals for Paris, which had been interrupted by the Franco-Prussian War. His recommendations were not implemented. Only at the end of the 1940s was a large forested area laid out near the highway connecting Buenos Aires with Ezeiza International Airport.

Between December 1925 and March 1930, under contract with the Cuban Ministry of Public Works, Forestier prepared a general plan of Havana. This was during the dictatorship of Machado, when the local middle classes, made wealthy by land speculation, the bank, and association with North American capital, which by the 1920s controlled most of the Cuban economy, strengthened the settlement of the city's western suburbs, developed the neighborhoods of Vedado, Miramar, and Country, and promoted the modernization of Havana in an attempt to convert it into a tropical Paris. As in other cities where Forestier worked, his major contribution was to redesign the old Paseo del Prado and to leave Havana a system of parks, by which he increased the value of the shoreline, the bay, and the areas surrounding the new avenues and highways. He also left plans for various existing squares and parks and for the civic center (Segre 1984). But even nearly completed projects were postponed when Machado's dictatorship fell in August 1933.

As with other Latin American urban plans of that period, especially in those cities that were growing rapidly, the absence of proposals for working-class neighborhoods and their amenities is noteworthy. Nor was there in Havana "the boldness of a middle class financially eager to invest large sums of money in the construction of new neighborhoods; the State concentrated its resources on the construction of symbolic buildings—the capitol, the university, the model prison, among others—and no office was created that was capable of attaining the necessary technical structures that a modern city required in order to function" (Segre 1984, 193).

The cities of Latin America adopted only a few of Haussmann's ideas, using them in a piecemeal way without any attempt to draw up a comprehensive physical plan for a city—an avenue here, a diagonal there, some monumental grouping, the redesign of a square, the groundwork for a civic center. Only in the siting and design of parks and certain squares and in the laying out and ordering of certain avenues in the new middle-class neighborhoods, where houses were set in large gardens, with front gardens as well, were good quality urban spaces developed.

LE CORBUSIER'S VISION

In 1922, at the Salon d'Automne in Paris, Le Corbusier (1887–1965) presented his study for a "Contemporary City for Three Million Inhabitants." The first part of the study was devoted to "a theoretical model of the city," which, as he insisted, was not in the least utopian. The second part was a study of a housing unit based on his Citroen 2 model. Le Corbusier's city plan had four main aims: to relieve congestion of the city center, to increase living density, to enlarge green areas, and to widen the streets. The proposal included a center made up of twenty-four sixty-story skyscrapers, each to house from 10,000 to 50,000 office workers or to be used as a hotel. Around the shopping and administrative center, an intermediate area was to be filled with multiple housing units of six stories for 600,000 people, with roofs to double as sun rooms. Beyond this, a series of garden cities was to house two million people. The whole was to be crossed by two straight rapid-transit, elevated traffic axes. The strict grid layout of rectangular superblocks was to be crossed by diagonals that would be used as direct access to the airport, industrial zones, and railroad station, all located outside the city. An enormous English garden would serve as a reserve for later expansion of the city (Le Corbusier 1946, 38–39).

Three years later, at the International Exhibition of Decorative Arts in Paris, Le Corbusier presented his "Plan Voisin," a proposal for redesigning the center of Paris along the Boulevard Sebastopol, which would be financed by the greater value the land accrued from increasing the density of the population from 600 to 3,200 per hectare. "To urbanize," Le Corbusier wrote, "is to increase values. It does not waste money, it makes money, it creates money" (1946, 111). The Plan Voisin followed principles hinted at in the Contemporary City for Three Million Inhabitants and is a forerunner of Le Corbusier's project for the Ville Radieuse. Le Corbusier wanted to redesign the old part of Paris, raising the population density three or four times and decreasing by a factor of three or four the traveling distances to work, thereby reducing fatigue proportionately. Buildings would cover only 5 to 10 percent of the ground area. One of his major concerns was urban traffic movement along highways that would also be true architectural creations. Mixed in with the highways and the giant office and apartment towers on a cruciform plan tens of stories high would be a Henri IV-period mansion or a Gothic church, an "amusing" Greek portico or a pedestrian walkway that used the existing Rue de la Paix. The buildings incorporated the five elements that Le Corbusier put forward for a new architecture—the pillar, the roof garden, the open plan, the free facade, and the panoramic window—all made possible by technological developments (Le Corbusier 1946, 112).

Another concern of Le Corbusier's (1939, 20), connected with traffic flow, was the use of the twenty-four hour clock: "The twenty-four hours of a normal day are not used to proper advantage, and . . . as a result of indifference and the all-consuming power of money, irresponsible enterprise has been the controlling influence on town control planning. The great task of city development is being tackled on a purely profit basis to the ensuing detriment of the individual. Only by bringing this unnatural situation to an end can the essential joys of life be found." A third concern was the rediscovery of nature, which had been attenuated by streets, stations, offices, and houses. "There are millions," he wrote, "who want to feel green turf under their feet. Millions who want to see the clouds and the blue sky. They want to live near trees, those immemorial friends of man" (1945, 20). The inefficiency of cities is paid for by the four unproductive hours taken up every day in getting to and from the work place and in the costly running of transportation systems. In a lecture in Chicago on the inefficiency of the modern city, he reiterated his proposal for a compact city without suburbs that would take up less space because identical buildings fifty meters high, with parks at their feet, would allow for densities of 1,000 people per hectare (400 per acre)—a city, in fact, whose sectors were planned according to function. Le Corbusier called for the harnessing of the community's collective energy, with its capacity to motivate action, to generate enthusiasm among individuals, and to create a civic spirit. He accused the promoters of garden cities of being responsible for the chaos of our great cities by relying on philanthropy to create "little individual houses and gardens for everyone as a way of securing their freedoms" (1945, 20).

Le Corbusier sketched general plans for the transformation of Moscow, Stockholm, Barcelona, Algiers, Rio de Janeiro, and Buenos Aires. The Algiers plan (1931–33) is considered by several authors to epitomize Le Corbusier's ideas on urban planning. Le Corbusier put before the municipality of Algiers a series of proposals, each of which he felt to be more detailed than the previous one and in which he suggested the creation of a city of shops at the far end of the bay. This city was to be linked to a high-rise garden residential city by a highway supported on a reinforced concrete structure that would rise between sixty and ninety meters above ground level and under which would be built dwellings for 180,000 people (Le Corbusier 1936, 174–177). This plan is a synthesis of Le Corbusier's "La révolution architecturale apportant la solution au problème de l'urbanisation des grandes villes."

These ideas were previously developed in sketches made by Le Corbusier during short stays in Rio de Janeiro, São Paulo, and Buenos Aires in 1929. His intention, particularly in Rio, was to link the various bays without disturbing the existing city. Hence, his ideas for an elevated highway that would solve the traffic problem, for high-rise housing under the highway, and, subsequently, for the creation of landfill areas, which would provide the main source of funding to finance the work. In his sketches for São Paulo, he persisted with the idea of a greatly elevated highway built upon multifamily housing, this time laid out in a cruciform pattern, possibly in the belief that the natural landscape of São Paulo, lacking the features of Rio de Janeiro, could provide for unlimited expansion. In his plan for Buenos Aires, he suggested building out over the river to create an airport and a landfill area on which he would site "a new city of shops" separated from the existing center by the breakwaters and jetties of the port. On those he proposed to build railroad lines to cross the city.

The last of Le Corbusier's urban plans during the period immediately before the Second World War was a theoretical model that he called La Ville Radieuse, published in 1935 (Le Corbusier 1935). The ideas that culminated in La Ville Radieuse were first developed five years earlier, and they included, among other things, a plan for Moscow, which was his first effort at a "socialist garden city." La Ville Radieuse contained no luxury apartments or basic dwellings as had The Contemporary City for Three Million Inhabitants. All the apartments had fourteen square meters of floor space per person, with accessible communal facilities. The general design of this city contained a single residential area, consisting of continuous lines of monoblocks set in the middle of green areas and facing in different directions, but tightly arranged in a grid of superblocks. The "Unit for Living," in Marseilles, may be considered a practical experiment in the form of living suggested by Le Corbusier in La Ville Radieuse, although on a much smaller scale. The closest realizations of Le Corbusier's concept are the first superblocks and monoblocks built in Brasília almost thirty years after the publication of La Ville Radieuse.

Le Corbusier's influence as architect, urban planner, and writer on the generation of Latin American architects who began work during the 1930s was selective but all-pervasive. This influence stemmed from his visits to the Atlantic port cities; his series of lectures in Buenos Aires in 1929, collected in his book Précisions (1930); and his chief written works, Urbanisme (1924), La Ville Radieuse (1935), and Quand les cathédrales étaient blanches (1937). His role as a founder of the congresses of the CIAM (Congrès International d'Architecture Moderne) in 1928 and as a drafter of the Athens Letter in 1933, which embraced his four main ingredients for the modern city (living, recreation, work, and getting about) also influenced later architects. Moreover, several young Latin American and Spanish architects worked in his Paris atelier in the years immediately surrounding the Second World War—among them, the Spaniards José Luis Sert and Antonio Bonet; the Argentines Jorge Ferrari Hardoy and Juan Kurchan; and the Colombians Germán Samper and Rogelio Salmona. Le Corbusier's influence on urban planning in Latin America is visible in the following instances:

- José Luis Sert (in association with Paul L. Wiener) prepared basic plans for a number of Latin American cities. The best known are those for Havana (in the years before the revolution), Bogotá, Chimbote (Peru), and a new industrial city (Cidade dos Motores) near Rio de Janeiro. In some of these plans Le Corbusier was the adviser. All except the last were soon forgotten.
- In 1947 the municipality of Buenos Aires commissioned Ferrari Hardoy and Kurchan to prepare a basic plan. Consisting of the redesigning of the city into superblocks four blocks long on each side, this plan had been worked out beforehand by the two Argentine architects during their stay in Le Corbusier's atelier in Paris in 1938 and 1939. Many young architects worked on the Buenos Aires plan for five or six years, but none of their proposals were ever implemented.
- In 1956 the municipality of Buenos Aires commissioned Antonio Bonet to redesign the Barrio Sur. Superblocks, high-rise buildings, reclamation of land for green areas, and traffic flow were priorities in the general design Bonet and his large team put together. The project, which was to be financed by the increase of land value as a result of increasing the population density, came to nothing.
- In Brasília, Lúcio Costa's urban plan, which won the prize in the national competition for a framework for the architecture of Oscar Niemeyer and other architects, incorporated some of Le Corbusier's principles. These included the division of city space into functional zones, the use of superblocks and tower blocks, the importance allocated to the flow of vehicular traffic, the maintenance of large green areas, and the severity of the architectural masses in relation to their function.

But the real impact of Le Corbusier and his ideas came through university teaching. Many of his collaborators and disciples occupied teaching positions in universities in North and South America, such as Harvard and the universities of Montevideo, Buenos Aires, and Rosario, as well as universities in Colombia, Chile, and Brazil. The first director of the UN Center for Housing and Planning was the Yugoslav architect Ernest Weissmann, a former Le Corbusier associate. The result of all this teaching was not always a faithful copy of Le Corbusier's ideas. His followers turned toward the design of the city, groups of buildings, and isolated buildings rather than to a discussion of the validity of Le Corbusier's principles in urban situations that were totally different politically, socioeconomically, culturally, demographically, and environmentally. In my opinion, the fundamental mistake made by Le Corbusier and his followers was to believe in what I would call a "universal" application of city planning solutions to radically different problems that change from continent to continent, country to country, region to region, and city to city. Good will in urban design could not solve the problems of cities that doubled their population every eight, ten, or twelve years in a context of great social poverty, inadequate institutional mechanisms, and insufficient investment to undertake works of the scale of the proposals.

In my opinion, the majority of the members of the CIAMs, almost all western Europeans, did not understand Third World cities. Their dogmatism, combined with the personalities and individual roles of the participants, delayed any discussion of the major problems and any common search for solutions. In this sense, their paternalistic attitude is as reprehensible as the philanthropic attitude of the initial promoters of garden cities or those of the non-city, such as Frank Lloyd Wright, against whom the CIAM groups directed their most ferocious criticism.

The cost of constructing and maintaining the cities and the problems of labor were not taken into account by architect-city planners, who dreamed of a technological utopia applied uniformly to Algiers, Rio de Janeiro, Montevideo, and Buenos Aires. People in these cities were to accept living in high-rise buildings and in artificial climates planned thousands of kilometers away by professionals who did not stop to think about these peoples' customs, family organizations, or different uses of time. The creation of wealth through an increase in population density and the direct intervention of a benefactor-administrator state (municipal government, presumably) combined with a strong municipality led by honest, imaginative administrators, would permit the financing of the construction of cities that grew at a rate of hundreds of thousands of new inhabitants each year and in which poverty, informal subsistence economies, and illegal squatting were constant realities. These planners did not try to think of the city and its multiple roles as part of the economy and society of each country, still less of the city's relation to the changing cycles of international economics, which directly influenced through the marketplace and the exportation of technology the productive capacity of those countries and the roles of those cities. The city was seen as a multiple artifact whose use was determined by those who thought they knew how to build and administer it, with land use strictly segregated according to function, an artifact that could not and should not increase beyond predetermined limits. Thus an opportunity was lost just when, after the Second World War, Latin American cities began to grow at a rate without precedent.

UNFULFILLED DEMAND FOR HOUSING

Between 1900 and 1930 the rapid demographic and physical growth of Latin America's main cities continued apace. Buenos Aires's population rose above 2 million; the populations of São Paulo and Mexico City grew to over 1 million; and the populations of Lima, Santiago, Porto Alegre, Bogotá, and Rosario all doubled or tripled, although none reached the million mark. At the same time, Montevideo's and Rio de Janeiro's rates of growth went down in comparison to previous decades, while Havana's accelerated. Even in 1930 the populations of many of the capitals and principal cities of Latin America were no greater than those of a number of large semirural towns (Hardoy and Langdon 1978). Even cities that today have exceeded 1 million or 2 million, such as Guayaquil, Cali, Monterrey, and Guatemala City, or 4 million, like Caracas, then had only about 100,000.

The municipalities resorted to foreign credit for support or awarded concessions for development to foreign firms, carrying on the practice that had prompted the expansion of the drinking water, drainage, tram, and electricity systems in previous decades. Foreign credit was also used to finance street surfacing and to build public markets, welfare department buildings, municipal buildings, and municipal hospitals. Direct foreign investment was used, through development concessions lasting three, four, or more decades, to extend the railroads and construct stations and ports. Sooner or later, all the Latin American countries used direct loans, concessions, or bond issues in an attempt to modernize their cities. By then it was clear that the cities were expanding faster than the capacity of municipal governments to extend the most basic services to the new districts that they sanctioned and incorporated each year on the outskirts of the big cities. The municipalities enjoyed an autonomy that they have not matched since, but their real income was limited, in part because they lacked adequate updating mechanisms and failed to collect property taxes. The main autonomous national government agencies had not yet been established; after the Second World War, these agencies, for good or ill, took on the construction and administration of essential public services. With limited revenue and accumulating debt, many municipalities got into a critical financial state.

During those years some types of low-cost urban housing were duplicated in all the most quickly growing cities in the region. These included rooms rented in old, run-down houses that their owners turned into multitenanted housing almost without services and with windows only onto small courtyards; shanties, built by their inhabitants out of perishable materials and located in small groups close to the center or grouped on empty lots on the outskirts of the city (these heralded the massive settlements that are known today as *villas miserias*); and the tenements built by private entrepreneurs. Information about these kinds of low-cost housing is scant. No details exist on their evolution or on their precise location, still less on the effect of speculative renting on the family budget or of the living conditions and crowding on health.

Skilled workers, clerical workers, and nonmanual workers in general, whose monthly incomes were two or three times higher than those of peasants, waiters, and servants, found another solution. They bought plots offered by private speculative developers in outlying neighborhoods at prices that could be paid off in three or four years (Álvarez Lenzi, Arana, and Bocchiardo 1986). Having acquired the plot, the buyer could then build a house with a state bank mortgage or with credit from the savings and loan system. This choice was quite often taken in Montevideo, Buenos Aires, and Rosario from 1880 to 1890 and from 1910 to 1920, bringing about the physical expansion of those cities, but it was beyond the reach of low-wage workers. I do not think that this situation existed in other Latin American cities at that time, except perhaps, in some Brazilian cities, since salaries elsewhere were considerably lower.

At the end of the century, there was a good deal of confusion about the housing problem. Poor living conditions among working people were recognized by some legislators as well as by some newspapers, writers, and persons with wider vision. Some health experts called attention to the effect of bad sanitation on peoples' health and forced the passage of municipal bills and national laws in support of building regulations. As in the European countries, the first concern was to deal with fire risk. Gradually the municipalities established codes and standards regarding room size, height, and ventilation. The general aim seems to have been to prevent the existing situation from getting even worse and to keep the cities from growing out of control, but little attempt was made to interfere in the undertakings of private individuals. Thus, the municipality's first steps were to lay out the street system, to refuse permission for buildings that did not conform to the new regulations, to site the principal public buildings, and to decide on the architecture of central areas and the limits of urban development where transportation lines were being extended.

The first examples of housing constructed expressly for working-class sectors appeared at the end of the nineteenth century. In Montevideo, a private entrepreneur, Emilio Reus, built two housing projects for workers of 512 and 50 units, respectively, although because of their final cost, they were occupied by the middle class. The French-style architecture made these projects look like certain parts of Paris.

Much more important in that pioneer period were the initiatives of a number of philanthropic societies, most of which were founded by Catholic groups, who built generally small working-class neighborhoods in Buenos Aires, La Plata, and other cities. Their activities were not an attempt to solve the problem of working-class housing, but rather to provide examples of what could be done with limited resources.

The housing that urban workers and their families occupied at the end of the century was, in general, grouped in districts near the city center or in the center itself. Municipal governments encouraged the construction of tenements. These one- or two-story buildings consisted of rooms along a central or lateral corridor, with few communal sanitary services and those few of the worst quality, quickly built, often of cheap materials. Given their high rental potential, they attracted the interest of factories, businesses, and private investors. At that time some firms constructed tenements to rent to their workers. Usually they were built close to the factories to reduce the time lost in traveling in a period of inadequate public transportation. In other instances, old houses, vacated by their owners who had moved to less congested districts with better air, were converted into multitenanted housing for families on low incomes, with communal services often even worse than those of the tenements.

These multitenanted houses, both types of which had certain architectural features in common, were set out in lines along the streets of proletarian neighborhoods, and sometimes they took many years to complete. They were not planned as such. They simply reflected private initiatives with respect to maximum usage of ground area without any attention paid to basic services—shops, for example. The result of this continuous demand for housing in the central districts of the cities was overcrowding, very poor sanitation, and a lack of basic social amenities. In a situation of rapid demographic growth, such conditions escaped control of the municipalities of the time.

Nor did this type of housing offer the occupants any choice; it was the only option that the private market offered. These constructions were not the work of architects or engineers but of bricklayers or builders, who used endlessly repeated floor plans.

The municipalities lacked resources to undertake workers' housing, and many years went by before the national and provincial governments intervened directly. Their main concern turned toward the health of the city and, in consequence, to regulating the layout and alignment of buildings, fundamental conditions for incorporating water, sewage, and public transportation systems, and for paving the roads.

There were, however, some municipal initiatives. In 1883 the municipality of Buenos Aires authorized the construction of four model neighborhoods whose plans, significantly, were approved by the Department of Health. One of them was begun two years later in the middle of Buenos Aires's Barrio Norte—nowadays one of the city's most expensive residential districts—and was made up of units of from one to three dwellings fronting on and lined up along passages six meters wide, with communal bathrooms.

Some industrial firms tried to create working-class neighborhoods near their factories, but, in general, these undertakings went no further than the creation of allotments, with their central square, school, and church, leaving the construction up to the workers.

Less affected by European immigration than the cities of the Atlantic coast, Santiago de Chile nonetheless was inundated with migrants from the rural areas and the mining provinces of the north, when there was a crisis in production there. In 1912, 73,030 people congregated in the northern part of Santiago into 26,972 rooms, a situation that broke all the health regulations (Gross, de Ramón, and Vial 1984). The Chilean tenements, like those of Buenos Aires, Rosario, and Montevideo, were also arranged around a common courtyard or a blind corridor. Their demolition threw thousands of families into the streets.

In Chile the first initiatives for better housing came from philanthropic institutions and the activity of Catholic groups. Concentrated within the city limits, these efforts were intended to solve the demand of some needy families and to show the advantages of better quality housing. I do not think that these institutions tried to solve the problem of working-class housing in this way alone, but they tested some interesting points. With similar backing, in the 1890s small neighborhoods in Santiago were begun, among them Mercedes Valdés, San Vicente, Pedro Lagos, and another promoted by the Leo XIII Foundation. Altogether these represented a contribution of several hundred modest dwellings.

In 1906 the government, influenced by Belgian and French legislation, passed a law on workers' housing that backed the creation of departmental councils for such housing. In 1911, a neighborhood of seventy dwellings was inaugurated in Santiago—part of a larger project—financed by a special mortgage credit fund, and another hundred dwellings were given full services. In the following years similar projects were inaugurated, but they were too few to fulfill the increasing demand, which was exacerbated by the continuous demolition of tenements. Up to 1925 the initiatives of the philanthropic institutions were much wider than those of public institutions. In 1925, a law was approved for the promotion of low-cost housing; this replaced the 1906 law and served to launch some neighborhoods of public housing.

INADEQUATE PLANNING

The first official banks for housing date from the end of the century, although the first construction with direct state assistance came considerably later. The National Mortgage Bank of Argentina was set up in 1886 to counteract high-interest short-term credit, which made credit inaccessible to most of the population; its instrument was the mortgage contract, which could be privately acquired and was issued at an interest rate based on market values (Yujnovsky 1984). The Workers Bank of Venezuela was founded in 1927, but its activities were very limited until the 1940s, when it intervened directly in the demolition of several slum areas in the center of Caracas, replacing them with apartment blocks. Chile established a Peoples' Housing Fund in 1936; Colombia's Commission for Workers' Housing dates from 1932; the National Mortgage Bank of Guatemala, from 1935. Ecuador organized a pension fund and a fund for private-sector employees and workers in 1928 and 1938, respectively. These assisted in the construction of housing. The activities of these organizations were at first very limited and only from the 1930s on did some governments begin to give direct aid to the construction of housing. I believe that even today no Latin American country builds more than three units of housing per year per thousand people, taking both private and public sectors into account. I estimate that the need varies between eight and twelve units per year per thousand, according to country. Consequently, the housing situation has steadily worsened.

Since the 1920s in Buenos Aires and Santiago, and a little later in Lima, Caracas, and other cities, the working-class population has had to find its own solutions to the problems of housing.

The contemporary movement in city planning began in the 1930s and 1940s. Two parallel movements emerged, both backed by those municipalities interested in regulating growth in their jurisdictions and improving transportation and sanitary conditions. The following are instances of this.

In 1902 it was decreed that all Peruvian cities should draw up urban plans to deal with the narrowness of their streets, a lack of squares, and badly aligned frontages that resulted in poor sanitary conditions, inadequate air circulation and movement, and bad drainage. The responsibility fell on the municipalities, which, because they received no aid from the central government, interpreted the decree as well as they could or wanted. Similar legislation for La Paz, Bolivia, dates from 1914, but it was also ineffective. In 1929 Chile passed a law placing the obligation for preparing urban alteration plans on all municipalities of more than 20,000 inhabitants.

Some municipal planning offices were set up in the 1930s. The planning office of Buenos Aires was set up in 1932. In 1937 the mayor of Rio de Janeiro set up a city planning commission. Montevideo's Basic Planning Department was established in the same period.

But the municipalities also relied on consultants to prepare basic plans. These consultants, often Europeans, inaugurated a period that went on in some countries until the postwar years. They tried to provide a complete physical vision of the future city, including expansion in outlying areas that were already partly built up and subdivided, but they ignored several basic points. Their plans were theoretical, based on good will on a grand scale, and did little to address the cities' problems, which, in fact, were caused by administrative inadequacies at national and regional levels.

BREAKDOWN OF THE CITIES

From at least the 1930s on, breakdown began to occur in those cities that were the first to experience rapid urbanization—Buenos Aires,

Rio de Janeiro, Montevideo, São Paulo, and Santiago de Chile. From the 1940s and 1950s on, this also took place in Lima, Caracas, Bogotá, Mexico, and other cities. The breakdown was partly due to a concentration on individual projects that had been approved. In Buenos Aires, Montevideo, and in all the larger cities, the incorporation of suburban railroads and the rapid spread of tramline systems and later the bus service significantly widened the area that could potentially be urbanized. The construction and growth of the cities in those decades of accelerated physical and demographic growth was almost solely due to a combination of private initiative—mostly with speculative aims—in individual projects unconnected with the infrastructure. As a result, large numbers of inhabitants were left out. At the same time many serious problems pertaining to an expanding city were overlooked.

Advances in health and sanitation were significant, at least theoretically. But in practice, the working population, badly paid or unemployed, had to find its own solutions to basic problems of survival. The most recent solutions to the housing problem have been the land invasions (in organized groups or piecemeal), the buying of illegally subdivided plots, and crowding in tenements. The first two encouraged the horizontal sprawl of cities; the last, overcrowding. Settlers often occupied land subject to floods and landslides, endangering the safety of the occupants. Access to health services and to sources of work became more and more difficult. There seemed to be an apparent indifference or management incapacity to face these problems as a whole. At a time when neighborhood and district problems could have been attacked at a city level, planners chose to insist on uncoordinated individual projects.

This limited outlook continued after the 1950s. The construction of cities was still dominated by isolated projects, by regulations that tried to limit ground use of neighborhoods to a single function, and by building codes that a growing number of inhabitants, forced to construct or convert their houses without enough money, could not fulfill. This narrow vision was reinforced as the municipalities lost many of their economic and political powers, the result of lack of continuity in government policy and an increase in centralized power, particularly during the period of military dictatorships. The municipalities play almost no role in the economic and social development of their countries. Restricted to collecting rates and taxes that go into national and provincial budgets, reduced to waiting for the return of funds from centralized distribution points, the municipalities' access to investments has been further and further diminished. These signs were already evident in the 1930s and 1940s.

REFERENCES

Álvarez Lenzi, Ricardo, Mariano Arana, and Livia Bocchiardo. 1986. *El Montevideo de la expansión (1868–1915)*. Montevideo: Ediciones de la Banda Oriental.

Breitling, Peter. 1980. "The Role of the Competition in the Genesis of Urban Planning: Germany and Austria in the Nineteenth Century." In *The Rise of Modern Urban Planning, 1800–1914*, Anthony Sutcliffe, ed. London: Mansell.

Cerdá, Ildefonso. 1867. *Teoría general de la Urbanización*. 2 vols. Madrid: Imprenta Española.

Choay, Françoise. 1969. *The Modern City: Planning in the 19th Century*. New York: George Braziller.

Collins, George R., and Christiane Collins. 1965. *Camillo Sitte and the Birth of Modern City Planning*. London: Phaidon Press.

Forestier, Jean C. N. 1925. Report to the Mayor of Buenos Aires, 1924. *Proyecto Orgánico para la Urbanización del Municipio: El Plano Regulador y de Reforma de la Capital Federal*. Buenos Aires: Intendencia Municipal, Comisión de Estética Edilicia, Talleres Penser. Pp. 367–423.

Giedion, Sigfried. 1955. *Espacio, tiempo y arquitectura*. Barcelona: Hoepli S.L.

Gross, Patricio, Armando de Ramón, and Enrique Vial. 1984. *Imagen ambiental de Santiago, 1880–1930*. Santiago: Ediciones Universidad Católica de Chile.

Hardoy, Jorge E. 1972. "Las formas urbanas europeas durante los siglos XV al XVII y su utilización en América Latina. Notas sobre el transplante de la teoría y práctica urbanística de españoles, portugueses, holandeses, ingleses y franceses." *Actas del XXXIX Congreso Internacional de Americanistas*. 2:157–90.

Hardoy, Jorge E., and María Elena Langdon. 1978. "Análisis estadístico preliminar de la urbanización de América Latina entre 1850 y 1930." *Revista Paraguaya de Sociología*. 15:42/43, 115–73.

Haussmann, Georges-Eugène. 1890. *Mémoires du Baron Haussmann*. Paris: Victor Havard (especially vol. 2, ch. 12–16).

Lavedan, Pierre. 1952. *Histoire de l'urbanisme*. vol. 3, ch. 3. Paris: Henri Laurens.

Le Corbusier. 1935. *La Ville Radieuse*. Boulogne-sur-Seine: Editions de l'Architecture d'Aujourd'hui.

———. 1936. *Oeuvre Complète de 1929–1934*. Zurich: Les Editions d'Architecture, Erlenbach.

———. 1939. *Oeuvre Complète de 1934–1938*. Zurich: Les Editions d'Architecture, Erlenbach.

———. 1945. *Oeuvre Complète, 1934–1938*, 2nd ed. Zurich: Les Editions d'Architecture, Erlenbach.

———. 1946. *Oeuvre Complète de 1910–1929*. Zurich: Les Editions d'Architecture, Erlenbach.

Needell, Jeffrey D. 1985. "La belle époque carioca en concreto: las reformas de Rio de Janeiro bajo la dirección de Pereira Passos." In *Cultura urbana latinoamericana*, Richard M. Morse and Jorge E. Hardoy, eds. Buenos Aires: Ediciones CLACSO.

Pinkney, David. 1958. *Napoleon III and the Rebuilding of Paris*. Princeton, N.J.: Princeton University Press.

Poëte, Marcel. 1924. *Une vie de cité: Paris de sa naissance à nos jours*. Paris: A. Picard.

Saalman, Howard. 1971. *Haussmann: Paris Transformed*. New York: George Braziller.

Schorske, Carl E. 1981. *Fin-de-Siècle Vienna: Politics and Culture*. New York: Vintage Books.

Segre, Roberto. 1984. "El sistema monumental en la ciudad de La Habana: 1900–1930." *La Habana: 465 aniversario, Revista de la Universidad de La Habana*. No. 222 (January–September).

Sutcliffe, Anthony. 1981. *Towards the Planned City, Germany, Britain, the United States and France, 1782–1914*. Oxford, England: Basil Blackwell.

Tarn, John Nelson. 1980. "Housing Reform and the Emergence of Town Planning in Britain before 1914." In *The Use of Modern Urban Planning*, Anthony Sutcliffe, ed. London: Mansell.

Wagner, Otto. 1895. *Moderne Architektur*. Vienna: A. Schroll.

————. 1911. *Die Groszstadt*. Vienna: A. Schroll.

Weber, Adna. 1963. *The Growth of Cities in the Nineteenth Century*. Ithaca, N.Y.: Cornell University Press.

Yujnovsky, Oscar. 1984. *Claves políticas del problema habitacional argentino*. Buenos Aires: Grupo Editor Latinoamericano.

3

Transitional Cities

Bryan Roberts

One of the most confusing images of Latin American cities is that of urbanization itself. Although a neutral term, referring to the proportions living in urban and rural places, the word conjures up a picture of an ineluctable process by which people progressively move to live in cities; the village, the "world we have lost," is replaced by the permanent new world of the city. The image is one of a historically discrete period of high mobility—the period of rapid urbanization—in which people make the change between two worlds, each with its peculiar culture and different demands on its inhabitants. For Latin America, the problem with the image is that the transition it depicts from one steady state to another obscures a salient feature of population history—the fact that mobility is a constant feature of the way the population copes with its environment, whether rural or urban.

My topic is the contemporary spatial mobility of the Latin American urban population. Population mobility continues even though the large-scale displacements of people from rural to urban areas are, in many areas, now coming to an end. In the contemporary cities of Latin America, people cope through moving, seeking out new opportunities, at times returning to their original homes, at times shifting, more or less permanently, their base. This movement, within cities and between them, is, I will argue, unlikely to be a temporary phenomenon because it results from inherent instabilities in the region's pattern of economic and political development.

Urban-based population mobility is not the same as rural-based mobility, nor does it have the same consequences. But there are continuities that should be recognized. Amidst apparently far-reaching changes in ways of life, some historical constancy appears in the basic strategies and elements of social structure. In coping with an unstable and unpredictable social and economic environment, contemporary Latin Americans use the same basic strategies as their predecessors in the colonial period.

STAGES IN POPULATION MOBILITY

Some time ago, Morse contrasted the centrifugal and centripetal stages in Latin American urban development. One characteristic of the centrifugal stage, the colonial period and the nineteenth century, was that the cities served to organize the economic exploitation of the rural hinterland. This hinterland was the major area of settlement, subsistence, and wealth creation. It was, however, an unstable source of livelihood, as areas flourished and declined with the vagaries of export agriculture and changes in cropping patterns. As Morse (1962, 368) put it, "Latin American rural settlement, however, was exploitative, badly articulated and, we might say, of a provisional nature."

Though there were settled areas, the opening up of the rural hinterland entailed considerable population movement, a movement that has continued to this day as the frontier regions of Latin America have been brought into production. Recurrent agricultural crises led landowners to eject dependent peasants, and peasants to seek their fortunes far afield (Scardaville 1977). The urban centers were firm points amid this mobility, concentrating charity and wealth and offering the prospect, at least, of subsistence for those unable to survive in the countryside.

Population movement in these cities was undoubtedly high, since the cities served as bridgeheads for colonization. Migration to the city was a continuous process, reflecting not only rural instability, but also the continuing demand of the urban economy for labor in the face of high urban mortality. The economy of the colonial city generated only a relatively small amount of stable employment. Apart from a few textile centers and tobacco factories, there were few large-scale industrial enterprises. The core of the colonial urban economy was servicing the resident elites. The administrators, landowners, mine-owners, and important merchants employed a vast retinue of servants and hangers-on, and were the main customers of the urban craftsmen and traders.

The variety of crafts was enormous. Many of these were organized into guilds, which ensured some occupational stability because children could, with less time and expense, take up their parents' craft. But guild organization was weak, facing competition from immigrant, often Indian, craftsmen, who were tolerated by the colonial regimes. Most work was to be found in construction activities or the services, and in unskilled and unstable jobs. Mining and textile centers offered more stable and better-paid employment, but in these, also, there was a substantial number of service workers whose jobs and residence were unstable. In addition, all colonial cities had a contingent of workers who came in daily or seasonally from nearby villages in search of work. The resulting social structure was a fluid one, with relatively little spatial segregation between different classes and high intermarriage between ethnic groups (Van Young 1987).

A different type of population mobility appeared in the centripetal stage of urban development, which began in the early twentieth century in countries such as Argentina and Brazil, and as late as the 1950s in countries that were slow to industrialize. The cities grew relative to the rural areas as industry became an important source of job opportunities. Economic modernization went hand in hand with political centralization and pro-urban development policies, leading to a rapid expansion of urban infrastructure and the urban-based state bureaucracy.

Mobility was mainly the one-way movement of individuals and families from rural areas and small towns to the cities. There was return migration, but now the "permanent" urban population increasingly included large numbers of migrants seeking to subsist in the city. One of Morse's points is that the urban migrations brought to the cities people whose patterns of coping were based on rural structures that were as fluid as the urban structures. Kinship and fictive kinship linkages, rather than age-old corporate allegiances, had been the major source of solidarity and getting-by in the countryside, as they had been in the cities. These flexible instruments were the means by which families would cope in the cities. With the important exception of Lima, regional or ethnic solidarities were not institutionalized as means of adapting to urban life (Roberts 1974). Caste-like differences between migrants and natives in residence or economic position did not appear in the Latin American city. In the various studies of occupational mobility in the cities of this period, which was one of general economic expansion, migrants and natives showed similar patterns of mobility (Balán, Jelin, and Browning 1973).

The cities were not anonymous and impersonal places, but absorbed large numbers of migrants who made their way with the help of kin and friends. Family was not undermined, but strengthened. Religious observance continued and perhaps was more assiduous in the city, especially if the new sectarian groups are taken into account.

What was lacking was the formal paraphernalia of cities, as described by the sociologists of modern urban life: voluntary associations, class-based organizations, settled neighborhoods of owners and renters. The growing cities were not, however, filled with a disorganized mass. Rather, as Morse (1962, 372) wrote, "there is archaic, paternalistic centralization of control at the top and a multitude of quasi-familial, potentially vital social cells at the bottom, with weak structures of organizations mediating between them." This account was written about thirty years ago, and this is a good opportunity to review the changes since that time. What can be learned about the future of the Latin American city from knowing what has happened to the cities since that first period of massive urban growth based on internal population movements?

In the third and contemporary stage of population movement, migration from the countryside becomes less important as a component of mobility—more of the city population will be born in the city and less will be born elsewhere—if only because the reservoir of rural population declines and cities inevitably become the major sources of new population. A different type of mobility emerges under these conditions. Now the cities export their population, usually to other cities. Mobility becomes more an inter-urban (and intra-urban) phenomenon. Thus, while the percentage of Mexico City's population born elsewhere declined steadily from 1950 to 1980, the percentage of the population born in that city who reside elsewhere in Mexico increased from 1950 to 1980. Cities also become the place of residence for rural workers, as in the case of the *boias frias* of Brazil who live in the towns of São Paulo and the northeast, and commute to work in the coffee and sugar plantations.

RURAL COLLAPSE: THE CITY AS SUBSISTENCE BASE

The present stage of population mobility occurs alongside the collapse of peasant farming in face of economic growth and changes in the organization and relationships of the international economy. Agriculture has been modernized to produce new export crops, such as soya, and to produce the old ones more efficiently. It has also been modernized to produce foodstuffs for the internal urban market, which has multiplied tenfold in the last twenty years. Modernization has meant mechanization and the use of technological packages whose costs demand a commercial attitude to farming. Peasant farming is ceasing to be a viable option throughout the continent, although its demise is obscured by variations between countries and regions in the rate of growth of commercial farming. Where subsistence farming continues, as in the case of the "repeasantization" of areas of the north and northeast of Brazil, it is made possible by government handouts, such as pensions or subsidies, that are paid for political reasons, often to stem rural outmigration.

Previously, in the centrifugal and, to an extent, in the centripetal stage, migration had been a time-honored strategy used to complement subsistence farming. The migrants often returned to their rural base. The more permanent migration of the centripetal stage made return migration a less common event, but the most common form of migration was that of individuals, usually young males and females, who, without family, sought better opportunities in the cities. Other family members might follow later, but, in this centripetal stage, the household of origin usually remained based in the village, maintaining contacts with those of its members who had left for the city.

In the present stage of mobility, these rural-urban relationships are likely to weaken and disappear. This claim may appear premature in face of the lively exchanges between town and countryside that still occur in countries such as Peru, Bolivia, and Mexico. But two factors, even in these countries, suggest the gradual ending of rural-urban linkages based on kinship and former membership in an existing rural household. One factor is the death of the older generations who had remained behind, but more significant is the fact that their role and linkages are not reproduced. Second, contemporary migrations are increasingly likely to consist in the exodus of whole households as rural areas cease to meet the subsistence needs of family members.

This exodus occurs because in many areas of Latin America there is no longer the local means to maintain even part of a household in rural areas, even with remittances or savings from migrant household members. Rural areas are increasingly losing their capacity to service the needs of subsistence households: crafts disappear; foodstuffs are imported from the city; local systems of credit, mutual aid, and even health care weaken. Whole families get up and go because the basis of household subsistence is now more easily found in the city. There, members of the household in addition to the main breadwinner can find some paid work, even if it is part-time and poorly remunerated. Health and educational services are more readily available in the cities. The density of urban relationships, based on crowded neighborhoods and cheap transport systems, provides systems of mutual aid.

Rural means of coping with a subsistence economy are, in effect, transferred to the city. This is a metaphorical rather than a real transfer, since the astute combination of self-help and mutual aid, based on using migration and the labor inputs of most members of a household, is also an age-old coping device of urban households. Indeed, where labor migration is used as a strategy of household survival, even among farm workers, the permanent base of the household is now often a city or town. I referred above to the phenomenon of the *boias frias* in Brazil, in which the household's base is urban because of the facilities and income opportunities the town or city offers, while the "main" employment is that of rural laborer. Another example of this pattern of survival is found in the towns close to the fruit-producing areas of the central valley in Chile.

THE INSTABILITY OF URBAN ECONOMIES

The "push" factors leading to permanent migration to the cities are not the only ones accounting for that migration. Urban economies in most Latin American countries have grown rapidly in the decades since the 1950s. This economic growth has usually been sufficient to ensure rising real incomes for urban workers, including categories, such as domestic servants, that are mainly drawn from rural migrants (Gregory 1986). Despite fears to the contrary, there was little evidence in the 1960s and 1970s that substantial sectors of the urban population were unemployed or otherwise marginal to the urban economy as a result of an oversupply of labor, in part due to the migration of the rural poor.

This optimistic picture always needed to be qualified in the case of the Southern Cone, and became increasingly inapplicable elsewhere with the debt-linked recession of the 1980s. Also, economic growth, where it occurred, did not guarantee stable employment or the prospect of upward social mobility through job careers in large-scale enterprises. Urban economic growth was based on the proliferation of small-scale enterprises. It entailed, in large as well as small enterprises, flexibility in hiring and firing labor, provided little social security, and, despite rises in real incomes, still left half the urban population living at or below the poverty line. Even in the growth years, the urban economies of Latin America were characterized by the readiness of their inhabitants to accept part-time employment at low wages, by the frequency of self-employment, and by the common phenomenon of unpaid family labor. The household, not the individual, became the basic wage-earning unit, and membership in a household was both essential to, and part of, an individual's wage-earning strategies.

In certain countries and cities more than others, these trends were offset by the continued strength of labor unions, by the presence of large-scale enterprises such as automobile factories and steel mills, and, perhaps above all, by the growth of state employment. The state, in most Latin American countries, offered low-paying but secure urban employment. Indeed, an important strategy for families struggling to make ends meet in the city was to secure one stable and protected source of employment that would not only guarantee a steady, if low, income, but also provide social security benefits.

The instability of urban job opportunities is thus a caricature of the Latin American labor market, but it is a useful one because the Latin American urban economies are unlikely to offer the types of stable work opportunities that would encourage families to settle permanently in any one city. The present trend is for labor to be treated as provisional. Labor is provisional from the point of view of employers when they are not prepared to commit themselves to particular workers and/or their skills. As people age they are replaced. As technology changes, so too can the gender, age, and skill profiles of the labor force. From the perspective of workers, their labor is provisional when they do not expect to commit themselves to careers in particular lines of work or are not interested in improving those skills that are specific to a particular job. A work history becomes opportunistic, with workers shifting jobs depending on relative pay and conditions of work, fluctuations in the urban economy, and changing family circumstances. Although these changes are often forced upon workers, they are, in part, a result of their expectations—of what is likely to happen as they grow older, of the need to prepare in advance for job loss, of fitting jobs to changes in their needs for income as expenditures temporarily increase or decrease.

The prevalence of informal employment is part of this context. This type of employment is not regulated by the state, receives no social security coverage, and is unprotected by labor contracts that guarantee some stability of employment. Informal employment opportunities are found throughout the urban economy, and large as well as small firms have recourse to them (Escobar 1986). The reasons for informal employment are various and familiar. The rapid expansion of the urban economies has been based on capital-intensive strategies of industrialization in which the supplies of unskilled and semiskilled labor are usually first absorbed through labor-intensive activities of low productivity: construction, service activities of various kinds, or small-scale "sweat shops." The profitability of these activities depends on an intense exploitation of labor and on cutting down overhead costs such as social security, taxes, and facilities. Market uncertainties and the seasonal or cyclical nature of demand for certain products and services further ensure that even large, formal enterprises employ informal workers, who can be taken on or laid off depending on the state of the market.

Even the formal labor market is unlikely to compensate by increasing its offer of secure jobs as the urban economies improve. Instead, the uncertainty of urban employment is likely to increase. In the manufacturing industry, the major sources of urban employment in the future are likely to concentrate in types of production demanding unskilled and semiskilled labor and in which labor turnover is high. Assembly plants are becoming more representative of manufacturing industries than are those industries that demand craft skills of their workers and offer internal promotion opportunities. Of even greater significance for employment prospects is the preponderance of service jobs. Professional and technical staff may appear to epitomize such services as banking or the social services; but even in these sectors, many jobs are dead-end, such as those of janitors, cooks, cleaners, and secretaries. State employment, long the mainstay of the growth in secure white-collar work, will become a less dynamic source of employment as budget crises and new economic models aimed at liberalizing the economy force cutbacks in state expenditures. Other service sectors such as retail and consumer services are even more weighted to low-paying jobs with no prospects of advancement. This is the reality behind the trend to the service economy in the United States, and it is a trend that is likely to be more intense in the Latin American economies (Noyelle and Stanback 1984, 230–31).

The low-paid and insecure jobs that are being created in the urban economies are often for women. The increase in the proportions of women working for pay results less from the emancipation of women from their traditional roles and their pursuit of a career, than from the demands of industry for a cheap, adaptable, and essentially provisional labor force. The new economic role of women is often little more than the intensification of domestic labor, working outside the home as domestics for others, sewing, preparing food for sale, and so on. Assembly work in the new high-technology industries is becoming concentrated among young, unmarried women who will work for a number of years at routine tasks with no promotion prospects and substantially lower pay rates than male workers performing similar tasks. Women are easily cast in the role of temporary workers—either filling in the years before marriage or as part-time workers—because of prevailing norms, especially among low-income families, that their earnings only supplement other sources of household income and that their main responsibility is with domestic chores.

MIGRATION AND THE URBAN SYSTEM

The consequence of provisional structures will be population movement within cities, between them, and across international borders. Little is known about the frequency with which people change their residences within Latin American cities, and impressions are contradictory. The prevalence of rental housing of various kinds, the *vecinidades, cortiços, inquilinatos, conventillos,* and *coralones* in city centers probably encouraged movement when cities expanded rapidly in the 1950s and 1960s, as individuals and households sought more spacious accommodation or places nearer to their jobs. Yet, in many cities, frozen rents must have contributed to keeping the poor in central city rental accommodations. Furthermore, the networks of mutual aid that arise in the dense environments of these tenements are also likely to discourage movement. As self-help housing became an increasingly important part of the housing stock—in squatter settlements or semi-legal subdivisions—there was the appearance of greater stability in the housing market, even if the buildings themselves were provisional, allowing for additions and subtractions depending on the needs and resources of their occupants. Once a family was established in a squatter settlement, it was unlikely to give up the space that it had fought for and in which it had invested so much time and resources.

However, there are indications of growing instability in respect to housing. As the cities get larger, and the journey to work grows longer, the pressure mounts for people to move more frequently to be nearer to work. People also move out of the cities to find work elsewhere. These movements are predominantly to other urban places, since those are where the job opportunities are. In certain times and places, some urban migrants may return to the countryside, especially when they retain some economic links to rural enterprise. For most, however, the countryside offers few possibilities for subsistence in comparison with the other cities of the urban system. All these movements are themselves provisional in nature, as people test out new ground and new opportunities, deciding perhaps to stay or, in disillusion or because of information from remaining kin or friends about better opportunities, to return to their original neighborhood or city.

The broader reasons for the population movement are both political and economic. The land and housing markets in the Latin American cities are, in practice, unregulated and unconstrained by popular needs and demands because these have no effective political channel. The problem of providing adequate housing and infrastructure for the mass of the urban population is handled by manipulating space and the rights of different groups to it. Granting titles to land to legitimize and promote self-construction is a more common form of meeting the housing needs of the poor than is providing them with cheap housing or needed infrastructure such as sewage disposal or a water and electricity supply (Gilbert and Ward 1985).

The politics of housing in Latin America consists in the lobbying activities of land speculators and the construction industry who are primarily interested in profitable projects, and these do not include low-income housing. As Kowarick (1977) pointed out some years ago, the disorder of the Latin American city has a consistent logic. It is a logic based on land speculation and the politics of providing urban infrastructure. The construction or urban infrastructure that benefits business, such as transit systems and highways, is more profitable than the building of low-cost housing and is therefore given priority. As the cities expand, central low-income neighborhoods are torn down or remodeled, and their inhabitants must seek accommodation where they can. The housing to which many dwellers in Rio's shantytowns were relocated in the 1970s was so distant from the center and their places of work that most soon left.

The process is not one of orderly expansion, in which outlying zones gradually acquire different residential characteristics as the central business zone expands. Rather, urban space is being recycled constantly through the uncoordinated actions of speculators, landowners, businesses, and people desperately seeking accommodation within their means that will cut down the journey to work (Batley 1983). Rental has become prevalent in squatter settlements too, and, as various authors have pointed out, such settlements eventually become a normal part of the housing market of a city, with people buying, selling, and renting according to changes in their life cycle and economic circumstances (Gilbert and Ward 1985, 246–50).

Economic forces affecting the region's urban system are additional factors creating population movement. The contemporary economic growth of Latin America has stimulated not only the growth in size of the urban system, but its diversification. Cities specialize in different types of production or are locked into regional economies whose fortunes depend on varied forms of insertion into the national and international economy. In times of national growth, some cities will expand faster than others, and in times of recession, there will be differences in the degree of stagnation. Nor are these variations likely to be consistent, so that the places that benefit from expansion are best able to endure recession. There is a constant flux in the fortunes of Latin America's cities. Heralded growth points, such as the oil-related towns of Mexico or Peru's fish-meal city of Chimbote, attract migrants for a period but are superseded by new boom places, which shift the balance of the national economy.

This flux is likely to be an enduring feature of the Latin American economies. Their increasing openness to international trade and investment in the manufacturing and service industries, as well as in the extractive ones, encourages a form of economic development akin to slash-and-burn agriculture: intensive, but often brief, experimentation with virgin urban territories attractive not because of their fixed resources, but because of more temporary resources, such as an amenable and abundant labor supply.

A further consequence of the diversification and volatility of the urban system is international migration. The phenomenon is continent-wide, although most attention has been given to migration from Mexico to the United States. The growing heterogeneity of economic development in the Americas, and between the countries of Latin America, juxtaposes rich and poor regions, labor-scarce and labor-abundant economies. Migrants flow from Bolivia to Argentina, from Colombia to Venezuela, and from most Latin American countries to the United States and Canada, despite the distances involved. Migration to the United States has long been part of the way individuals and communities supplement the livelihoods they can make locally. Despite the substantial accumulation of migrants who take up permanent residence in the United States, most of this migration has been, and is, temporary. People leave periodically, or for a period of years, to try their fortunes in U.S. labor markets, but the intention is usually to return; many migrants leave families behind who depend upon them for some or all of their subsistence.

In recent years the migrants from Mexico and their destinations have changed; rural migrants to agricultural areas in the United States are giving way to urban migrants moving to U.S. urban areas. While labor flows from Mexico to U.S. cities, capital and goods flow in the reverse direction. These cities are becoming part of the same system. The international migration from other parts of Latin America reflect in a similar fashion the increasing incorporation of both rural and urban areas into a continental, even worldwide, urban-based economic system. As the city, not the countryside, becomes the major basis of subsistence and the principal dormitory of Latin America, so the region's inhabitants become more dependent on, and sensitive to, the linkages and opportunities of the international urban economy. The goods residents purchase, the media to which they are exposed, and the networks they use to find work increasingly make foreign cities, whether elsewhere in Latin America or in the United States, appear as a normal part of their labor market. To many small-town inhabitants of Jalisco, Los Angeles is as much part of their labor market as is Guadalajara. For many people in Bolivia, Buenos Aires is a more realistic labor market than La Paz.

An appropriate image for the future of the Latin American city is given by one of the United States' most provisional, but visually spectacular, cities, Houston. That image needs to be merged with the image of a labor camp providing temporary accommodation for workers who can be flexibly allocated according to shifts in the national and international economy. Labor camps usually have relatively few permanent structures apart from those designed for control, administration, and production. The fine structures are designed to house and meet the needs of others than the nighttime denizens of the camps. Infrastructure is basic, mainly to ensure that the essential economic functions are maintained with minor concern for the welfare or comfort of the inhabitants. This vision is premature, and is still distant from Latin American reality, especially in the older and more sedate cities of the continent, but it helps account for the general climate of disregard for planning and developing the city to fit the needs of its inhabitants.

THE INCREASING POPULATION CONCENTRATION

The migrations of recent years have been associated with increasing population concentration in a few cities (Browning 1987). Urbanization in Latin America has not resulted in an even spread of towns and cities, hierarchically ordered in terms of population size and the flows of goods and services. It has been a disordered process in which the large cities deal directly with the smallest villages, often bypassing intermediate places, whether trading or administrative centers. Likewise, the dominant flows of population have been to the large centers, so that, for rural migrants, provincial towns are often no more than a temporary stopping-place on their journey to the distant metropolis.

The smaller cities have often shown faster rates of growth than the metropolis, but that has not produced a more even distribution of population. These smaller cities are of two types: essentially satellite towns on the fringes of the metropolis, or new growth centers fostered by external planning and investment. These latter centers depend on political whim, as in the search for new capitals in several Latin American countries, or on the opportunistic location of large foreign or domestic enterprises seeking "green field" sites, such as the Ford Motor Company in Hermosillo, Mexico.

Neither type is indicative of even regional development powered by cities and towns of diverse sizes performing different but interdependent functions within the regional economy. Instead, their growth reflects, and contributes to, the volatility of urban systems that have shallow roots in their own regional markets and are increasingly dependent on the international economy.

Population concentration—the continuing primacy of the Latin American urban systems—does not create a stable population. The large cities grow ever larger, both through natural increase and migration, but their population is a changing one. Cities export their populations to other cities or abroad in search of new opportunities or as a consequence of economic interdependence, as when banks or large industrial corporations send their employees from one place to another. Primacy, under modern conditions, entails the disappearance of regionally specific work skills and traditions. The concentration of industrial production and producer services in a few metropolises, reduces the autonomy of provisional places. Local decisions over credit, for instance, are less likely to be decided by the village moneylender or town banker and more likely to be referred to the central bank or government agency. Increasingly, industrial production at the local level is carried out through branch plants of firms headquartered in the large city. These are familiar processes in the developed world, and in the years from 1960 to the present, they have become integral features of the Latin American economic landscape.

As economic concentration and interdependence strengthens, there is little to anchor people in any one location. Their work skills are transportable nationally or internationally. With time, their social networks, even those based on kinship, will include a number of other large cities, both foreign and national, facilitating movement. The continuing and, in some cases, strengthening of primacy is thus a factor in the mobility of the Latin American populations. Primacy is, essentially, a structural relation, reflecting the imbalance in power and economic resources between the major urban center(s) and the rest of the country. It is a constantly destabilizing relation, encouraging movement within a country and between countries. Although economic opportunities are concentrated in primate cities, their power of attraction is much greater than their capacity to create stable jobs for all their inhabitants. Their very dynamism leads to a recycling of their population. So too their sensitivity to external linkages contributes to their instability.

THE BASES OF ORDER

Mobility has been one of the chief bases of order of the Latin American urban populations. The expansion of the urban economies has been, in most cases, sufficient to bring a rise in living standards for all the population. The rise has, to be sure, been greater for the upper and middle classes, but even the poorest segments of the population have seen some improvement. This improvement has been the more significant because the comparisons are not made with more affluent urban groups, but, usually, with rural inhabitants. The rural living conditions of Latin America were, and are, much inferior to the urban, whether the measure be that of housing, amenities, or health and educational facilities. Rural life is, with some periodic exceptions, one of drudgery in which from the very early years until old age, people work long hours in home or field. Even the conditions of the slums of Latin America do not present such difficult living conditions. Studies of squatter settlements and the migrants in them consistently report that most compare their situation favorably with what they had in the countryside.

This type of social mobility is, however, coming to an end in Latin America. As part of the population becomes urban, so the new generations can only compare themselves with their urban counterparts. The slow rise of living standards from one generation to the next may not continue. Certainly, the recent recessions have resulted in a drop in standards. Job prospects are not likely to bring much chance of occupational mobility—the major transformations and upgrading of the labor force are over. In this context, spatial mobility becomes the main base of social order, generating institutions that become an integral part of Latin America's urban culture.

For people to maintain mobility, old institutions must take on new forms. Family and household continue as essential units of survival, but their form and significance change. The variety of household types increases to accommodate the economic instability, and consequent movements, of the breadwinners. Single-parent households become more common. Parents and children leave and rejoin households as their circumstances change or they are called upon to replace missing household members.

Networks, rather than community and class, become the bases of identity. People define their possibilities, both good and bad, in terms of their networks, and spend time and ingenuity in maintaining and expanding them.

Collective action is not easily organized in cultures based on spatial mobility. Common interests are likely to be temporary and common action short-lived. Countervailing tendencies are at work, however. The instability of work and residence undermines patron-client relations in politics and economic life. Patronage systems are, after all, built on stable relationships of exchange of favors, and in the emerging Latin American city, neither patron nor client is likely to be the same person from one month to the next. Moreover, based on experience, people have in common a shared experience of how the agencies of government fail to handle their problems, this at a time when community forms of welfare are weakening and the need for public welfare is becoming more apparent.

There are signs that precisely because of the instability surrounding their personal lives, people are ready to join neighborhood and other forms of association, such as soup kitchens or church-sponsored *comunidades de base*, which act as channels for grievances and serve as a means of cooperating to make some improvements. These associations are as available to newcomers as to long-time residents and provide a ready means of assimilation into a new neighborhood. They are more accessible to women than formal political organizations, since their activities can be viewed as a "natural" extension of the woman's role. Studies in Buenos Aires, São Paulo, and Lima show that women in poor neighborhoods learn to act collectively and politically through such associations and see their participation as a natural and necessary extension of their domestic role (Jelin, 1987).

This new basis for order contains the seeds of conflict and change. This type of order is unlikely to be the basis for formal political action through traditional political parties. But the action it promotes is not easily suppressed by authoritarian government. It is too firmly rooted in the everyday experiences of city dwellers. This order also has its anarchic face. Common interests and identity based on stable work and place of residence are essential supports for successful urban planning; they create identifiable constituencies with which city government can enter dialogue. The culture of Latin America's cities becomes every day more hostile to this form of planning. Zoning regulations and development plans are ignored by people using numerous collective and individual strategies to seek necessary, but short-term, improvements in their life-style. There is very little coordination across a city in what is given or what is achieved.

I can return to Morse's point about the ways in which the institutions of a provisional rural structure found a ready home in the contemporary urban culture of Latin America. These have now become generalized and reinforced, linking cities and crossing national frontiers. They permit an astonishing degree of social and economic flexibility that is almost sufficient to sustain a flagging optimism about the survival of the Latin American city. There is, however, an unresolved tension between flexibility and the sustained organization needed to govern a city and make it work to everyone's benefit. Understanding the roots of community organization and how it can link into the formal political structure is one of the most urgent practical and academic research topics.

REFERENCES

Balán, J., E. Jelin, and H. Browning. 1973. *Men in a Developing Society.* Austin: ILAS/ University of Texas Press.

Batley, R. 1983. *Power through Bureaucracy: Urban Political Analysis in Brazil.* Aldershot, Eng.: Gower.

Browning, H. 1987. "Characteristics of Urban High Primacy Systems and the Case of Mexico." Population Research Center Occasional Paper, University of Texas, Austin.

Escobar, A. 1986. *Con el sudor de su frente: Mercado de trabajo y clase obrera en Guadalajara.* Guadalajara, Mexico: El Colegio de Jalisco.

Gilbert, A., and P. Ward. 1985. *Housing, the State and the Poor.* Cambridge, Eng.: Cambridge University Press.

Gregory, P. 1986. *The Myth of Market Failure.* Baltimore, Md.: Johns Hopkins University Press.

Jelin. E. 1987 (ed.). *Ciudadanía e identidad: Las mujeres en los movimientos sociales en América Latina.* Geneva: UNRISD.

Kowarick. L. 1977. "The Logic of Disorder: Capitalist Expansion in the Metropolitan Area of São Paulo." IDS Discussion Paper, 102. Falmer, Sussex, Eng.: Institute of Development Studies.

Morse, R. M. 1962. "Latin American Cities: Aspects of Function and Structure." *Comparative Studies in Society and History.* 4:4 (July) 473–93.

Noyelle, T., and T. Stanback. 1984. *The Economic Transformation of American Cities.* Englewood Cliffs, N.J.: Rowman & Allanheld.

Roberts, B. R. 1974. "The Interrelationships of City and Provinces in Peru and Guatemala." In W. Cornelius and F. Trueblood (eds.), *Latin American Urban Research,* Vol. 4. Beverly Hills, Calif.: Sage Publications.

Scardaville, M. C. 1977. "Crime and Urban Poor: Mexico City in the Late Colonial Period." Ph.D. Thesis, University of Florida.

Van Young, E. 1987. "Islands in the Storm: Quiet Cities and Violent Countrysides in the Mexican Independence Era." *Past & Present* 118 (Feb. 1988): 130–55.

4

Latin American Urban Studies: Beyond Dichotomy

Matthew Edel

The literature on Latin American urbanization has long been organized around dichotomies. The early cultural theories presented folk-urban and traditional-modern distinctions. These somewhat moralistic categories were later linked to an economic distinction between primary and secondary sectors of production and were reified by census cutoffs between urban and rural places. More recent work has tended to be guided by, or to react to, dependency theory—itself a dichotomization of geography into autocentric and exocentric places. Along with this new view, a central distinction has emerged between formal and informal sectors. This distinction has been applied to labor markets and types of businesses, to housing arrangements, and to systems of social support and political mobilization.

A final distinction, implicit in the neo-Marxist literature and lurking implicitly in other models, is that between the city as a locus of production and the city as a locus of consumption. Manuel Castells (1977) distinguishes production's "regional question" from an "urban question" concerning consumption issues and the "social reproduction" of the working class. Other forms of this distinction inform (or weaken) much of the urban literature on developed and underdeveloped countries.

Taxonomy, it must be allowed, is a necessary and useful stage in scientific inquiry, and a dichotomy is nothing but the simplest form of taxonomy. But it is also limited in its nuances. Even smoothed into a continuum, it is still one-dimensional. Initially, it reinforces a rigid either-or form of thinking that can feed a Manichean moralism. And so dichotomies tend, eventually, to be superseded by more sophisticated frameworks. If all goes well, these keep and expand the kernel of the ideas expressed in the original dichotomy but do so in a more useful way.

FROM FOLK-URBAN TO INFORMAL-FORMAL

The evolution of the *folk-urban* dichotomy is well known. Initially, it presented opposed ideal types, presumably embodied in actual societies. These types represented opposing moral orders, each admirable yet subject to patronization. Those venerable stereotypes, the noble savage and the restless Faustian modernizer, were lurking in the background. Never the twain could meet and mix (Redfield 1930, 1941). But Lewis (1951, 1952) found elements of "urban" complexity even in Redfield's rural Tepoztlán and "urbanization without breakdown" in Mexico City. Redfield's teacher, Park (1915), had found elements of folk community in the North American urban neighborhood, and Gans (1962) took that view even further. Eventually Redfield (1947) relaxed his dichotomy into a continuum. More and more, cities seemed to be mixtures of folk traditionalism and urban modernity.

The related underlying distinction between *traditional* and *modern* was also deeply rooted in the development literature of the 1950s and 1960s. Indeed, modernization, a notion influenced by the sociological tradition culminating in the work of Parsons (1960), became the key notion in the mainstream view of development (Rostow 1960). But this school came under attack for positing a too simple and conflict-free view of change. Eventually, it reduced itself to absurdity in the debate over whether bombings in Vietnam were to "bomb them into the Stone Age," or, as some of the modernizer school had it, "bomb them into the twentieth century" by enforcing a flight to cities. The seventies saw the search for appropriate technologies, with hints that small might be beautiful and only partially traditional. A simple and unambiguously beneficial movement from the traditional "small" society to a modern era of large-scale production was shown to be erroneous. Cities came to be thought of as potentially overgrown, as overurbanized rather than modern. The eighties have even seen praise for "archaic" paternalism as the height of modern Japanese management practice. The good and the useful thus lost their old dimensions of space, scale, and temporality.

A third aspect of the weakening of old distinctions has been a historical blurring of the line between *urban* and *rural*, as well as the weakening of the association of industrial (secondary) production with urbanization. Within the developed countries, it has become clear that the industrialization of the countryside has gone far. This involves, on the one hand, the movement of some industry from metropolitan to small-town settings and, on the other, the rise of agribusiness and the shift of small farms to capital-intensive production.

(Small farms have been market-oriented for a long time in the United States and Europe.) Thus, the notion of an economically precapitalist rural culture has become obsolete. In the cities, what is more, elements resembling Third World culture have been cited by recent commentators, although a modern, not a traditional, Third World is meant. Thus, both urban and rural areas of the country have come to share more and more of a common situation and fate, although important elements of regional differences in culture and outlook remain (Edel and Edel 1985).

In the Third World itself, similar processes have gone on, although many areas of peasant agriculture, with elements of traditional family life and culture, do remain. But more and more of the peasantry is caught in a web of market production, debt, contracts, and a need to supplement income through off-the-farm work. The rural proletariat and the peasantry are no longer as separate as they once were (de Janvry, 1982). The transfer to cities of ostensibly rural handicraft activities, as well as family patterns, is central to both Lewis's (1952) original critique of the Redfieldian view and the later conception of an urban informal sector, of marginal activities by "peasants in cities" (Roberts 1978).

Censuses in both developed and underdeveloped areas have traditionally demarcated the urban-rural distinction by establishing certain thresholds for classifying places as urban or rural. The more recent proliferation of different thresholds for classifying urban places as metropolitan or nonmetropolitan, or assigning them to other subcategories, suggests a realization that the dichotomy is obsolete.

Perhaps most important is the breakthrough of a conception of similarity into the public policy debate. As one who has worked on both rural land reform and urban housing issues, I have long noted similarities in the political economy literature of the two fields. Although some scholars have moved back and forth between the two, there have nonetheless been separate traditions of work by "land reformers" and "housers," to use the semiofficial self-designations of two groups of reform-minded institutionalist scholars. To bring the two traditions together was long overdue. Herein lay the importance, ideologically at least, of the Vancouver Conference on Human Settlements, HABITAT. For the notion of human settlements as encompassing both rural and urban settings helps to highlight their common problems and suggests some similarity of approaches to the study of the two.

As urban-rural, or folk-urban, and traditional-modern dichotomies weakened, a new dichotomy came to replace the old. *Autonomy,* or autocentrism, which could be envisioned in collective or individualist terms (compare, for example, Paul Baran [1957] with John F. C. Turner [1976]), replaced modernity as the favored virtue. *Dependency*, or exocentrism, rather than traditionalism, was the malevolent fate to be resisted or endured. The marginalism of Third World cities was attributed to distortions of dependency rather than to lack of pull from the modern sector. (Armstrong and McGee 1985; Gilbert and Gugler 1982; Portes and Walton 1976, 1981; Roberts 1978).

The weaknesses and strengths of dependency theory are by now well known. It is too static; it reifies regions; it overemphasizes exchange relations over production relations. But to its credit, it has focused attention on underdevelopment as itself a product of development, rather than a traditional state of nature, and has reintroduced the study of conflict to the development literature.

It is within this theory that dependent nations and their cities were conceived of as having separate but interconnected *formal* and *informal* sectors. These sectors in some ways paralleled the modern and traditional sectors described in earlier writing. But the formal and informal sectors were different because each had a long ancestry and because one could not presume a historical progression from informality to formality as one could from traditionality to modernity. Indeed, informal sectors were likely to expand under conditions of dependent urbanization. Similarly, the informal-sector notion included the possibilities of informal activities being both a manifestation of superexploited dependence and a source of independent strength and freedom for the poor. These polar views are particularly explicit in the respective positions on housing of Emilio Pradilla Cobos (1976) and John F. C. Turner (1976), or those on small industry of Alejandro Portes (1978) and Hernando de Soto (1986).

This view of informal sectors represented a useful focus on activities within the city that had been described first in the context of a critique of modernization and folk-urban theories. Oscar Lewis's initial work on Mexico City—particularly his article "Urbanization without Breakdown" (1952), but also his initial description of the culture of poverty in *Five Families* (1959)—was designed to counter the view of cities as modern-but-anomic. He showed that traditional elements of family life, brought to the city by rural migrants and preserved there in a new cultural milieu, survived the move and helped the urban poor to cope.

Unfortunately, Lewis's initial presentation of coping strategies got lost in a paradigmatic trap. Seeking to defend the poor from the anti-urbanists' charge of being without culture—a serious charge for an anthropologist—Lewis (1959, 1961) honored their activities with the designation of "Culture of Poverty." But "culture" seemed to imply learned behavior. From coping mechanism, these behaviors were reinterpreted as a learned whole. And when some dysfunctional attributes of this whole were pointed out, it was easy to move to the view (as Moynihan did) that a transmitted culture of poverty was itself a problem (Rainwater and Yancey 1967).

It was not until the 1970s that the explicit problem of coping strategies again came to the fore, in the anthropological work of Carol Stack (1974), Larissa Lomnitz (1977), and others on families' use of networks. By then, literatures had also grown up on squatter and self-help housing, on small-scale or "secondary sector" enterprises and jobs, and on social movements from below. These four strands clearly referred at least in part to the activities of the same people. They came to coalesce in a general view of "informal sectors."

This formulation in turn was strengthened by the evolution of dependency theory. This theory had initially postulated that large areas and groups were made marginal by the growth of export and financial sectors and by inappropriate technology imposed by monopoly or by culturally dependent modernization. As evidence mounted that the poor were not marginal to the working of this process, but were rather exploited by it, "informal sector" descriptions of coping mechanisms and of surplus extraction replaced the description of the poor as entirely expelled from the system. This linking of informal sectors to dependency has led to an increasing focus on links between these sectors and the outside world economy. But often the attempt has been to establish the connection of the bottom to the top (to New York banks and the like), underplaying links with intermediate actors such as local formal-sector businesses, unions, or governments. Indeed, when these actors are looked at, at least provisionally, they appear to be so interlinked with the informal sectors that the borders of the latter are quite debatable. Thus, one is left with a new dichotomy, that of formality and informality, that may need to be modified.

LINKING PRODUCTION AND SOCIAL REPRODUCTION

A second major set of dichotomies affects the urban literature both in Latin America and in the developed nations. That is the split between the study of the city (or region) as a productive system and the study of the city (or community) as a locus of consumption or "social reproduction." The split between the two is apparent if one compares studies of farmer or peasant life with urban life. The typical peasant study, be it in anthropology, rural sociology, or agricultural economics, discusses both the farm's production and the living arrangements and survival of the farm family. The typical urban study, however, discusses the location of an industry or its labor organization and labor process, or else it deals with family life, neighborhoods, housing, social services, and the public expenditures that pay for the latter. Either the production side or the consumption side is featured. Only the study of the journey to work seems to link the two, and even that is really part of social reproduction—the process of getting the workers and managers up to the workplace gate.

This separation reflects an actual separation of residence and workplace in modern cities. Since their origin, cities have included some "unproductive" consumers (at least if the work of ruling society is deemed unproductive) who acted only in the residential sphere. But most artisan workshops, and, indeed, governmental or ecclesiastical palaces, served both as residence and workplace. Only with the rise of commercial capitalism did larger cities, with dormitory communities separated from business and factory districts, replace the earlier agglomeration of occupational quarters (Mumford 1961). This separation led, eventually, to a social science that handles home and work as entirely separate spheres.

Thus, the study of urban economics has come to be dominated by a model of residential location and land values, with a geography whose workplaces are abstracted down to a single-point central business district. Meanwhile, the rest of "location theory," dealing with the siting of industry and employment and the multiplier effects of investments, is elaborated in a regional economics that can also be applied to cities. The only significant point of linkage has occurred in the discussion of economies of agglomeration, and even there much of the discussion involves economies of scale in providing services, although some discussions, including a good study of Mexico City (Garza 1985), encompass benefits of agglomeration to industries.

Similarly, urban sociology and anthropology have fragmented, compared to the comprehensive agenda outlined by Robert Park (1915). But it is not merely that many studies take on small, empirical topics. Even those seeking a broad, historically rooted overview of the urban problem encounter the basic split.

The key work in this respect is Manuel Castells's *The Urban Question* (1977), meant as a Marxist critique and reformulation of urban sociology. Castells complains, with some reason, that previous studies, ranging from orthodox sociological treatments to Lefebvre's general defense of a "right to the city" (1968), have reified the concept of "the urban" with the presumption that a variety of questions can be settled by the appeal to an invariant object of study. As an example, he shows that the analysis of capitalist investment in urban locations, which he terms "the regional question," has considered issues different from those of what he terms "the urban question." The latter is the question of how cities are organized to structure the social reproduction of the labor force. This question, or set of questions (which might perhaps better be called "the community question") is central to Castells's (1977, 1983) contributions on issues of contemporary urban social movements. These, as he points out, are primarily concerned with issues of consumption or reproduction. Castells's critique thus extends from a sorting-out of definitions to a practical critique of Marxist views that only the organization of production workers around production issues was central to the class struggle.

In addition to making a distinction and a political argument, Castells also created a vocabulary. And here the kind of intellectual dialectic that reversed Oscar Lewis's view of poverty has also reversed, at least partially, Castells's critique of rigidity in urban research. For if the primary urban question concerns social reproduction, then issues of production (the regional question) are separated from it by a gulf between fields of study. A similar gulf is opened by the debate between Weberian and Marxist housing scholars about whether housing classes as defined in the consumption sphere are logically coequal to classes as defined by positions in production. (See, for example, Rex and Moore 1967, Edel 1982).

Fortunately, not all scholars of urban life accept this split. In the United States and England, the new field of "labor and community" studies focuses on the relationship between culture in the working-class community and resistance at the workplace. For example, Kornblum (1974) and De Fazio (1986) have studied communities in which specific workplaces dominate the local culture and the linking of the two spheres is unavoidable. But the interest in the relation of workplace and community extends to other contexts, too, especially when issues of gender and race, which cut across the two spheres almost by definition, are involved.

In Latin America, there have been some studies of labor-community links in isolated mining centers (Nash 1979) or border industrial enclaves (Fernández Kelly 1983). Further potential for overcoming the gap may be found in the informal-sector studies. Originally, these studies tended to look at single categories of activity: squatter or "pirate" housing, small-scale commercial and artisan enterprises, irregular jobs not covered by social benefits, or organizations of politically unrecognized neighborhoods. Only later did the notion of partial overlap between these different types of informality begin to develop. The interactions are yet to be worked out, but the promise is great.

AN AGENDA FOR RESEARCH

These reviews of theoretical history lead to certain suggestions for research and theory.

First, if both traditional-modern and dependent-autocentric categories are not rigid dichotomies but ideal types, with actual societies showing mixes of attributes somewhat like theirs, then there is some validity to developed country–underdeveloped country comparative studies. Obviously, differences in national wealth and power must be kept in mind in these studies, but parallels can be fruitfully explored.

For example, New York has more underused infrastructure and less ability to allow squatter settlement of vacant land than does Lima. But New York can allow squatting in city-owned buildings seized for the tax arrears, tolerate illegal third apartments in houses zoned as two-family, and otherwise use some "informal" activities in the face of its housing problems, and these can be compared with Latin American housing "solutions."

Similarly, parallels can be drawn between the processes of class conflict and compromise that led to state policies for housing expansion in the United States, Britain, and Sweden (Edel, Sclar, and Luria 1984; Dickens, Duncan, Goodwin, and Gray 1985) and those that led to the explicit toleration of squatter or informal housing in Mexico and Peru (Perlo 1981, Collier 1976).

Second, if the rural-urban distinction is seen as weakened, a more careful paralleling of rural and urban observations is needed. An intellectual history of the parallels between the literature of "agrarian reformers" and of "housers" might be instructive. I suspect the two traditions have influenced each other more than the participants usually suggest. One might look, for example, at the literature on peasant or village markets and on small-scale production in comparison to the literature on the new urban informal activities, not in order to suggest that parallels prove urban activities are "peasant" in origin, but to learn from a wider sample about the advantages and difficulties of small-scale enterprise. Or one might look at the relative mechanisms of party patronage and control in urban and rural sectors of a country to better understand mechanisms of political domination and dependence.

Third, if production and consumption are not to remain isolated units of study, the "labor and community" approach needs to be extended to the study of Latin American cities. More studies of the relation of workplaces to their workers' communities and families are needed. Studies of women's roles in factories and in their surrounding communities, in Mexico's *maquiladoras* and elsewhere, are one place where these connections are beginning to be explored. So are studies of peasant villages, some of whose workers commute to urban jobs. Studies of informal-sector activities in urban shantytowns sometimes bridge the limits. But too often studies stop either at the factory gate or the threshold of the home. They need to be extended further. And they need to be complemented by broader studies of the links between economic sectors and households, as for example, in Weisskoff's (1985) extension of input-output modeling to take separate account of demands for male and female labor.

Fourth, the excellent proliferation of recent studies of "informal" activities need to be complemented with studies of the "formal" sector. There have been some industry studies and a few studies of central government services. Little, however, has been done on formal local government (apart from a few studies of public finance) since the late 1960s, when a number of studies were done to test the applicability of rival power-elite and pluralist theories (see Portes and Walton 1976). At present, it is not unfair to suggest that the social science literature deals more with neighborhood leaders than with the mayors with whom they negotiate.

Within these studies, to be sure, scholars need to be alert to aspects of informality in the formal sector (such as political factors in the distribution of public housing or city contracts). But they cannot study only the informal side.

Fifth, related to this, scholars need to conceptualize better the role of local government in the theory of the state. It may be that the lack of recent study reflects a lack of importance, as either market forces or national policy have preempted any power local elites or municipal agencies may have had. But with continuing economic crisis, new demands on informal community organizations, and a process of democratization at work, new roles may be thrust on local government. I do see some increasing importance, at least symbolic, in recent developments: the presidential candidacies, even if unsuccessful, of mayors in Peru and the Dominican Republic; the institution of mayoral elections in Colombia; the attention paid to mayoral races in Brazil's democratization process; and even the extent to which small-town mayors literally have their lives on the line in El Salvador and elsewhere.

This importance, or lack of importance, may be examined in relation to the growing literature on the local state emanating from England, the United States, and elsewhere. This literature, following on the more general literature on theories of the state, suggests several possible interpretations, including the notion of the local state as the instrumentality of specific elites or a ruling class, and that of the local state as an arena for class conflict (or interest-group conflict). Behind these are theories of structural determinants of the autonomy or of the inactivity of governments.

These theories suggest that, as industry and finance have become more internationalized, local (and even national) governments lose the ability to solve problems internally, either by ruling-class imposition or by creating an area for compromise. This seems to have happened to local governments in the United States as national corporations and capital markets emerged in the 1880s. A similar notion, of "Sovereignty at Bay" to use Vernon's term (1971), emerged in the 1960s with the rise of multinational corporations, and capital mobility on a world scale.

In such a system, several possibilities still exist:

- Government can cease to do much. U.S. local governments often ceased to do much except help local real-estate interests, whose assets were not mobile. Today some believe that national Keynesianism is dead because of capital's ability to flee social expenses.
- Government can become more repressive, because each jurisdiction must "shape up" to compete with others. This is one aspect of O'Donnell's (1978) explanation for the rise of authoritarianism in Latin America. In the United States, where municipal reform movements have been analyzed as reshaping cities in the interest of capitalist competitiveness, control of the working class or the poor is a principal attribute of these programs.
- Even though control over one government locally cannot accomplish much, as "socialist" control of Burlington, Vermont; Lima, Peru; or Bologna, Italy, demonstrates, it has the potential to play a role in legitimizing further working-class policies or parties, which could develop power at a more appropriate scale. Federalism in the United States sometimes allows states or cities to play a bellwether role, on either the right or the left. The reemergence of federalism may lead to something similar in Brazil.

The role of local government in Latin America is not yet clear. But these possibilities suggest that scholars should not write off local government as an area of study.

Sixth, the lesson of the whole culture-of-poverty debate must be remembered. What began as an investigation of coping strategies and a critique of a dichotomous paradigm was sidetracked for a decade into an ideological debate over how much to blame the victim. It is important that scholars avoid a similar sidetracking of work on informal sectors and community self-help. Prevailing intellectual and political winds could easily transform a concern for these activities into one or another of the following dogmas.

- *The use of "informal sector" as a simple surrogate for "culture of poverty,"* *with the implication that it is informality (that is, illegality) that keeps the* *poor in their poverty.* A popular U.S. literature that identifies an "underground economy" of tax avoidance and other illegal activities suggests such "informal" activities may have short-term economic advantages. It is a short step from that to a position that the unemployed need no help because they can get "underground" incomes, and then to the view that these activities themselves perpetuate an underclass culture. Such a view is less tenable for Latin America, where informal activities are so visible and sometimes so clearly unlucrative, than it is for the United States, but it plays to old fears of disorder and the "dangerous classes," and hence its own danger cannot be disregarded.

- *The use of informal-sector activities to suggest that a market is working* *properly and, hence, that nothing need be done in the way of policy.* The identification of small-scale peasant trading with a laissez-faire optimum has been around in the development literature for some time. Sol Tax (1953) used the term "penny capitalism" in describing Guatemalan village economies, and P. T. Bauer and B. S. Yamey (1957) used a similar view of peasants as the foundation for a free-market onslaught on any government development effort. The energy and resourcefulness of actors in the informal sectors can, of course, mean these actors do respond to market opportunities. At times a bit of deregulation may be good policy (De Soto 1986). But it is highly exaggerated to suggest that this entrepreneurialism would automatically lead to Pareto-optimal allocation and high growth if only government would vanish completely. (De Soto may or may not really be making such a strong version of this argument, bit it accounts for some of the reception his work has received.) Nonetheless, this farcical view is propounded quite seriously by enthusiasts of the Korean, Hong Kong, or Singapore model of development, who manage to ignore considerable government intervention (mostly designed to ensure low wages) in those economies.

• *The exaggeration of the degree to which it is possible for communities of the poor to drop out of the wider society and create some sort of anarchist utopia. (This exaggeration is then matched by a critique that suggests that any such localized activities are reactionary attempts to forge new chains for the masses.)* The debate between Turner (1976) and Pradilla Cobos (1976) is an example of these positions: both well stated, but essentially reprising the Engels stand of a century ago (Engels, n.d.). The implication is that community self-help and informal activity are either the cardinal revolutionary activity or not revolutionary at all. The search for a simple rule for radicals is appealing. But urban reality may not allow for such simple formulas. Theory and analysis must allow for more complexity.

Seventh and finally, to go beyond this last point and back to the issue of transforming the Latin American city, it should be asked whether all of these discussions about research and theory have implications for practice. Obviously, I think they do. At the least, there is the need to avoid the creation of ideological traps like the culture-of-poverty theory, or a version of dependency theory or structuralism that "proves" nothing is possible. At best, I expect not exact blueprints, but some guides to exploratory action.

Here, the discovery of great strength and resilience in local communities and networks within the informal sectors is of great importance. This strength suggests a fundamental source of energy and drive for transformation and a hope that transformation can allow for decentralized autonomy. But the study of the overall international and intranational division of labor suggests how much needs to be overcome for meaningful results. The complexity of interaction between the spheres of production and reproduction indicates that the "urban" and "regional" questions will not stay separate. And the brief consideration of the theory of the state and a history of limits to peasant organization and local organizing in both developed and underdeveloped countries suggests that localism is not sufficient. Coordination and links to formal organizations—be they unions, parties, governments, federations, or whatever—are also necessary. The study of both informal and formal sectors, both rural and urban, developed and dependent, can *at its best*, but only *at best*, provide inputs to political thinking.

This research was supported in part by grant number 666218 from the PSC-CUNY Research Award program of the City University of New York. The author also thanks the Charles H. Revson Foundation and the William and Flora Hewlett Foundation for their support of his research at the Bildner Center for Western Hemisphere Studies, CUNY. The section of the paper on "Linking Production and Social Reproduction" expands on a suggestion made by David Barkin at a meeting at the Bildner Center.

REFERENCES

Armstrong, Warwick, and T. G. McGee. 1985. *Theatres of Accumulation*. London: Methuen.

Bauer, P. T., and B. S. Yamey. 1957. *The Economics of Underdeveloped Countries*. Chicago: University of Chicago Press.

Baran, Paul K. 1957. *The Political Economy of Growth*. New York: Monthly Review Press.

Castells, Manuel. 1977. *The Urban Question*. Cambridge, Mass.: MIT Press.

———— 1983. *The City and the Grassroots*. Berkeley, Calif.: University of California Press.

Collier, David. 1976. *Squatters and Oligarchs*. Baltimore, Md.: Johns Hopkins University Press.

DeFazio, William. 1986. *Longshoremen: Community and Resistance on the Brooklyn Waterfront*. S. Hadley, Mass.: Bergin & Garvey.

De Soto, Hernando. 1986. *El Otro Sendero*. Bogotá: Editorial Oveja Negra.

Dickens, P., S. Duncan, M. Goodwin, and F. Gray. 1985. *Housing, States, and Localities*. London: Methuen.

Edel, Kim, and Matthew Edel. 1985. "Dialogue, Utopia and the Division of Labor: Reflections on Some Themes by Harry Magdoff." In *Rethinking Marxism*, S. Resnick and R. Wolff, editors, 83–98. New York: Autonomedia.

Edel, Matthew. 1982. "Home Ownership and Working-Class Unity," *International Journal of Urban and Regional Research*. 6:2, 205–222.

Edel, M., E. Sclar, and D. Luria. 1984. *Shaky Palaces: Homeownership and Social Mobility in Boston's Suburbanization*. New York: Columbia University Press.

Engels, Frederick. n.d. *The Housing Question*. New York: International Publishers.

Fernández Kelly, María Patricia. 1983. *For We Are Sold, I and My People*. Albany: State University of New York Press.

Gans, Herbert. 1962. *The Urban Villagers*. New York: The Free Press.

Garza, Gustavo. 1985. *El proceso de la industrialización en la ciudad de México (1821–1970)*. Mexico: El Colegio de México.

Gilbert, Alan, and Josef Gugler. 1982. *Cities, Poverty, and Development*. Oxford, Eng.: Oxford University Press.

Janvry, Alain de. 1982. *The Agrarian Question and Reformism in Latin America*. Baltimore, Md.: Johns Hopkins University Press.

Kornblum, William. 1974. *Blue Collar Community*. Chicago: University of Chicago Press.

LeFebvre, Henri. 1968. *Le Droit à la ville*. Paris: Anthropos.

Lewis, Oscar. 1951. *Life in a Mexican Village: Tepoztlán Restudied*. Urbana, Ill.: University of Illinois Press.

———— 1952. "Urbanization without Breakdown." *Scientific Monthly*. 65 (July), 31–41.

———— 1959. *Five Families: Mexican Case Studies in the Culture of Poverty*. New York: Basic Books.

———— 1961. *The Children of Sánchez*. New York: Random House.

Lomnitz, Larissa. 1977. *Networks and Marginality: Life in a Mexican Shanty Town*. New York: Academic Press.

Mesa-Lago, Carmelo. 1978. *Social Security in Latin America*. Pittsburgh, Pa.: University of Pittsburgh Press.

Mumford, Lewis. 1961. *The City in History*. New York: Harcourt Brace Jovanovich.

Nash, June. 1979. *We Eat the Mines and the Mines Eat Us.* New York: Columbia University Press.

O'Donnell, Guillermo. 1978. "Reflections on the Patterns of Change in the Bureaucratic-Authoritarian State." *Latin American Research Review.* 12 (Winter), 3–38.

Park, Robert. 1915. "The City: Suggestions for the Investigation of Behavior in the Urban Environment." *American Journal of Sociology.* Vol. 20, no. 5.

Parsons, Talcott. 1960. *The Social System.* Glencoe, Ill.: The Free Press.

Perlo Cohen, Manuel. 1981. *Estado, vivienda y estructura urbana en el cardenismo.* Mexico City: Universidad Nacional Autónoma de México.

Portes, Alejandro. 1978. "The Informal Sector and the World Economy: Notes on the Structure of Subsidized Labor." *Bulletin of the Institute of Development Studies.* 9 (June), 35–40.

Portes, Alejandro, and John Walton. 1976. *Urban Latin America: The Political Conditions from Above and Below.* Austin, Texas: University of Texas Press.

———— 1981. *Labor, Class, and the International System.* New York: Academic Press.

Pradilla Cobos, Emilio. 1976. "Notas acerca del problema de la vivienda." *Ideología y Sociedad.* 16, 70–107.

Rainwater, Lee, and William L. Yancey. 1967. *The Moynihan Report and the Culture of Poverty.* Cambridge, Mass.: MIT Press.

Redfield, Robert. 1930. *Tepoztlán: A Mexican Village.* Chicago: University of Chicago Press.

———— 1941. *The Folk Culture of Yucatan.* Chicago: University of Chicago Press.

———— 1947. "The Folk Society." *American Journal of Sociology.* 52:2, 282–308.

Rex, John, and Robert Moore. 1967. *Race, Community and Conflict.* London: Oxford University Press.

Roberts, Bryan. 1978. *Cities of Peasants.* Beverly Hills, Calif.: Sage Publications.

Rostow, W. W. 1960. *The Stages of Economic Growth.* Cambridge, Eng.: Cambridge University Press.

Sennett, Richard, ed. 1969. *Classic Essays on the Culture of Cities.* New York: Appleton–Century–Crofts.

Stack, Carol. 1974. *All Our Kin.* New York: Harper and Row.

Tax, Sol. 1953. *Penny Capitalism.* Washington: Smithsonian Institute of Social Anthropology.

Turner, John F. C. 1976. *Housing by People.* New York: Pantheon.

Vernon, Raymond. 1971. *Sovereignty at Bay: The Multinational Spread of U.S. Enterprises.* New York: Basic Books.

Weisskoff, Richard. 1985. *Factories and Food Stamps: The Puerto Rico Model of Development.* Baltimore, Md.: Johns Hopkins University Press.

II

Frameworks for Policy

5

The City: Its Size and Rhythm

Manfred A. Max-Neef

Aristotle in *The Politics* and, before him, his teacher Plato in *The Republic* said that a city "should grow so long as in its growth it consents to remain a unity, but no further." When Aristotle pointed out that "it is necessary that the citizens should know each other" and Plato stressed the importance of unity, they revealed a common concern. Put in today's terms, they were advocating the fullest possible communication among citizens as the quintessence of the good life, which, to the ancients, was a life guided and governed by justice and virtue. Both these ideals would therefore seem—again in contemporary terms— linked to the notion of scale.

As a mathematician, Plato was meticulous on the subject. For Plato, everything had an ideal number, and a city was no exception. He was quite specific when he set the number of citizens in his ideal city at 5,040.

These two great teachers are not the only ones to link quality of life with size of population. None of the famous utopias, it should be pointed out, finds merit in sheer size. Thomas More suggested that the ideal community consists of 6,000 families. Fourier's phalansteries were limited to 1,600 people. Robert Owens's parallelograms sheltered from 500 to 2,000 members, and similar numbers were involved in Horace Greeley's cooperative communities. In all these cases the basis is the same—the Platonic unity or the Aristotelian necessity that the citizens know each other. That is to say, that communication among people should be possible and effective.

The advantages of a society whose size was on a human scale were felt both in Athens and Sparta. The city-states of Renaissance Italy are examples of more or less the same idea. The prosperous free cities of the Hanseatic League are another example. These cities, as cities alone, generated a cultural wealth and diversity greater than the vast Holy Roman and Austro-Hungarian empires which in the end were brought down by the very weight of their absurd and humanly untenable size.

Europe's many-faceted culture rose out of specific, localized identification—that of the citizen with his city and not that of the subject with an empire. This multiplicity of identities bequeathed so rich a rhythm of diversity that it still amazes the traveler who makes his way through Umbria and Tuscany, who sails down the Rhine or Danube, or who journeys over the Pyrenees and across the Low Countries.

For more than two millennia, empire and city—each in its widest meaning—have confronted one other as alternative ways of life, alternative sources of identification. Unitarianism or federalism, integration or balkanization, centralization or decentralization, nationalism or regionalism—these are merely some of the manifestations of the confrontation. All are options and each has advantages and disadvantages. Nevertheless, for Plato and Aristotle it was not a question of options. Communication and the personal participation and responsibility that arise from it was a matter of size. It is obvious that unlimited size is the natural enemy of communication. Man *is* insofar as his surroundings belong to a human—and therefore humanizing—scale.

The ideal size for a city is debatable and, in fact, is hotly debated. The ancients to whom I have referred were clear on the matter. They believed natural laws governed the size of any system, no matter what it was.

Many centuries later—far more than would have been necessary to invalidate a spurious argument—Galileo, with extraordinary scientific precision, strengthened Aristotle's theories using mathematics. His argument for limitations to the size of all natural things was his belief that the natural order was based on laws of proportion which could be calculated with proper measurement.

The mathematical law put forward by Galileo in his arguments is clear and simple, showing that if the length of a bone is tripled, its width will have to be increased ninefold. He suggests, in other words, that to maintain the ratio between momentum and resistance, the diameter has to be proportionate to the square of the length.

Galileo's hypothesis takes the notion of ideal size a stage closer to my current concern. He holds that every system that grows beyond a certain size has to change its structure.

So much for ancestral voices. The modern world is different. It has engines, radio, and television. Materials are stronger, and ships no longer use oars. Those with the talent to be town criers are employed in other jobs. Everything nowadays is different—but is it? How much of what the ancients talked about is invalidated by present-day gadgetry?

It is Galileo who serves as a bridge between the arguments of the past and the concerns of the present. Galileo does not mention gadgets but talks about structures, and it is by a discussion of structures that we will bridge the gap between ancient and current views of the matter which this essay will try to elucidate.

GIANTISM IN CITIES

When the technology of communication was poor, the most splendid cities were relatively small. Now that communications are almost instantaneous and can reach out long distances, more and more cities tend to giantism. If one accepts that the potential for communication among people is linked to a city's size, then one must agree that communications technology has become more and more obviously a substitute for genuine human communication. Technology is not to blame for this paradox; rather, the problem lies with the structural change of the spaces in which human beings establish their chains of relationship.

In spaces of huge size and density, where David Riesman's "lonely crowd" is scattered, many live out their personal dramas, trying to identify—and imagining they have succeeded—with characters in television soap operas rather than with their fellow men, who become invisible and seem indifferent in the unfriendly horde heading nowhere and achieving nothing at full speed. Sought-after identification, the need to compare one's experience with that of others, confrontation with deeds and events as well as with the fearful, distressing confirmation of the value put on their own behavior are only as far away as a program schedule and a remote-control button. Experience filtered through television can be seen, felt, sensed without participation or involvement. They are substitutes for that communication which human beings find hard to relinquish.

As a city grows, not only does human communication weaken or change, but other distortions become evident. Aristotle's ideal city, in which citizens know each other, turns—during what might be called an "intermediary stage"—into a place of anonymity. Soon, however, the development of administrative techniques, which growth makes necessary, especially in matters of policing, ends up by destroying the pervading anonymity. But there is no return to the prior condition. On the contrary, the less the citizens know each other, the more they are "known" by the police, who zealously build up, expand, and perfect their files. When everyone is under surveillance by the authorities, human beings have less eye contact with each other. In this connection, look at what available statistics reveal. In large cities, the number of police increases proportionately more rapidly than that of the rest of the population. Despite this, crime figures tend to be greater where the ratio of police to population should suggest the reverse. Later, I will try to explain the reasons for this paradox.

Another aspect of giantism seldom taken into account is a purely economic one. More and more compelling statistical evidence shows that as a city grows, a decreasing percentage of each new unit of the gross national product per capita is spent on improving living standards. The rest is swallowed up in changes demanded by side effects of growth itself and by the disposal of waste products. In any given country the large city centers, in solving their problems of growth, use up increasing proportions of the economic surplus generated by surrounding areas. That this phenomenon increases and exacerbates the problems of the metropolis is another paradox that will be dealt with later on.

Another well-known and also paradoxical problem in big cities is traffic congestion. The planners keep coming back to the same solutions—wider roads, elevated highways, underpasses, one-way traffic systems, etc. What is the result? After each supposed improvement, the congestion becomes worse. One has only to drive through a few Latin American cities to experience this at first hand. In every case, a kind of law of "unforeseen consequences" seems to operate, wherein the end result is the opposite of the aim.

These are only samples of the distortions evident in large metropolitan centers. What is the reason behind all this? Merely to attribute the problem to size is to say very little. Rather, one must investigate specific changes that take place when a construct, in this case, the city, exceeds prescribed limits and reaches a point where paradoxical distortions arise. To do this, quantitative mechanical analyses must be set aside and aspects relating to proportion explored instead.

Analyzing a city's physical dimension is not enough to show how such an organism works. Its social or functional dimension must also be recognized. While the physical dimension is determined by the number of inhabitants, the social one is a function of four factors: size, density, administrative unit, and acceleration. As Kohr (1965, 24–25) shows,

> a denser society is, in effect, a bigger society than one of equal size but with a lower density of population, since the former will generate greater energy. For the same reason, a more highly structured society is, in effect, larger than a less structured one and a faster society larger than a slower one. In this way, the physical size of Great Britain, being much smaller than that of India, Britain's social dimension, reflected by its power ranking, is much greater precisely because of the amplifying effect of a stronger adminis-

trative structure and of its greater acceleration thanks to the higher technological development of its population.

One aspect of Kohr's analysis could be further clarified: acceleration as a determining factor in the effective dimension of a social conglomerate. Kohr (1965, 18) explained this when he wrote that

> according to the law of physics, a change in velocity produces the same quantitative effect as a change in the number of particles in motion. Thus, a greater number of people moving in a larger space represents the same mass as a smaller number moving faster. Emergency exits in theaters are larger while people use them normally, but this is necessary so that in the event of panic the door can cope with the effect of the increase in mass produced by the movement of people.

This principle is known in the tactics and strategy of warfare. Blitzkrieg (lightning war) is simply a way in which a smaller number of troops compensates by greater speed of movement.

Anyone familiar with the basic principles of monetary theory will find analogies between the above discussion and the equations of Irving Fisher. These show that an inflationary process can be generated not only by the amount of money circulating in respect to disposable goods and services but also by an increase in the speed of circulation of the same money. The inclusion of the speed of circulation as a relevant factor gives to these theories not only a quantitative but also a qualititative aspect. The same is true of what Kohr (1973) calls his "theory of demographic acceleration." This theory is worth examining in some detail.

Consider a purely quantitative demographic viewpoint. The mass of people (mass in Kohr's sense), M, is determined by the number of the population, N, in ratio to the available physical living space, S, and thus coincides with its density. This can be expressed in the equation: $M = N/S$.

From this it is easy to deduce that if the mass of population increased beyond what is estimated as appropriate, there are only two possible solutions to the problem: to reduce N, the number of inhabitants (by birth control or emigration); or to expand S, the available living space (by conquest, colonization, or war). Until now this has been the orthodox theory of population, and ample evidence of these two solutions exists. There is, however, an interesting third possible solution, which has not yet been tried.

If, as the above examples show, the velocity, V, of the population has an influence that is in direct proportion to its mass, the corrected equation can be expressed in the following terms: $M = N \times V/S$.

It is immediately deduced that to change the demographic mass, one has only to modify the velocity with which the population is displaced (as in the example of people leaving the theater).

Kohr enlarges upon his formula in conceptual, not mathematical, terms. Nevertheless, the mathematical approach is worth trying. Look at how the velocity of the population is determined. Velocity is obviously a function of distance traveled, D, and the time available to travel it, t. Thus: $V = f(D, t)$, which can be expressed as: $V = D/t$.

In turn, distance (D) is a function of space (S) and will increase in proportion to any expansion of S.

What exactly does time (t) mean? Substituting the expression for V into the equation for M, we obtain: $M = N \times D/S \times t$.

Time (t) does not correspond to the total of hours in the day. It is only the time it takes for people to move about, say, from their homes to their places or work. If it is assumed that people sleep for eight hours, work for another eight hours, and spend six or seven hours on meals and other tasks essential for a minimally satisfactory life, that leaves an hour or two for moving about. Thus, t can—and should—be considered a constant if it is not to diminish the quality of life. Here is a very simple example.

Suppose a city expands so that the distance between my house and my place of work increases by one kilometer. This kilometer means, in fact, two kilometers—one going and one coming. If I lunch at home, the distance becomes four kilometers. If the increase affects my wife and two daughters in the same way, each kilometer causes my family to increase its movement by sixteen kilometers a day—all in the same available time, t, or, in other words, at greater speed. If the process continues, we shall no longer be pedestrians and because of the imposed restriction t, we shall have to travel by car. If it continues further, there will be more and faster cars. All this increases the demographic pressure, even when the absolute number of inhabitants has not changed. And if, as is probable, the absolute population increases, the whole process will increase correspondingly. A moment will come when the pressures become extraordinary and solutions in situ completely impossible.

Two basic conclusions can be drawn: 1) although a city expands in arithmetic progression, effective distances progress geometrically, as do the costs that stem from the ensuing effective movements; and 2) any system that expands beyond a certain limit breaks down irreversibly. Thus the development of multiple processes seems to present the most sensible way out.

Note the similarity between the first conclusion and Galileo's law for the growth of a body. As for the second conclusion, irreversible breakdown beyond a certain limit presupposes some recognizable critical size for a city. Although this size cannot be expressed in absolute terms, Kohr's relative definition seems satisfactory. Kohr (1965, 25) wrote that a city is too big when its

> problems are brought about not by some human or organizational deficiency but by its proportions. Just as at a known altitude breathing difficulties occur simply as a result of the altitude and not as a result of some pulmonary disorder, or just as a critical quantity of uranium explodes because of its mass and not because the isolated particles of uranium have altered their substance.

Every system has a critical dimension. This varies according to the principal functions of that system. Kohr (1965, 25–26) demonstrated that the concept has a degree of "mutability" according to the nature of the given problem. "With respect given to war," he said,

> the critical dimension is that which prompts the State to believe that its power is superior to that of any possible rival. With respect to theft, assaults, and violent crimes, the critical dimension is reached when the number of people is so large that it is beyond police control. With regard to economic fluctuations, the crisis point is reached when markets become so large that governments . . . can no longer regulate them.

So what should the functions of a city be? There are at least four: the distribution to its residents of companionship, welfare, security, and culture. Some of these aims are attainable in the degree to which communication among people is satisfactory and adequate and citizen participation is full, responsible, and effective. Human communication was the main concern of this chapter. Now I should like to set forth this matter of communication in theoretical terms as a function of human time and space.

SUBJECTIVE HUMAN SPACE

Every system is made up of a set of interrelated elements that operate together to achieve a common objective, such as an established goal. Unless there is an objective, the set never becomes a system. An individual person can be studied as a system in the same way a society or a city is. When the city is the system under consideration, people are the elements or subsystems. If a city is a system whose function is to bestow on its inhabitants companionship, welfare, security, and culture, the achievement of these objectives depends on how its citizens (or elements) relate to each other and with the rest of the elements that make up the system (or city). The other elements may be natural or artificial objects or other living creatures, such as animals and plants.

Any interrelation between elements in which one or more persons come together (person to person or person to object) can be considered as a communication link in the broadest possible sense. Whether the communication works well or badly, is necessary or pointless, is not important for the moment. To say that all human communication takes place in time and space may seem a truism, and so it would be if I were referring only to chronological time and physical space. But because I am more interested in a subjective meaning, this statement takes on a special significance. With this in mind, space and time may be defined as subjective human phenomena.

Beginning with space, I suggest the following definition: *Space*, as it is perceived, *is the combination of abstract relationships that define an object.* These relationships can be classified according to shape, distance, proximity, depth, etc., all of which presuppose the existence of other objects. Distance means distance in relation to something else; proximity is proximity to something else; size is greater, the same as, or less than some other object. An object cannot be defined nor does it make sense without reference to other things. Wittgenstein said that "just as we are quite unable to imagine spatial objects outside space or temporal objects outside time, so too *there is no* object that we can imagine excluded from the possibility of combining with others." He goes on to say that "each thing is, as it were, in a space of possible states of affairs. This space I can imagine empty, but I cannot imagine the thing without the space."

Human beings have classified objects and thus defined the abstract relations that characterize objects. This is the way in which humans perceive space and, in perceiving it, are actually creating it, or, to be more exact, creating it for themselves. Their link with space is therefore a link with a subjectively perceived reality. Physical space is only a useful convention for measuring, evaluating, and classifying those changes and distortions that affect subjective human space. This point can be illustrated with some simple examples.

Anyone who has seen a building under construction will have seen the following phenomenon. When one looks at the foundations, the future rooms seem smaller than they did on the plan. Once the walls are up, one has the odd impression that the rooms have grown. In the same way, when the rooms are finished but empty, they look smaller than they do after they are furnished, so long as there is not too much furniture. What causes these different perceptions?

Perhaps the most plausible theory is that the perception of spatial size is a function of the quantity of information that the brain receives and stores in relation to the space in question. In other words, an empty room, with a limited amount of information, places a minimum of abstract relationships in the brain. A furnished room increases the number of abstract relationships and, therefore, the brain stores a larger amount of information and the space is perceived as greater.

Here is another example. A person lying on his back to look at a night sky full of stars perceives an immense space. The vast number of stars represents an enormous amount of information, while the simultaneous perception of their number absorbs almost all of the stargazer's attention. If he were to look at only one star, the sensation of the immensity of space would sharply diminish. Finally, if he were surrounded by total darkness, the sensation of space would disappear almost completely. This is why perceived spatial dimension does not depend on the physical distance at which the objects under observation are located but on the quantity of information that the said space delivers to the brain.

That there is a relation between perceived spatial size and the amount of information stored by the brain seems to me probable, even though I cannot back up my theory with hard evidence. In any case, the relation that I suggest does not seem to be linear. That is to say, the sensation of spatial size grows with the increase of information but with less intensity. The function may be logarithmic or, if there is a point of saturation, a negative exponential.

These speculations may seem an unnecessary digression, but in fact they are essential to my point, since subjective space exerts a major influence on people's behavior. Very little physical distance may separate individuals living and working in overcrowded cities, but in fact the amount of spatial information is so great that the chains of communication have become very difficult or impossible. People find themselves separated by great subjective spaces. In small cities the opposite happens, as anyone's experience can confirm.

I conclude, therefore, that urban solutions based solely on physical spatial concepts do not confront the real problem.

SUBJECTIVE HUMAN TIME

To define time and to penetrate its essence has been the aspiration of countless philosophers and scientists. I shall not be so intellectually arrogant as to try to give a definition here. Instead, I shall merely advance the idea that in addition to chronological or astral time, one can also talk about subjective human time. I mean the sense that people have of the duration of any particular event. A five-minute toothache seems longer that five minutes spent in pleasant company. I shall therefore define subjective human time as the aggregate of abstract relationships that link a human being with an event.

Robert Ornstein (1969, 21–22) defines this form of temporal experience as "our normal experience of time passing, of hours lengthening or shortening, of a recent event seeming 'a long time ago,' of one interval passing more quickly for one person than another or more quickly for one person at one instance than another. It is the continuing, persevering, time in which we live our lives." His book confirms the subjectivity of people's experience of time. He tests the validity of what he calls "the Metaphor of the Dimension of Storage," which he defines as that which "relates the experience of duration of a given interval to the dimension of the storage space for that interval, in terms used for the processing of information. In the storing of a determined interval, increasing the number of stored events and the complexity of the said events will increase . . . the dimension of the storage space." In proportion to the increase in the size of the storage space, the experience of duration is "lengthened." The same might be said for what I have called the "intensity" of the information, which has nothing to do with the number of stored events nor with their complexity. A good instance is the endless time it takes a watched pot to boil. The impatience with which a person waits for a given event to happen represents an increase in the storage space that the brain has reserved to process the information. My theory is that the storage space really grows, because impatience forces one to reprocess the same information several times over. I suggest that the processing of an event in a determined interval rather than a number of different events is more or less the same as processing, in the same interval, the same event "n" number of times.

Léniz and Alcaíno (1980), from another viewpoint, suggest that in planning the welfare of people, subjective rather than chronological time should be taken into account. They maintain that, with all its changes and impressionable events, a year passes slowly for children, while it tends to pass more rapidly as one grows older. This, they claim, is because adults compare the period with other periods already lived through instead of treating the year as a fixed unit. Léniz and Alcaíno suggest that the perception of the duration of time is proportional to the square root of the perceiver's chronological age.

Ornstein is talking about microexperiences—that is, the experience of individuals—while Léniz and Alcaíno are interested in whole-life macroexperience. The two complement each other. During research into these matters, Professor Carlos Mallmann, of the Bariloche Foundation, and I concluded that an additional element should be taken into account. It seemed to us that a cultural constant ought to be included in any formula that claimed to interpret an individual's sense of passing time. We called this sense "the cultural constant of time evaluation." Its justification as an essential component of any general formula springs from the fact that cultural differences, including environmental ones, establish different kinds of links between the being and the event. Cultural anthropology presents evidence to corroborate this. The link, for want of a better term, that places a person in the time continuum that surrounds him, bears him along, and determines what happens to him in particular and in conjunction with others is not the same for a settled rural dweller and a nomad. Thus, too, the peasant's link with time is different and has different meanings and consequences from that of a city dweller, especially one who lives in metropolitan industrial surroundings. It is obvious that the famous (and quite destructive) phrase "time is money" has no meaning to the peasant. He is linked to a time determined by the metabolism of natural systems, while the city dweller is linked to a time determined by the metabolism of industry.

TIME-SPACE DISTURBANCES

I have said that a city is a system whose function is, at the very least, that of distributing companionship, welfare, security, and culture. The nature and quality of the links that people establish between each other and with the other elements that make up a city and its surroundings determine the likelihood of the city's fulfilling this function. I also said that communication links present themselves in subjective time and space. Now is the time to define these links. My aim is to supply a few arguments for establishing those characteristics and conditions that will humanize a city. My as yet incomplete theory I call *the theory of time-space disturbances*. It develops along the following broad lines.

People who live in a city live in a space. This gives them two alternatives: to exist in the space or to become integrated with it. To become integrated means to be part of the space generated by oneself as a determining part of the self and therefore created for oneself. I label such a condition *the human spaceless state.* In other words, I am part (object-element) of a space that is *my* space because, while I contribute to its creation, simply by being present and by making it definable through my presence, by being an element that *exists* in it, I reach for and acquire identity.

Being alone in a space represents an absence of identity. That is to say, I walk and move, I float, so to speak, in a space that I cannot understand and in which I am too insignificant to aspire to be an essentially definable element capable of generating space. I call this state *human spacelessness.*

People who live in a city live in a time. This means that they are permanently exposed to micro- and macro-experiences of time. The subjective element of both is influenced by the type and quality of the links of communication permitted by the environment. When subjective time, lived for a particular period, inhibits the ability to create and satisfactorily complete a chain of communication that the individual considers objectively possible for that chronological period, the individual is in what I would call a state of *human timelessness.* These timeless states produce varying degrees of anxiety and nervousness according to the importance given them by the person involved in the thwarted chains of communication, In this connection, I was inspired by the entry for January 16, 1922, in Franz Kafka's diary: "This past week I suffered something very like a breakdown . . . impossible to sleep, impossible to stay awake, impossible to endure life, or, more exactly, the course of life. The clocks are not in unison; the inner one runs crazily on at a devilish or demoniac or in any case inhuman pace, the outer one limps along at its usual speed."

Subjective time and subjective space could be treated as separate fields of investigation. When the problem is the city, however, this separation makes no sense, for each influences the other. I have chosen two examples. The first deals with the relationship between spatial and temporal microexperiences and is relatively minor. The second deals with space in relation to the temporal macroexperience.

Imagine a driver in a vehicle in a traffic jam on a metropolitan superhighway. Now examine everything that happens in light of the concepts that I have just set forth. First, a physically large space turns into a space that is subjectively small; second, this subjective reduction of space causes impatience; third, impatience leads to a continuous reprocessing of the same information—that is, the information that the brain processes is monotonic but of high intensity; fourth, the intensity of the information prolongs the sense of the duration of the event; fifth, this undesired prolongation blocks the capacity for establishing and diversifying the possible chains of communication with other people, the countryside, or oneself; sixth, this block brings about a breakdown linked to anticommunication—horns are sounded, insults hurled at fellow drivers; seventh, this anticommunication generates yet more impatience, and the cycle repeats itself with increasing intensity. In the end, the driver reaches home, where the annoyances continue. There is no time to talk to the children, and the slightest problem becomes disproportionately irritating.

This apparently frivolous example sketches the consequences of what I call *a human state of time-space disturbance*. I suspect that these states are responsible for a great deal of family crises in big cities. The resulting stress seriously impedes the success of chains of communication, which are indispensable for keeping human relationships in balance. In isolation, the example may seem trivial. Yet, however trivial these states are in themselves, they are repeated systematically day after day in most large cities so that their damaging effects are cumulative.

The second example deals with macroexperience of time. Everyone, wherever he or she lives, is affected by three simultaneous types of aging: chronological, biological, and social. I will concentrate on the last two, the first having only legal and bureaucratic importance. Biological age is comparatively simple and requires little explanation. Social age, however, is more complicated. It is the one that society assigns by its attitude to us. One feels it according to the way society treats one and in the growing number of opportunities that one is no longer offered. If biological and social age are not synchronized, the result may be disturbing, and this is exactly what I want to analyze.

Biological age may be influenced by, among other factors, heredity, environment, and customs. Social aging is chiefly influenced by environmental and cultural factors. If customs are considered a part of culture, then the influences of culture and environment are common to both forms of aging. Anyone who has lived in both a large urban center and a rural community or small city must have observed a subtle difference in the aging process between one and the other. In other words, the implications of aging differ. In urban-industrial surroundings, retirement is the social sanction that makes old age official. This practice is less prevalent in rural areas. What is more, if retirement goes hand in hand with a lack of choice of activities, the person may feel he is a useless burden on his family, who, in their turn, begin to think of him as an encumbrance. The upshot is the internment of a new patient in a home. This type of social aging can dramatically accelerate the process of biological aging.

In rural communities and in small cities, old people normally come to be respected for their wisdom; they are given new functions, they are listened to; they take an active part in and influence the making of decisions. Such old people continue to be active, to feel integrated into society and, therefore, useful.

Gerontologists and psychologists are in agreement that biological old age accelerates as a person feels more and more useless. The sense of being superfluous is certainly more common in big cities and urban centers than in small cities and rural areas. If social aging is more rapid than biological aging, a state of asynchronization can be said to occur. Furthermore, if social aging tends to be more rapid in metropolitan centers than in small cities or rural areas, a space-time disturbance is created that affects large urban conglomerations.

Cultural factors are also important. In Oriental and African countries, social aging is not so dramatic an experience as it is for Westerners, but even in the East and Africa it is better to grow old in a small place than in an over-large one.

A CITY FOR HUMAN BEINGS

I do not want to give the impression that I am a fanatic for smallness. Everything is relative. There are, for example, great cities and big cities. People feel better in the one than in the other, however similar their size. Why is that?

At risk of being repetitive, I want to review the four minimum conditions that a city should fulfill: companionship, welfare, security, and culture. I would venture to say that if the four conditions are satisfied in a big city, it is because that city has small spaces within its largeness. I should like to illustrate this by my own experience. One of the happiest periods of my life was the time that I lived in Montevideo. It is a large city, in which half of Uruguay's population lives; nevertheless, I consider that Montevideo satisfactorily fulfilled the four requirements. I should emphasize that I lived there twenty years ago; recent visits during the years of the dictatorship were a disappointment. When I lived in Montevideo, companionship was on every street corner and in every bar or café. Well-being could be felt in the relatively modest material ambitions that are so typical of Uruguayans. Security was guaranteed by a nationwide system of welfare and by a low crime rate, compared with other Latin American capitals. Poverty existed, but not destitution. Culture was accessible in all its forms and in great quantity. There were theaters and concerts to satisfy everyone's taste. A public library served people at any hour of the night or day. It was a city where walking was a pleasure; Montevideo was full of mysteries that begged to be explored. It was a city where one felt in a state of space-time coherence.

Buenos Aires also held great attraction for me at one time. I have thought a lot about these experiences, especially when I have found myself reacting unfavorably toward other metroplitan centers where I have lived. My conclusion is that the big cities that I have liked—that is, the ones where I have felt well—are big but contain a great many small spaces. Cities like Montevideo and Buenos Aires are made up of many neighborhoods, each with its own identity, traditional customs, and flavor of intimacy. There is a diversity about these neighborhoods that prevents monotony. This is what makes them attractive and, above all, pleasant to live in. But why are these characteristics found in some cities and not in others?

It seems to me that if one had to pick out other cities with the characteristics that I have just described, one would find that almost all of them had become large before the period of rapid industrialization. This is certainly so in Latin America. Cities that grew as a consequence of industrialization usually lack a distinctive stamp and appear oppressively monotonous. There are, moreover, other cities—São Paulo, for example—where all the preindustrial charm has simply been obliterated in the name of progress.

My image, then, of a city for human beings is that of either a small city or of one that offers the appearance of smallness within its largeness. Since humanizing dimensions are small dimensions, wherever big cities lack the charm of inner diversity, the sensible move would be to revitalize the small cities—victims of a mistaken idea of progress—that are struggling to survive.

REFERENCES

Kohr, Leopold. 1965. *El superdesarrollo: los peligros del gigantismo.* Barcelona: Editorial Luis Miracle.

———. 1973. *Development without Aid.* Llandybie, Wales: Christopher Davies.

Léniz and Alcaíno. 1980. Paper presented at a seminar on Time, Quality of Life, and Social Development, Bariloche, Argentina.

Ornstein, Robert. 1969. *On the Experience of Time.* New York: Penguin Books.

Wittgenstein, Ludwig. 1921. *Tractatus Logico-Philosophicus.* Berlin: Annales der Naturphilosophie.

6

The Right to the City

John Friedmann

they graciously gave me the inferior role of chronicler
I record—I don't know for whom—the history of the siege
                                        Zbigniew Herbert
                              "Report from the Besieged City"

I come from a city without streets. The dominant feature of Los Angeles is, without question, its freeways. And freeways are designed for rapid movement. We race in our private steel and glass capsules at sixty miles an hour. If someone cuts in ahead of me, I curse and yell, but the other driver, his windows rolled up, cannot hear me; I doubt whether he can see me in his rearview mirror. His radio is turned up, screaming with the insistent rhythm of punk rock. The music blurs out the roar of the columns of traffic on either side of us. No place is very far away in L.A. We go from somewhere to somewhere at a frantic speed, dipping under the city, now riding high above its roofs. The buildings next to the freeway are turned away from it, they are shielded by noise barriers eighteen feet high. From the freeways the city is invisible.

People make love on the freeways. Sometimes they also die there. Streets are meant to be places of encounter, but the streets of Los Angeles are empty. If you are caught walking the street, you feel guilty; chances are a squad car will pull up next to you, demanding to know what you are doing there at that hour, as if you had a god-given right to be there.

The other "dominant feature" of the city is the dozens of new shopping centers that have sprung up at strategic locations over the past ten years or so. The first few stories of each center are typically devoted to parking. (It costs more to build a parking space in Los Angeles than to house a working-class family in Latin America; a rough estimate is $15,000 per slot.) The rest is developed as a series of pedestrian malls. Shopping centers are air-conditioned mazes given over to the single activity of spending money. As you stroll from window to window, piped-in music relaxing any vestigial buyer resistance you may still offer, TV monitors discreetly observe your every move, their unblinking eyes rotating indefatigably in 120-degree arcs. And the ever-present Pinkerton guards in their blue uniforms can be seen to murmur secrets into their walkie-talkies, reporting to Central Control, ever watchful of the slightest irregularity in this environment controlled to perfection, this fascist utopia.

Because shopping malls charge merchants high rents, only the better sort of shop can open up along its dust-free corridors. Unlike the street, shopping centers are by their very nature exclusive. Only those who can afford to buy its luxurious merchandise are also allowed to contemplate its waterfalls and glittering mirrors.

There are only four streets in L.A. that are also places of encounter. One is Broadway, an Hispanic working-class street in the central city. Another is Hollywood Boulevard, which gets lively, especially on weekend nights, as punks, motorcycle gangs, street people, runaway kids, drug dealers, sightseers, and prostitutes are barely kept in check by extra contingents of the Los Angeles Police Department. The third is the boardwalk on Venice Beach, which has some aspects of a circus sideshow. And finally there are a few square blocks in the entertainment district of Westwood near the University of California that on weekend nights caters predominantly to raunchy teenagers and undergraduates.

Together with Tokyo, Los Angeles is the premier control center for the Pacific Rim economy. As a city, it is efficiently designed for this purpose. Its object is to facilitate movement—the movement of cars on freeways, of money through its banking system, of information through its system of computers, of people through its shopping and entertainment areas. People fantasize about life in L.A. They think they can experience there the ultimate freedom, "to do whatever you please so long as you don't hurt anyone else." And if you make lots of money, the fantasy comes true at least to this extent: you can spend it any way you please, because everything is up for sale. But as an environment, the city is more like Jeremy Bentham's model prison, a gigantic Panopticon, its famed diversity of life-styles barely managing to hide the fundamental uniformity of its movement patterns. Like prisoners tramping in a yard, the people of Los Angeles move monotonously in only one direction under the nervous scrutiny of the uniformed guards in the tower.

WHEN THEY TAKE TO THE STREETS

There are only two occasions when people take to the street and claim it as their own: when they arise in protest against the authority of an oppressive state, and when they celebrate. Protest and celebration are not very far apart. Perhaps it is because of this that the state is ever eager to maintain the drab, everyday uniformity of the city. Even the slightest crack in the enforced discipline is perceived by the authorities as an invitation to anarchy.

A few years back, a friend invited me to join in the festivities celebrating the anniversary of Saint Anne, patron saint of the city of Tudela in the Basque province of Navarra. For three nights and days, the ancient center of the city, with its rabbit warren of narrow streets clustered around the Plaza Mayor, sprang to life. As young and old poured forth into the streets to take possession of them, the city refused to sleep. *Taking to the streets* is a great celebration of the convivial life. For seventy-two uninterrupted hours, with their own ebb and flow of time, thousands of people, loosely grouped into small bands of friends and relatives, danced, ate, drank, conversed, sang, then danced again. In the mornings, collective breakfasts were improvised on the streets. Neighbors and friends shared long tables heaped with olives, tomatoes, onions, and crusty fresh bread; meats were roasted over small fires built on the pavement nearby; the red wine flowed copiously. Later, following mass in the cathedral, a solemn religious procession carried the patron saint's image through the city. And then came the running of the bulls.

It was in Tudela that I learned that a city can truly be called a city only when its streets belong to the people. Before they are traffic arteries to facilitate the city's commerce, streets are places of human encounter. It is in its streets that people express their sovereign right to the city as a political community, with a memory of itself and a name.

> The solidarity of the neighbors from the periphery and those
> from the Old City Center signals the path in search of the right to
> the city. If some group of governing municipal officials should, by
> chance, not accept this dynamics of the city into its program, it
> will be falling into the games of a petrified bureaucratic society. It
> will accept that urban space is merely a firm designed for producing more. (García Tabuenco et al. 1978, 31)

It is much the same in Recife or Rio during the season of carnival. In February of each year, the *favelados* come down from the hills. They come by busloads from the working-class suburbs to the heart of the city to celebrate life on the streets that, during the rest of the year, are effectively denied to them.

The convivial life of the carnival does not mesh well with the high velocity of money that is a prime indicator of success in our societies.

And when the holiday is over, the streets return to being traffic arteries with their carefully timed light signals of STOP and GO. Displaced from the street once again, the people return to their barrios and *favelas* on the periphery of the city of the rich. The glorious memories of the few days when they took to the streets in celebration of their sovereign right to the city will keep them going for another year.

ANOTHER FASCIST UTOPIA

Santiago de Chile in 1983 is a city stretched taut to the limit. Only a third of the population has steady employment. Hunger has invaded the city.

In the Calle Huérfanos young men and women from the proletarian suburbs are spreading their wares on the pavement. Carefully, they fold blankets on the sidewalk and arrange green and pink plastic toys, combs, mirrors, glass beads, batteries, and cheap watches in a display meant to invite the passersby. Some of the women keep small children, occasionally a swaddled baby, by their side. Their smiles are forced, but when it is a matter of eating or not eating, you learn to be hungry and to smile at the same time.

Suddenly, like wind rustling through leaves, tremors of agitation sweep down the row of hawkers. The carabineros are coming to clear the street! Blankets and babies are scooped up, and moments later the hawkers have vanished into the shadows of archways and alleys. It is the way the state lets them know that it alone shall decide who may use the street, for what purposes, and when. Calle Huérfanos is for the well-dressed shoppers and licensed establishments. In Calle Huérfanos, hawkers are in criminal violation of the state's pleasure.

It is some months later. A Belgian priest working in the suburbs is killed by a stray bullet. The bullet was intended for a Chilean worker, but it missed. Word of the killing spreads from barrio to barrio, as Santiago's workers rise up enraged. Unarmed they descend upon the city, that the entire world may know of their rage against political repression. For two days, the city becomes an ancient forum where people come to be seen and heard, speaking on matters of common concern. By the cathedral, a group of working people, both young and old, are holding hands. Defiantly, they sing the national anthem. And when the carabineros arrive, they hold their place.

In riot gear, complete with Lucite shields and visored helmets, the carabineros appear like hard-shelled beetles from another planet. They are coming quickly now, on the double, forming a phalanx.

Mercilessly, they swing their batons, cracking the skull of whoever crosses their path: old women, school kids, unemployed workers. Rapaciously, they pounce on any convenient victims, like God's avenging angels, beating them unconscious. Now and then, they capture an unlucky citizen, drag him across the street, and throw him into a waiting van. Weeks later, some of those captured will reemerge from the dungeons of the state, the marks of torture upon their broken bodies. Others simply disappear.

Random violence holds the city in fear. The streets of Santiago are empty. Still in their riot gear, small clusters of carabineros lounge at the corners, looking for victims. They can crush whomever they choose, whenever they choose. For in Santiago de Chile, the law is with those who hold a monopoly on violence, terrorism is officially sanctioned, no one is safe. Thus excluded from the city, the people retreat into the shelter of their neighborhoods.

THE RECOVERY OF POLITICAL COMMUNITY

In Peru, self-built working-class suburbs used to be called *pueblos jóvenes*. In Santiago, they are called *invasiones, callampas, barrios populares*. Excluded from the city by force and from earning a decent livelihood in the economy, workers have secured a small space for themselves. Their object is neither to accumulate capital nor to increase the velocity of money, but to survive as free and independent citizens.

And thus their neighborhood becomes the City. In hundreds of working-class barrios throughout Latin America, the idea of a "polis" is brought back to life without fanfare or even knowledge of the extraordinary nature of this event. A perennial idea is reawakening in the face of prolonged economic crisis and official terror. A revolution without violence, the polis is engulfing the ancien régime that ever more desperately clings to its privileges.

The emerging polis is a convivial society. In the course of its evolution, it is discovering its own forms and institutions. Dense social networks cross and recross the barrio, giving rise to those myriad activities that, taken together, sustain life. The barrio's inhabitants are engaged in building a self-reliant economy to produce, as much as they can, their own food, clothing, and shelter. Increasingly, they are engaged in cooperative ventures—*organizaciones económicas populares, comunidades de base*—that bring some cash into the community and strengthen internal social relations. Their celebrations mark the high points of the convivial life: fiestas and communal eating, anniversaries, and deaths. In some cities, special measures are taken to protect the autonomy of their life space and to limit the damage in the event the state succeeds in its periodic harassments and attempts at intimidation. In this way, the people secure for themselves the space they require for the production of their life and livelihood. In all these efforts, the barrio can count on only a few friends: the progressive church, one or another of the political parties, perhaps a handful of university students who have declared their solidarity with them and help to connect the barrio to the outside world (Arendt 1965).

The new polis is still a fragmentary space; its limits are the limits of its social networks. What used to be one city, ruled from above, is now becoming many. By force of circumstance the polis remains small. Being small, it lacks power. And lacking power, it cannot provide material benefits in excess of simple physical survival.

THE DISCREET CHARM OF THE BOURGEOISIE

The country club El Golf looks out upon vast expanses of verdant green, assiduously cared for by scores of gardeners who clip the grass and trim the hedges in the English fashion. Under the yellow and blue canopy of the terrace, tables and chairs are artfully arranged. Members of local elite families are engaged in casual conversation, as waiters wearing jackets of starched white cotton silently serve the afternoon tea. One can hear the ice tinkle in the glasses. Off to one side are the tennis courts, where the younger generation is still engaged in desultory exercise. A hawk glides gracefully across the cloudless sky. The scene is worthy of a Gainsborough. As the late afternoon sun casts its golden glow over this idyll, a tall man in grey uniform wearing dark glasses, his hair clipped close in military fashion, steps out onto the terrace from inside the main building. A senior member of the military junta that has recently seized power, he takes his seat at one of the tables. There are *abrazos* all around. And the vice-president of the local Citibank branch exclaims: "Ah, Colonel. How happy I am to see you. We have really missed you here."

The purpose of this little sketch is to make a point. The country club looks away from the city. It is cut off from the city by a security gate. What the elite most crave is the illusion of rustic tranquility. What they most crave is to talk with replicas of themselves. What they most fear and despise is the city and its streets crowded with people who are quite unlike themselves and whose movements are barely controlled by the official terror. What they most fear and despise is the polis, because the polis is also their nemesis. And so they must gag its voice and, in the park-like, rustic setting of El Golf, try to forget that the polis exists.

THE ECONOMIST AS MAGICIAN

Several years ago, I was a member of a World Bank mission that surveyed a number of the smaller centers in the surrounds of Mexico City, places such as Pachuca, Toluca, and Querétaro. In a typical visit, we would be given a technical briefing in the morning and, after lunch, the mayor would take us on a guided tour. Invariably, we would end up on a small hill above the town and from a convenient lookout would gaze down upon the city whose splendid panorama extended before us. Proudly, the mayor would point out to us the principal landmarks and comment on the problems he and the city council were facing. Afterwards, we would inspect the critical sites. And I thought, how fortunate the city that can still be surveyed from a hilltop and where the eye is actually connected with an object on the ground.

The dominant view of the city today is not the view from a hill. Let's listen to how economists talk about the city among themselves. Here is a current example from an economic geographer:

> The paper opens with a redefinition of the urban question in terms of the logic of industrialization. It is shown how processes of vertical and horizontal disintegration lead to increasing external economies of scale, and how these then translate into a basic urban dynamic (Scott 1986, 25).

One might be tempted to conclude from this quotation that economists do not like to talk about cities at all. As if by magic, they have made the city disappear into thin air. What they make visible instead is a presumptive universal process; in the case just cited, it is the "logic" of industrialization that, in turn, gives rise to a "basic urban dynamic." This process is described as being independent of the city; although it shapes the city, it is a global process that comes from within itself, a part, for example, of the "international division of labor."

To the economist, then, the city is at best a point location in an abstract space that displays certain characteristics important for capital accumulation: a docile labor force available at a low price, accessibility to other economic activities ("economies of scale"), a connection to the international system of markets, and a "climate" conducive to making a great deal of money. In the economist's language, particular cities are dissolved into market configurations, their history is replaced by something called the urban dynamic, where people disappear as citizens of the polis and are subsumed under the categories of abstract urbanization processes, while human concerns are reduced to property, profits, and competitive advantage.

I don't want to be misunderstood. Urban economic analysis may indeed lead to new insights. But these will be of use primarily to the managers of the "urban dynamic," the large transnational corporations and the *comprador* elites who work for them. Efficiency is the managers' watchword, as they consider the velocity of money and their returns on investment. Where cities are planned with managerial principles in mind, they are designed to share the fate of Los Angeles and to become cities without streets.

But in Latin American cities, most of the people do not work for the transnationals; increasingly, they do not seem to be working much at all. In order to survive, they need their barrio, their polis, their life space, their bastion to defend as best they can. They need a territorial base.

GENERATIVE OR PARASITIC CITIES?

More than thirty years ago, the economic historian Berthold Hoselitz (1955), one of the pioneers of development studies, posed the question whether cities in what were then still called the "backward" economies would turn out to be "generative" or "parasitical." Would these cities, he asked, have a favorable impact on economic growth or produce the opposite effect, draining their respective regional and national economies of resources for the enrichment of privileged urban classes who render no productive services in turn?

Since then, a good deal of energy has been spent on this question, as development economists have speculated on the existence of "growth poles," and anxious planners, too much in a hurry to wait for the evidence, have devised policies to concentrate investments in cities they believed likely to sustain long periods of economic expansion. Historically, urban-based industrialization was indeed spatially concentrated. In this sense, growth-pole theory was merely stating the obvious. But the theory went beyond the historical record to argue that economic growth would not only be spatially concentrated; it would diffuse *outward* from "poles" to the regions surrounding them and *down* the urban hierarchy, from large to small. Couched in the language of spatial diffusion theorists (which was a geographic specialty), growth-pole theory was an almost metaphysical concept. In the 1960s, it nevertheless had a great deal of credibility. From South Korea to Chile, regional policies were based on it.

The growth-pole or *pôle de croissance* was the brainchild of the French economist, François Perroux, who, in turn, had adapted it from Joseph Schumpeter's entrepreneurial model of economic growth. According to Perroux, cities displayed dynamic economies not merely because they housed highly interconnected and rapidly expanding industries, but also because they were powerful centers of innovation. To put the innovations in place, Perroux relied on a local entrepreneurial class, backed by appropriate technical knowledge. The notion that most relevant innovations in production would actually be imported from abroad formed no part of his theory. Latin American dependency theory which came later would take a strongly critical view of growth poles for precisely this reason (Coraggio 1972). Growth poles were thus thought to be "generative" cities in Hoselitz's sense. They would stimulate the development of their regions and, beyond them, the national economy as a whole.

The growth-pole approach to spatial planning remained popular for about a decade. By the early 1970s, however, it came to be challenged on both theoretical and empirical grounds and, by the end of the decade, it was all but abandoned. New understandings were emerging about the nature of the transnational economy, the restructuring of the older industrial regions of Europe and North America, and the new international division of labor that rendered the theory of growth poles obsolete.

At issue, in part, was the meaning of economic growth. Growth poles had been conceived in terms of the sectoral volume of production. But when one considers cities as places for making a living, it is the criterion of employment that is relevant. And in respect to employment, the record of Latin American cities is a somber one.

Three sets of data are telling. First, in the twenty years between 1960 and 1980, overall manufacturing employment in Latin America showed scarcely any increase at all relative to the total number of jobs. Remarkable gains were registered only in the residual services sector, which grew from 33 to 45 percent over the same period (Pinto 1984, table 2). The employment-generating capacity of new manufacturing investment, despite large gains in production, is therefore disappointing. Services, on the other hand, also have limits to their capacity for productively "absorbing" labor. In countries where there are no "safety nets," and where the cruel dictum "If you don't work you don't eat" holds, open unemployment stood at 10 percent in 1983, and another 20 to 50 percent of the labor force was irregularly employed in relatively unproductive occupations. The most dramatic development, however, has been the decline in real wages. In many countries, urban wages were less in 1983 than they had been in 1970 (García and Tolman 1984, table 6). This means that labor productivity was probably declining during these years (and because of disinvestment, will further decline in the future), and that there was increased labor exploitation as well. In socially relevant terms, major Latin American "growth poles" did not grow at all over the past decade or two, but actually declined.

Nor have any of the theoretical assumptions about growth poles been empirically substantiated. More often than not, entrepreneurs turned out to be foreign corporations that made their investments from boardrooms in New York, Los Angeles, or Tokyo. Most production and process innovations came from overseas as well. Local elites acquiesced in this "style" of development because they preferred elegant consumption to the uncertainties of entrepreneurial risk. Their investments tended to flow into real estate or were channeled abroad. The Latin American bourgeois thus had little in common with his Euro-American counterpart so highly admired by Schumpter.

Neither did growth poles spread development into their hinterlands. On the contrary. Wealth tends to be transferred from the periphery to the center through a series of mechanisms that include migration, policy bias, transport subsidies, a differentiated pricing system favoring urban producers, and direct capital transfers. As a result, the income gaps between large metropolitan regions and the rural periphery have been increasing.

In sum, I am obliged to conclude that Latin American cities, located as they are on the periphery of the global economy, are more correctly regarded as "parasitical" than as "generative." Expressed in human and social terms, their growth is an illusion. This situation is likely to remain unchanged until a new development, not exclusively based on outside control, unlimited accumulation, and vast social inequalities, comes to replace the model currently in force.

TOWARD AN AUTHENTIC DEVELOPMENT

The development paradigm still popular with Latin American elites is in deep trouble. There are hopes for its speedy revival, but this is an unlikely prospect (Sunkel 1985). If there is to be another development, it will come neither from the state nor from the powerful international organizations that represent the old order of things, but from among the people themselves, as they perceive new possibilities for action.

In many of the working-class barrios of Latin America, a new polis is taking shape. What appears to be happening is an extraordinary revival of people's power (*poder popular*). Instead of seeking a violent solution, however, as in classical revolutionary practice, people's power is, at least for now, engaged and increasingly conscious of itself in the daily struggles for physical existence, in processes of collective self-empowerment, and in the continuing defense of its territorial base. Emerging new forms of people's organizations may be interpreted as prefiguring the future of the Latin American city, with its strength in the barrios rather than in the institutions still symmetrically arranged around the Plaza de Armas, or the more recent citadels of oppression. Despite its Spartan circumstances, life in the barrios is a generous and optimistic life, based on mutual aid, cooperation, and democratic self-governance. And for the first time in history, women are taking an active and even leading role in its regeneration.

As a form of development, the new barrio organizations are deficient, because they are trapped in production at the lowest level without the possibility for significant accumulation. The next step, therefore, must be to move toward a regional confederation of barrios and the joint undertaking of large-scale production. Reflecting their different origin, these new forms of production will be geared less to individual consumer demand than to socially recognized needs that are so much more urgent. The goal of a confederation of barrios would be a politically engaged, productive, and convivial life. Its staging area is the city itself, which, by ancient right, belongs to the people. Historically, the city has always been a place of both oppression and fierce struggles against it. An alternative development that addresses people's genuine needs appears as a form of liberation that demands a frankly political solution. Its promise is to give people a genuine voice in their affairs and to transform the city from parasite into a stage for the creation of a culturally authentic and socially progressive life.

To some, this extension of current regenerative efforts in the barrios of Latin America may seem a pipe dream, a comforting thought in times of great trouble. Much will depend on the outcome of the present economic crisis. If unemployment should deepen, if the economy should fail to make a strong recovery over the long pull, an alternative development grounded in *poder popular* may well be the only alternative to mass starvation. A visionary leadership and the unity of the people will be needed to confront the challenges of their new situation in a politically creative way. If the economy should miraculously stage a comeback, the question will still have to be faced whether the Latin American city wants to imitate streetless Los Angeles or recover its public spaces for a new polis.

REFERENCES

Arendt, Hannah. 1965. *On Revolution*. New York: Viking.

Coraggio, José Luis. 1972. "Hacia una revision de la teoría de los polos de desarrollo." *Revista Latinoamericana de Estudios Urbano Regionales*. 2, 24–40.

García, Norberto, and Victor Tolman. 1984. "Transformación ocupacional y crisis." *Revista de la CEPAL* 24 (December), 103–16.

García Tabuenca, Antonio, Mario Gabiria, and Ptxi Tunón. 1978. *El espacio de la fiesta y la subversión. Análisis socio-económico del casco viejo Pamplona*. Pamplona: Hordago.

Hoselitz, Berthold F. 1955. "Generative and Parasitic Cities." *Economic Development and Cultural Change*. 3 (April), 278–94.

Pinto, Aníbal. 1984. "Metropolización y terciarización: malformaciones estructurales en el desarrollo latinoamericano." *Revista de la CEPAL*. 24 (December), 17–38.

Scott, A. J. 1986. "Industrialization and Urbanization: A Geographical Agenda." *Annals of the Association of American Geographers*. 76 (March), 25–37.

Sunkel, Osvaldo. 1985. *América Latina y la crisis económica internacional: ocho tesis y una propuesta*. Buenos Aires: Grupo Editor Latinoamericano S.R.L.

7

War on Waste and Other Urban Ideals for Latin America

Enrique Browne

There is a clear need to rethink Latin American cities. In the near future the number of poor living in large urban centers will probably grow at a rate that will double the population of every major city. Geisse and Sabatini (1988) have pointed out that when the unofficial influx of migrants becomes the rule rather than the exception, it is "time to change our concept of the city and of development." True, but to put forward new concepts of development and of cities is beyond the scope of this essay. I therefore propose the somewhat more modest objective of setting out a few ideas about development in the Latin American city.

First, will the so-called unofficial influxes constitute the largest part of the urban population of Latin America? According to the Latin American Center of Demography of the United Nations (CELADE), between now and the year 2000 some of Latin America's largest agglomerations will double their populations. Two of these cities, Mexico City and São Paulo, will be the largest conurbations in the world with 26.3 million and 24 million inhabitants, respectively.

The total urban population of Latin America will increase by 160 million between 1985 and 2000. Cities with populations already over 1 million will absorb about 100 million of this increased population, raising their share of the total urban population by almost 50 percent. Although the remaining 60 million will constitute an enormous problem for the smaller cities in which they will live, I shall concentrate on those masses that will be absorbed by the metropolitan areas.

It is useful to know how much every new resident in a city costs. This would include housing, water, sewage, and electricity, plus the per-capita expense of setting up workplaces, roads, parks, and other amenities. In the new city of Milton Keynes, in England, this cost was calculated, in 1985 prices, at $23,000 per person (Milton Keynes Development Corporation 1970, table 4). Using World Bank data, I have estimated (Browne 1978) that the minimum cost in a Third World country would be just under $3,000 per capita (at 1985 prices).

Therefore, $300 billion would be needed if the increase in population of the large metropolitan areas is to be accommodated even at the most modest standard. Such funding is out of the question, particularly when one takes into account that most of the expenditure of these cities goes to maintaining existing services. In addition, there are huge accumulated deficits. The crisis implies, then, that in the coming years fewer resources will be available for housing, services, and urban infrastructure—even fewer if the need to settle millions of new inhabitants in smaller cities is taken into account.

It is quite likely that the influx of unofficial migrants will increase. At the same time, the number of people in the region living below the poverty line set by the United Nations is expected to increase from 40 percent in 1985 to 66 percent in 2000 (Sachs 1985). The proportion of the work force engaged in the underground economy is expected to grow from 23 percent in 1950 to 51 percent by 2000 (Castells 1985). It is probable, then, that the proportion of the population of metropolitan areas living in shantytowns, which was 35 percent in 1975, will exceed 50 percent by the end of the century (Van Der Rest and Browne 1976). These makeshift settlements will thus be the rule rather than the exception in Latin America.

That is why ordinary Latin Americans are sceptical about large-scale plans for urban development. They may well be right. With few exceptions, most of these grandiose long-term plans have moved no further than the drawing board. This is not uncommon. Political and economic instability is the norm in a region where institutions work in their own idiosyncratic ways. Large-scale developments require resources that are unavailable. Long-term projects need either a sustained consensus that is seldom achieved or authoritarian regimes that no one wants. Moreover, those in charge of carrying out such projects normally remain in their positions for only a short time. Those who take over rarely wish to inherit their predecessors' plans. "Wipe the slate clean" is the usual cry.

If all the above is true, it may be sensible to alter the focus. Why not simply suggest wide-ranging perspectives or permanent objectives and then concentrate on medium- and short-term programs, which can be translated into concrete projects in a relatively brief span? This would be a more flexible, efficient, and credible way of proceeding. A consensus on the long-term objectives, which would give them a certain degree of continuity, would be easier to achieve. (Such a method works in other fields. Notwithstanding the different positions and polemical sources in the field of economics, one notices a certain consensus about permanent objectives such as "promoting jobs and savings," "redistributing income," and "combating inflation.") This approach would also facilitate public policy by stirring the population into action. At the same time, medium- and small-scale projects would be more in keeping with available resources.

WAR ON WASTE

Commenting on the crisis in Latin American cities, Ignacy Sachs (1985) said that "the cities of the future will have to use their resources with care. . . . It is quite clear that however difficult the situation may be, it is never completely beyond hope so long as there are human and physical resources which are idle or under-used or run down. . . . This enormous degree of waste paradoxically offers some reason for hope. . . . [One could develop] a strategy for growth based on a genuine war on waste. We shall see that in the field of urban planning there are many such opportunities." He listed several forms of waste, from technology, where carelessness, inexperience, or ostentation leads to excessive use of resources, to the failure to conserve energy or recycle waste products. Finally, he noted, "The worst form of waste is, increasingly, the failure to make use of the potential of human labor."

Sachs is right. War on waste should be one of the principal urban policies in Latin America. The factors that he selects are vital, though there are no objective criteria by which to measure them. However, he fails to mention an increasingly common form of waste that is huge in economic terms and that can be objectively demonstrated: the increasing misuse of the city's physical resources. The evolving demands of city dwellers, combined with the modern concept of the specialized use of space, turns the running of cities into a bottomless pit (Browne 1978).

In order to evolve, urban activities need time and space. The process can be compared to the setting up of a conference. One needs a conference hall of a certain size for a certain number of hours a day. These requirements may be expressed in terms of *time/space use*, measurable in square meters multiplied by hours ($m^2 \times h$), or days, and so forth. The spatial level varies according to a curve. (See Figures 1 and 2.)

The physical resources destined to absorb these demands also have a time/space relationship. The difference is that over short periods, the spatial dimension is constant. The way in which fluctuating demands

Figure 1
Highway Use by Month

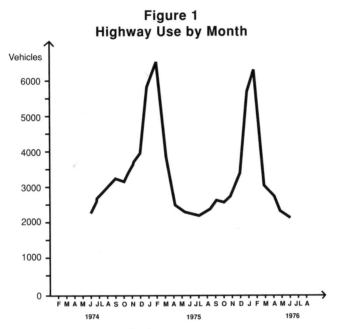

Source: Ministry of Public Works.

adjust to constant resources is the nucleus of the functioning of a city. The area that lies below the demand curve is time/space use. The area that lies above that curve but below the line of availability is time/space disuse. Finally, the demand area that exceeds the level of availability is time/space congestion. (See Figure 3.)

In contemporary cities—with variations of season and place—the demands of use have been affected by three changes. Their combined effect in Latin American cities today is explosive. These changes are:

1. *The rapid growth of urbanization,* which results in large increases in the level of demand;

2. *The progressive differentiation of the social division of labor,* which causes the number of activities requiring space to fragment and multiply, even when the total population remains constant. For example, if a group of craftsmen decides to split its work up into production, administration, and marketing functions, more space will be required to satisfy these demands. On a global level, this means that cities increase in size and decrease in density even though the population as a whole remains constant. This has happened in most modern cities (Doxiadis and Papatoannou 1974, figure 8). The effect is similar to what happens

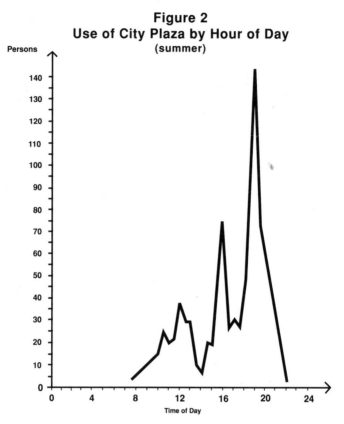

Figure 2
Use of City Plaza by Hour of Day
(summer)

Source: J. Matas, A. Necochea, P. Balbontin: "Las Plazas de Santiago."
Ed. Universidad Católica de Chile - 1983.

on a much smaller scale when a family is no longer willing to accommodate several domestic activities in a single area and separates the spaces devoted to resting, eating, sleeping, and so on. Figure 4, which illustrates an actual case, shows that the minimum quantities of space required increase dramatically even though the size of the family remains unchanged.

3. *The progressive simultaneity of the social division of labor.* Synchronization means that city dwellers get up, go to work, perform their work, and rest at increasingly specific hours of the day. As a result, the demand curves fluctuate more and more from peak to trough. The peaks correspond to an internal displacement of demand (from the axis of time to the axis of space), although these demands remain

Figure 3
Use and Availability Demands

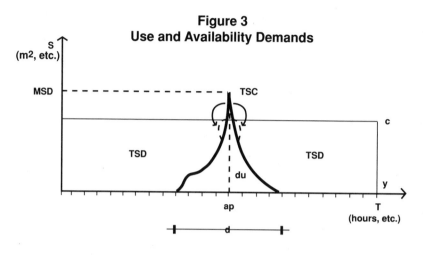

S	space	TSD	time-space disuse (obsolescence)
T	time	TSC	time-space congestion
MSD	maximum space demand (peak load)	d	duration demand
y	period of time considered	ap	axis point
du	time-space demand for use	c	constant

Figure 4
Effect of Disaggregation of Activities on
Demands for Space in Dwelling

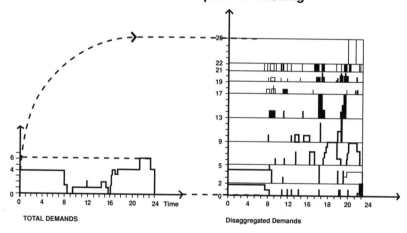

Source: Enrique Browne: "El uso de las ciudades y de las viviendas,"
Ed. Siap-CLACSO, 1978.

constant in terms of time/space. A small-scale example illustrates the point. For a poor family of five living in the country, all of whom eat breakfast at different times, one small table is enough, and it is used for a long period each day. In an urban middle-class family of the same size, the mother gets up first and prepares breakfast for her husband and children. When it is ready, they eat together and leave for their various tasks. They need space for a table large enough for five. Figure 5 illustrates the internal displacement from time axis to space axis while individual elements of demand remain constant.

Such changes as those, which began to operate in European cities after the Industrial Revolution, all make greater demands for habitable urban space. In Latin America, however, the combined effect of these changes is particularly explosive. For some time, the rate of growth in urban population has been much greater than the world average, and forecasts indicate that this situation will continue until the end of the century, with a corresponding increase in demands. These increases will be accompanied by a drastic decline in resources.

The progressive differentiation and simultaneity of the social division of labor in activities connected with the formal sectors of the economy result in qualitative changes in demand and increased basic needs. These last two changes operate less forcefully in the informal sectors of the economy and in unofficial settlements. However, if one

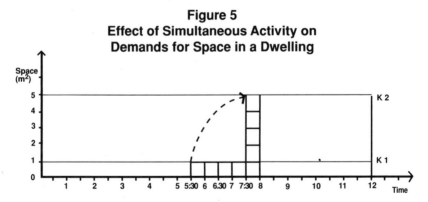

Figure 5
Effect of Simultaneous Activity on
Demands for Space in a Dwelling

Source: Enrique Browne: "El uso de las ciudades y de las viviendas," Ed. Siap-CLACSO, 1978.

attacks successfully—or at least with partial success—the causes of extreme poverty, these demands automatically diversify and increase simultaneously. For this reason, every effort to eliminate poverty takes for granted the absorption at one and the same time of the increased demands that result from the three changes in composition of urban demands—increased demands due to urbanization, diversification, and simultaneity. This is what makes the problem so difficult and explosive.

Table 1
AVERAGE ANNUAL GROWTH RATES OF URBAN POPULATION
BY REGIONS, 1960–2000

Region	1960–70	1970–80	1980–2000
The World	3.6%	2.7	2.5
North America	1.9	1.1	1.2
Latin America	4.2	3.7	2.9

Source: United Nations Population Division. Urban, Rural, and City Projections.

The theory underlying plans for development and urban legislation in Latin America comes from the International Congress on Modern Architecture (CIAM) and in particular from its Letter from Athens (1933). Point 15 of the letter states that "each individual will be given his own place within a city by the division of the city into zones. This division is based on a necessary discrimination between the various human activities, each requiring its particular space." In other words, the theory postulates specialization of use as a possible means of tackling the problems of urban chaos and congestion. In practice, as will be seen later, this is not the only possible method. In any case, it is the combination of specialization of use with the qualitative changes in demand (particularly its progressive simultaneity) that makes it almost impossible to solve the problem.

Using the same example of the breakfasts of the poor rural family and the middle-class urban family, suppose each member needs one square meter of space and half an hour to have his or her breakfast (0.5 square meters per hour per head). The total demands of the two families will be 2.5 square meters per hour. But to avoid congestion, in both cases the space available must be at least equal to the point of highest demand—one square meter for the poor family and five square meters for the middle-class family. If the period of time considered is half a day, 12 square meters per hour will be available in the one case and 60 square meters per hour in the other. The use falls from 20.8 percent for the rural family to 4.2 percent for the urban family, with a corresponding increase in disuse. (See Figure 5.)

This example can be applied on an urban scale. As physical resources increase with specialization of use—at a very high cost—their
utilization diminishes, and the yield from investment decreases. Paradoxically, then, investment and waste go hand in hand. As resources
are always limited, the problems are intertwined. Resources that satisfy some demands inefficiently reduce the effectiveness with which
other issues are resolved. Thus widespread urban crisis comes as no
surprise.

There are two possible solutions—a reduction in simultaneity of
urban activities, and changes in the way cities are used.

A Reduction in Simultaneity of Urban Activities

The synchronization of demand for the use of resources does not
presuppose simultaneity. Simultaneity is the most basic form of synchronization, but with modern techniques it is possible to spread
demands over different time periods. These measures can be used to
distribute activities over any period of time. A week is the most favored unit of time that has evolved because it does not correspond to
any physical phenomenon. Historically there have been several attempts to change the length of a week. After the adoption of Chris-
tianity, the Romans changed the week from eight to seven days. During
the French Revolution a new calendar was tried, and each month was
divided into three weeks of ten days each, the tenth day being a holiday. In 1929, the Soviet Union instituted a "continuous week" of five
days. The objective was to keep the labor force working without inter-
ruption. This force was divided into five groups, each with a different
day of rest. The system led to domestic and labor problems, and in
1940 the country returned to the seven-day week.

Since 1970 several new proposals have been put forward in various
parts of the world. Yona Friedman (in Cook 1971) suggested that the
Industrial Revolution produced a change in the organization of society from family groups to groups based on determinate factors. That,
Friedman argued, should allow for a change of rest days within the
seven-day week according to job. The result would be the decongestion
of cities.

The Argentine Carlos Varsavsky (1977) also rejected the principle of
simultaneity. He proposed a continuous nine-day week, all days being
exactly the same. He suggested that the population be divided into
three groups, of which two would always be working and the third
resting. The nine-day week would make better use of capital assets,
such as buildings, where investments of hundreds of millions of dol-

lars are wasted because the buildings are empty for two out of every seven days. With a continuous week, their use would rise by 40 percent. Something similar would happen with leisure facilities, industrial and service buildings, and other facilities. Moreover, the changeover "peaks" would be reduced by a third.

Kevin Lynch (1975) suggested that imposing uniform times when certain activities must be performed reduces freedom. For everyone to get up, eat, and go to sleep at the same time is not the general preference, Lynch argued. Western society has shown itself to be rigid in its attitude toward the clock. It has extended the needs of production into other areas. There should be some flexibility in the structure of time to satisfy different preferences. Different timetables for eating and teaching could be tried. It is feasible for offices to remain open during unconventional hours, and employees could then be allowed to choose their own hours of work. If some people prefer to shop on Sundays or at night, they should not be prevented from doing so. Essential services such as transportation, food shops, public conveniences, medical services, and communications should be available at all times, as fire-fighting services are. This reduction in simultaneity, Lynch said, would offer the additional advantage that employment would be better distributed and facilities used more efficiently.

Jacques de Chalendar (1973) observed that at peak times there is not enough room for everyone. This occurs daily, weekly, and annually. The cost of providing buildings and facilities to meet these peaks of demand is disproportionate. In Paris, for example, the Syndicat National des Chemins de Fer has 1,500 extra coaches that are used only at Christmas, Easter, and at peak holiday periods. To reduce these peaks, he proposed flexible and personal timetables, only a very small part of which would overlap for all the employees of any particular company. He also suggested changing over from the seven-day week to the fortnight, keeping Sundays free and allowing wage-earners to choose three consecutive rest days one week and to rest only on Sunday the following week. The same system would be used in schools. He suggested dividing the year in two: one period of "intense activity" (seven months, including the winter), in which schools, businesses, and services would work at full capacity, and another period of "lesser activity" (five months, including the summer), during which a varying number of personnel would be on holiday at times of their choice.

Changes in the Way Cities Are Used

Urban waste can be attacked in another way—by dispensing with the idea of "specialization of use" as a nucleus for programming, design, and construction of cities. Three forms of use have existed throughout history: superimposition, specialization, and alternation.

In superimposed use, the same space is used for two or more activities at one time. This tends to occur in situations where demands are not synchronized and construction resources are scarce. In specialized use, each space is used for only one activity all the time. This tends to be found where demands are synchronized and resources are freely available. In alternating use, a space is used for two or more activities in rotation. This tends to occur in circumstances where demands are synchronized and resources are limited. The first of these three kinds of usage is indiscriminate; the second introduces discrimination in the use of space; the third discriminates in the use of time.

Changes in the way cities are used should lead to a new generalized concept of the city itself. Such changes make room for the peaks, taking advantage of their characteristics to reduce congestion and make a city function more efficiently. Simultaneity of activities means that conflicting demands would coincide less often and for shorter periods. Space could then be used for two or more activities at different times daily, weekly, or annually.

Urban *generalization* could adopt alternating uses of space as another option, but not necessarily an inflexible option. All forms of use would be brought into action, according to specific circumstances. Specialized use would be confined to activities that are dangerous or cause some nuisance or that require highly specific or numerous facilities (such as laboratories, underground transport, airports). Specialized use would also apply to activities that take place for short periods or at unpredictable times (such as emergency services). Such use would also apply to activities with relatively stable demands (public health, for example). Because of a scarcity of resources and a pattern of demand that is not simultaneous, superimposed use would be the prominent form of use in the unofficial settlements of Latin America. In this way, demands could be brought into balance, somewhat precariously, with the availability of space. For this reason superimposed use should be encouraged. But if extreme poverty is fought successfully, these demands will diversify and synchronize simultaneously, increasing the fluctuation between peaks and troughs. At this point the emphasis should change to alternating use.

Because this last form of usage produces considerable economies of space, it is beginning to be tried in many cities of the world. It can be applied in various forms. During Chile's pre-1973 democracy, an institution was formed to educate adults and intermediate leaders. The institution had 103 centers and 60,000 students, but it never owned its own classrooms. The students used empty church halls, union meeting rooms, and the like. Thousands of square meters of space were saved in this way. This type of concentration results in economies in transport and public services. The variations in use also give variety to urban life. Running costs decrease, but programming techniques have to be perfected, and current legislation has to be improved.

The generalization of cities facilitates permanent changes in their use. It smooths over the disparity between the fixed stock of physical structures and the sudden variations in demand. This results in further economies, because it checks the cycle of construction-destruction-construction found in the cities today and works to preserve cultural heritage.

CONQUERING THE CENTER

"The face of the contemporary city is to a great extent found on its outskirts, which brings together the new work forces that are the craftsmen of urban development," Aldo Rossi wrote (1977).

> The challenge is to integrate these forces into city life, to achieve a coordinated development of the urban structure, to eliminate poor and isolated areas as well as slums, which, as if they were in quarantine, have become no-go areas. . . . It is like living in a border town between city and country, without roots or prospects. . . . The general negative characteristics of city outskirts can be summed up as a totally irregular and diverse network, which gives rise to a neighborhood that lacks the natural harmony of the countryside and does not share the dignity and spaciousness of the urban landscape, which was created before the last century. . . . We must try to find a place and a role for all those who form part of the expansion of a city population, since it is only when employment has ousted the misery of unemployment that the city will have truly integrated its outskirts.

These remarks vividly indicate that the outskirts are the crucial problem of the modern city. Moreover, this problem will not be solved completely so long as a city's inhabitants are unemployed.

The solution is neither easy nor quick. One of the main obstacles is the lack of any theory about the outskirts of cities. There are no such theories in Europe, let alone in Latin America. Speaking specifically of Italy, Rossi (1977) said: "The sad state of our city outskirts . . . is a symptom of more than just a political and technological vacuum; it is a symptom of a complete lack of vision. . . . These mistakes are of recent origin and continue to occur, thanks to an impeccably justified policy that takes hold at the far margin of coherent understanding. There is no way of preventing this except by putting forward a new idea . . . sufficiently powerful to constitute a genuine alternative."

Rossi tried to show this kind of vision in his book *L'Architettura della città* (1966). His focus on well-established networks and urban monuments may be useful for European cities, but I cannot see how they can be applied to the two extreme cases of American cities—New York, where the network is in itself a monument, and Latin American "unofficial settlements," where there is no network or monument.

For Latin American city outskirts, a comprehensive vision should arise from an empirical and critical analysis of the city itself. The fact that none exists should not bar one from proposing some tentative hypotheses.

The fact is that Latin American cities have not one but at least two outskirts. The first of these is the integrated upper- and middle-class suburbs. Although they live in suburbs, people from these areas enjoy all the features of integration. They have a certain degree of autonomy with regard to the city center because of their good educational, commercial, and other facilities. They also have good communications with the rest of the city, by virtue of infrastructure—a road network, transport, and telephones. This relationship is one of accessibility to the center of the city. Rather than outskirts, these areas are really new parts of the city.

The other outskirts are quite the opposite—poor, alienated, and far more populous. They have scant social and commercial services. Because the strength of a market is determined by the size of the population's income, these areas are fundamentally poverty-stricken. A new administrative or recreational center, a new school or church or small shopping center (often run-down), does little to improve the area.

Another feature is perhaps even more important—poor access to the city and its center. The links with the networks of water, sewage, electricity, and telephones are weak. Road and transportation connections with the center are also bad. A lack of autonomy and a poor relationship with the city proper and its center make its condition one of alienation.

There is also the distinction between homes built by the state or with state subsidies and those built by the residents of these outskirts themselves. The dominant characteristics of the former are monotony and the dinginess of very low-grade housing. The features of the latter are the diversity and precariousness of the dwellings, whether built of logs, timber, brick, or some sort of scrap material. (However, for the moment I propose to deal with this marginal periphery as a whole, without making any distinctions.)

The truth is that as long as the economics of cities do not provide for full employment for their marginal population, all solutions will be only partial. The root of the problem is poverty and not the poor living quarters themselves. Meanwhile, something must be done. The extreme scarcity of resources requires that clear priorities be set.

Before trying to establish their own autonomy in terms of physical facilities, the marginal areas must "conquer the city center." This means installing better road and transport connections with the city center. These links with the city proper are essential, for they will form the basic structure of any future urban network. This is an essential task for architects and planners.

An outlying area that is integrated but not autonomous would start by using the existing facilities provided by the city center. All the inhabitants of a city have a fundamental, historic right to use of the city center. For the poor who live on the edge of the city, it is less important to have services within their own neighborhoods than to have access to work, education, health, and other services, wherever these may exist. Survival depends crucially on access to opportunities to work, which are generally found in the central areas of the city, since that is where well-established facilities are usually located. Of course, these facilities can often be overloaded and congested. Nevertheless, congestion tends to occur at certain hours of the day and on certain days of the week. For the rest of the time these facilities are underutilized. Perhaps ways can be found to use them more efficiently without having to enlarge them. If necessary, with small additional running costs, these facilities could be used during the hours or days when demand is normally low.

To give priority to the conquest of the center does not mean that the poor suburbs will always be dormitory areas. One should accept that basic facilities and commercial activity would then improve as part of a spontaneous, gradual, and logical process. The prerequisite for this development is a change in the rigid rules that now govern the location of urban services.

FOUNDING THE CITY'S OUTSKIRTS

Giving priority to communication links between the center and the outer edges of a city does not mean that action within these areas should be neglected. Suburbs built with government funds are dominated by dull and repetitive housing schemes. To assist suburban integration into the existing urban network, plans should be limited to medium- and small-scale projects.

Here I am concerned above all with the shantytowns. In these areas the principal figures are not bureaucrats, city planners, or architects, but the people living there. If it is agreed that the problems of these slum dwellers cannot be solved without their own efforts, it must also be admitted that they should take part in any decision concerning the work involved. The making and carrying out of plans by experts should only be in support of plans worked out by the inhabitants— something that bureaucrats and experts, who are accustomed to making plans that others will implement, may find hard to accept. I am not talking about a romantic notion of "cities without planners" nor of "architecture without architects" but of cities and architecture with professional backup after the planning stage.

It should also be recognized that cities are not works of art. They may contain works of art, or even have some small areas that are works of art, but cities as a whole are not works of art. Consider Rome. The Campidoglio, the Piazza di Spagna, and the Piazza Navona are works of art. Rome as a whole is not a work of art. Urban spaces that in the course of history or as a result of modern intervention (which is relatively infrequent) have achieved a delicate spatial and dimensional balance represent an unusual achievement. But the very quality of these spaces sets them apart from the rest of the city, which is in a continuous state of flux. The vitality and growth of a city presupposes a certain disorder, a certain blend, a certain lack of definition, a certain imperfection. Although some artistic movements may have demystified many traditional beliefs, works of art still maintain an abstract, exclusive character that is not like that of real life.

Why is this? Ramshackle constructions of planks, logs, bricks, matting, cardboard, tin, and other scrap materials, which make up the *favelas, callampas,* and *villas miserias,* understandably bring to the minds of middle-class professionals images of temporariness, chaos, and disorder. That any positive undertaking could spring from this state of affairs seems impossible. Therefore, such a state of affairs must end. This implies that all the hard work of the past must be discarded. To paraphrase Sarmiento, it is a question of "barbarity or civilization."

If the city as a whole is not a work of art, however, but simply a place to live, the slums, no matter how makeshift, must contain some seed of creativity and poetry. The aim is to discover these qualities without prejudgment. Poverty is neither ethical nor aesthetically attractive. It is ugly. Poverty is only acceptable if it has been adopted voluntarily, and in Latin American cities this is not the case. One tries to understand from the confused sociocultural reality of poverty what potential it has to achieve a higher level of harmony and well-being. Three factors stand out:

1. Family ownership of property is a basic requirement for the development of slum areas. An identity card and a home address are essential for new inhabitants and for their integration—however precarious—into city life. Any kind of loan or job requires both.
2. A home is not a finished product or an isolated unit. It is part of a changing environment that, among other things, adapts to the mechanics of life, such as work, food, clothing, or education. Access to opportunities in these other areas of subsistence determines the character of the home.
3. The recycling of waste material and the heavy use of labor, which are features of continuing growth, contribute to the efficient use of scarce, disposable resources.

Several things can be done about these factors. First, one should accept that continued growth implies an unfinished product—which, paradoxically, is one of its most permanent characteristics. This can be seen in situations typical of the Latin American middle classes. For example, it is common to have two or more homes—for parents or close relatives—on one site. A business or a service within the home is a normal way of increasing family income and it allows housewives to have their own income. The size of the rooms is not determined by some abstract notion of minimum requirements but rather by old and large pieces of furniture. Living with domestic animals requires secure fencing around one's property; front gardens with thin hedges are inadequate. Living next to one's neighbors has more to do with personal relationships or practical issues, such as minimizing the danger of fire, than with aesthetics.

These and other possible examples can do nothing but confirm the need to accept an ad hoc form of urban development rather than to impose a poor imitation of pretentious middle-class garden suburbs.

As well as making the necessary changes in legislation for these communities, authorities could concentrate on the points of conflict between the needs of the city's outskirts and those of the city as a whole. One obvious conflict is the contradiction between a general need for family-owned property versus the unavoidable increase in the total density of city populations in the context of reducing the costs of providing infrastructure and maintaining services.

The foregoing point is valid, but it is not the most important one. The edges of cities—and this goes for the unofficial ones as well as those created by the state—have a fundamental weakness that must be overcome. They have not been formally laid out. They contain heterogeneous or monotonous groups of buildings and spaces, but they have no formal urban design. This is one of the crucial ways in which the development of Latin American city environments differs from those of Europe. In the latter, the hallmark of a city is its historical existence. In the sprawling suburbs of Latin American cities, character must be created in the context of a shapeless, growing mass.

By the term *creation of urban design* I mean a formal architecture, even if it is added to what already exists. Such building is a specific act intended to embody the latent spirit of certain spatial landmarks and to give meaning and unity to adjoining areas. The design could incorporate anything from utilitarian structures—a water tower, say—to some sort of later amenity, tree-planting and color, for example. In his book *Build, Inhabit, Think,* Heidegger maintains that the object of building is inhabiting. The act of inhabiting is one of man's basic traits. Heidegger asked himself what a construction was and he gave the example of a bridge: "The bridge and the river banks become, in every instance, an extension of the area immediately behind the banks. The bridge brings river, bank, and hinterland into proximity with one another. The bridge gives coherence to the land beside the river . . . it gives coherence to a landscape by defining an area. . . . The place did not exist before there was a bridge. . . . Thus the bridge does not first come into existence in a place, but rather the place comes into existence as a result of the bridge itself. When you have a place of that sort a space has been defined. Space is defined by means of a place. Thus space derives its essence from places and not simply from 'space.' To produce such things is to construct. Thus the creation of places is a process of founding and linking spaces." This sums up what I mean by the creation of urban features. It is the architecture of foundation.

The author is grateful to the architects Claudio Calveri, Jorge Wilheim, and Fernando Pérez O. for helpful observations and remarks.

REFERENCES

Browne, Enrique. 1978. *El uso de las ciudades y de las viviendas.* Buenos Aires: Ediciones SIAP-CLACSO.

Castells, Manuel. 1985. "Castells fala sobre metrópoles en São Paulo." *Projeto.* no. 79 (September), São Paulo.

Cook, Peter. 1971. *Arquitectura, planeamiento y acción.* Buenos Aires: Ediciones Nueva Visión.

De Chalendar, Jacques. 1973. *La planificación del tiempo.* Madrid: Instituto de Estudios de Administración Local.

Doxiadis, C.A., and J. P. Papatoannou. 1974. *Ecumenopolis: The Inevitable City of the Future.* Athens: Athens Publishing Center.

Geisse, Guillermo, and Francisco Sabatini. 1988. "An Alternative Development for the Large Latin American Cities." In *The Metropolis Era,* Mathew Dogan and John Kasarda, eds. Beverly Hills, Calif.: Sage Publications.

Lynch, Kevin. 1975. *¿De qué tiempo es ese lugar?* Barcelona: Ediciones Gustavo Gili.

Milton Keynes Development Corporation. 1970. "The Plan of Milton Keynes." March.

Rossi, Aldo. 1966. *L'Architettura della città.* Reprint, Milan, 1978.

———— 1977. "La ciudad y la periferia" and "El problema de la periferia en la ciudad moderna." *Para una arquitectura de tendencia. Escritos 1956–1972.* Barcelona: Editorial Gustavo Gili.

Sachs, Ignacy. 1985. "Encarando la crisis en las grandes ciudades: el trabajo, los alimentos y la energia en el ecodesarrollo urbano." *Ambiente y Desarrollo.* 1, no. 3 (October).

United Nations. 1985. *Estimates and Projections of Urban, Rural and City Populations, 1950–2025: The 1982 Assessment.* New York: United Nations.

Van Der Rest, Josse, and Enrique Browne. 1976. "La Conferencia de Caracas sobre Asentamientos Humanos." *Mensaje.* no. 243 (October), Santiago de Chile.

Varsavsky, Carlos. 1977. "Why Seven Days in a Week?" Unpublished manuscript, New York University, Department of Economics, New York.

III

The Political Process

8

Past, Present, and Future of Local Government in Latin America

Jordi Borja

My aim is not to recount the history of the various republics of Latin America in search of an explanation for present-day political and administrative centralization, but to sketch only those aspects of the background of local government organization that are relevant to an understanding of the current state of affairs.

LOCAL DEMOCRACY: A NONEXISTENT TRADITION

The Spanish system of strong municipal organization was formally transferred to the New World. In this way, the *cabildos* became the political instrument of the local people, not counting the indigenous population, the mestizos, the recent immigrants, or the lowest social classes. Colonization, however, did not produce an urban society (encompassing manufacturing, commercial, and cultural activities) like that of Europe, so the *cabildos* retained a distinct oligarchic character and, almost always, little tradition or capacity for setting up public services. (The great public works and principal political and governing functions were in the hands of authorities appointed directly by the Crown.) The colonial period left a municipal organization that was more apparent than real.

The modern state, which was founded after independence, adopted—perhaps inevitably—a strongly centralized form. That occurred for broad economic, administrative, and ideological reasons, as had been the case in Europe—the creation of a basic infrastructure and of a system of public administration is essential for the cohesion of an embryonic nation. But centralization also occurred for specific reasons. Political and military power, which had conquered the center, had to build the nation-state while in conflict both with its neighbors in consolidating frontiers and, even more, with local and regional *caudillos.* Sparsely and unevenly populated territories were already endowed with strong city-capitals or, as in the case of Buenos Aires, with a city that was to grow quickly. Dominant political groups were chiefly interested in consolidating the power of the state, not in promoting civil society or the participation of the people. On the contrary, most of the citizens were excluded, by law and in practice, from the formal political system.

The identification of the state with the capital city in many cases gives that city a special status that excludes it from the local general rule. Thus in Mexico and Argentina, the governing of the capital fell to the president of the nation, who appointed a regent or mayor to exercise power in his name. In other countries, such as Colombia, this system was extended to all cities, which were governed by delegates appointed directly by the minister of the interior or by a provincial governor. The authoritarian regimes that assumed power in the majority of Latin American countries throughout the last century and a half have gone a long way toward normalizing these undemocratic conditions. Unopposed by a tradition of local representatives, these regimes reinforced the custom of city administrators appointed by and dependent on the central power.

The type of state prevalent in Latin America in its nineteenth-century oligarchic-liberal form, or in its later bureaucratic-authoritarian form, did not in any way promote the social and political integration of the majority or favor the construction of strong local communities. Rather, the reverse was true. They were exclusive regimes that responded only to the interests of minority social groups and to the apparatus of the state itself. The experiments with national popular movements of the past fifty years were based on the mobilization of urban masses and on the monopoly of a highly centralized, personalized power. These movements did not promote decentralization, nor did certain reformist experiments of a democratic nature in the 1960s. Perhaps with the single exception of Venezuela, this failure to decentralize may have been due to lack of time and social basis.

In short, there is no solid tradition of local democracy in Latin America. Historical, theoretical, political, and specialist expertise in local government is poor. Intellectuals and social scientists have long grappled in considerable breadth and depth with worldwide social and economic problems, class and race conflict, and the larger ideological questions, as well as with analysis of the state or, more precisely, of its central apparatus. A number of specialists have analyzed the phenomena of the increasing concentration of the population in cities, general urban problems, and urban social movements. But seldom have they studied local government.

Practical politics in all its activities has given the centralized state total priority. Oddly enough, even democratic and progressive reform movements have neglected to use the local level of the state as the basic arena of popular participation and political and administrative action to benefit the majority. Cárdenas's Partido Revolucionario Institucional in Mexico, Peronists in Argentina, and the Unidad Popular in Chile did no significant work in this area.

Modernization of the state in Latin America is still in progress, and in the majority of the Latin American countries, relatively modern centralized administrations have been created incorporating techniques of contemporary public management. This is not generally the case in local administration, which lacks the necessary resources. Because of a dearth of technical and financial means and the scant political accountability allotted to it by the central government, local administration is mired down in outmoded procedures.

SOCIAL EFFECTS OF THE HISTORICAL WEAKNESS OF LOCAL GOVERNMENTS

Historically, in countries with a strong tradition of local democracy, the local powers have fulfilled a complex function of integrating and invigorating the social fabric. On the one hand, they enabled social groups that had lost a presence in central power, or that had never managed to achieve it, to find it to some extent at the local level. On the other hand, they gave groups out of power, including fringe groups, access to institutionalized politics, which is necessary both for setting up a dynamic balance and for revitalizing the political and administrative classes. In Europe, the representative political entities have played an essential role in the political socialization of workers, women, and young professionals, among others, and in the development of the politics of social welfare with popular participation.

In Latin America, the low level and fragmented nature of socioeconomic development and the shallow penetration of the state into society are at one and the same time the cause and consequence of the weakness of local governments.

Municipal governments have almost never acted as agents for development, not even in the service of the middle-class entrepreneurs of internal growth, much less as the instrument of dynamic social groups that consolidate their economic strength and acquire political force through local power. For this reason municipal governments are not even capable of creating the broad conditions favorable to economic

activity, but have limited themselves simply to ensuring certain basic
services (almost always technically and socially inadequate as well as expensive), to paving the way for speculative activities (in urbanization and
in service concessions), and to fulfilling the functions of political control.

Local administrations almost always have been economically inadequate and socially inefficient in the matter of services intended for the
welfare of the people and the functioning of the city. Among the most
relevant negative elements, the following should be singled out:

- The low qualifications required for technical and political positions (a dedication to local government has had low prestige) and
  almost total absence of career personnel at the local level or of
  institutions that train and assess local government personnel.
- Little experience in direct management of public services, which
  has impeded the creation of an entrepreneurial culture and civic
  amenities.
- Minimal technical resources for the organization and management of public services; the use of modern techniques of programming, civic organization, personnel and information management, control of expenditure, and cost-effectiveness analysis is
  more apparent than real.

These negative aspects are exacerbated particularly by the scarcity
of resources. In general, local governments have access to less than 10
percent of public expenditure, even in countries with a federal structure. In those where expenditure is more centralized, municipalities
and provinces barely have at their disposal one-third of total public
expenditure.

These local administrations are in no position to control the phenomenon of rapidly growing cities nor to make an even minimal
response to the demands of the people. Only two facts need to be
cited: approximately 50 percent of actual urban land has not been
properly surveyed and, in the majority of Latin American cities, a
large part of the population (much more than 50 percent) lives in
marginal urban conditions, where occupation of land is temporary,
houses are self-built, and basic services such as water, drainage, and
transport are lacking. That means that governments are unable to
legitimize some 50 percent of the land area of Latin American cities.

THEORY, DEMOCRATIC MOVEMENTS, AND THE LOCAL QUESTION

Until recently, analysis of democratizing processes has shown a significant theoretical and practical weakness in whatever relates to the local

question. This weakness is found both in intellectual circles and among social and political leaders, and the result has been an inability to promote a meaningful process of democratization and modernization of political institutions and public administration. No doubt exceptions exist, but in general, democratic and progressive thought in Latin America, as in Spain, has until recently had little impact on the local question. The most characteristic evidence of this failure is:

- An almost exclusively structuralist view emphasizing antagonistic contradictions between society and the city, and interpreting urban policies solely as functions destined to reproduce the socioeconomic system or to destroy it and replace it with another.
- An intellectual and political option that has given priority to the lower classes and excluded the urban middle-class.
- Omission of the political and institutional dimensions of democratization of the state and of local organizations. This is paradoxical considering the important role that social and urban demands have played and the intense political mobilization of citizens that has taken place in the last few decades in Latin America cities.

It is obvious that these three points are linked and that an excessively schematic understanding of the urban system has led to a political-social option that looked at only one part of the population and, sometimes, gave priority to marginal groups. On these bases it is understandable that representative political institutions, managed with the support of the state, have forgotten that they are responsible to all citizens and that they should practice their rivalries and activities in a legitimate manner.

Of these three features or weaknesses of political theory, it seems to me that political institutions, decentralization of the state, and the strengthening of local government should be emphasized.

The struggle against dictatorships put priority on democratic representation and national consensus as well as the mobilization of the popular sector toward immediate objectives and greater political participation. Only the existence of local democratic power will permit the synthesis of more heterogeneous procedures within it. Little by little, democratic political and intellectual sectors have begun to realize the importance of local government.

THE PRESENT SIGNIFICANCE OF LOCAL DEMOCRACY

In Latin America, even in countries with constitutional governments where state institutions have reached high levels of development, local institutions have little autonomy and often are not very representative. They have limited political prestige and make no attempt to train or incorporate new blood from the lower and middle classes or the professional classes in local and national political life. Thus, the competence and resources of local institutions are scant, and they do not provide the necessary services, urban organization, or economic and social development that, ideally, they should offer. As a result, intellectuals and progressive professionals and urban social movements have tended to develop radical extra-institutional ideas and practices, which take from democracy powers that should be basic to it and which sometimes generate social pressures and reactions at odds with the stabilization of democratic institutions.

Today, after a decade of traumatic experiences and bloody dictatorships, the democratic process is being consolidated in most Latin American countries. In every case, both in the countries that have formal, yet strongly centralized, democracies (Mexico and Colombia) and in those countries that have recently undergone transitions to democracy (Argentina, Brazil, and Uruguay), great interest is shown in local democracy, decentralization of the state is proposed, and more effective participation by the people is being attempted.

Demands are being made at three levels:

- Democratic governments (national, provincial, and local), which ask for training for elected and appointed political positions, retraining for bureaucrats, technical and political assessment for organizing local government, and technical assistance for carrying this out.
- Democratic parties, whose explicit legitimacy comes from the progressive, democratic, theoretical discussion, which is the root of local democracy, ask for decentralization of the state, local autonomy, greater popular participation, and urban social policies, to be carried out at the local level.
- Universities, research centers, and other academic institutions are exerting a growing demand for the study of urban subjects and local administration (through courses, seminars, participation in symposia and conferences, and establishment of postgraduate research courses). There is a vague awareness of the need to train university graduates to become experts and administrators in this field.

These demands show that it is understood, explicitly or not, that local government is important to the consolidation and development of democracy. This is because:

- Representative pluralistic democracy cannot be based on central-ized, personalized power in the first phase of the democratic pro-cess (even if, as in Argentina and Colombia, that power is pro-gressive and decisive). The interplay of society with institutions needs to be strengthened and made more representative in local government. Centralization and personalization of democratic political power makes that power more unstable and vulnerable, since it has to respond to all demands and resolve all conflicts.
- Traditional liberal, democratic, and socialist parties have never managed to take root at the popular level (except for populist demagoguery, which is hardly democratic). But in some cases there have been middle-class parties unconnected with the local oligarchy or with client groups. Other radical movements have almost always derived from minorities or from force of circum-stances. The working class has been too weak to breed socialist parties on the European model. Present-day social fragmentation has not made possible or desirable the forming of parties on a strictly class basis. It is through their presence and activity in local institutions that democratic and progressive parties can take root in the working classes and generate a reservoir of political representatives.
- Apart from the armed forces, the principal problem facing de-mocracy in Latin America is that of the contradiction between social expectations and political liberties on the one hand and, on the other, the administrative and financial ability of the public powers to respond. Only by promoting the decentralization of the state, by organizing locally the dialectic between demand and re-sponse, and by generating multiple mechanisms for public inter-vention and for building social cooperation can alienation and confrontation between the lower classes and democratic govern-ments be avoided. An economic miracle is not possible, but a more economically and socially efficient and participatory local political scene is.

ELEMENTS OF A NEW MUNICIPAL ADMINISTRATION

The municipality is the instrument of management most closely linked to everyday reality in local society. Its dynamic rests on its links with both local society and the state, of which it is part. On the one hand, the municipality reflects the specific characteristics of that local society: its history, its traditions, its culture, its production and consumption, its political and social conflicts and alliances. On the other hand, the municipality is that level of the state with the smallest territorial area and is therefore subordinate to an institutional hierarchy in which it occupies a low position. The characteristics and outlook of the state are reflected in the functioning and policies of the municipality. At the same time, the municipality acts with regard to its local society of reference. To some extent, the municipality is the point of greatest interaction between the state and civic society, the point where the logic of the state and the logic of daily life interact. The more democratic the state, the more open the local government will be and the more power it will have in proportion to the amount of political flow it transmits from the governed to those governing. Conversely, the more authoritarian and class-ridden a state is, the more local government is reduced to the role of a conveyor belt for transmitting the orders of the state apparatus for their execution at the lowest level.

This analysis helps explain the strategic role of local government in dealing with the urban crisis. For public policies and urban planning to represent the interests of the majority, the local government should be particularly sensitive to these interests. While this is more true of a democratic, progressive state, the same can also arise in a populist regime or even in an authoritarian state, which has to give in, at least tacitly, to popular pressure. In all these cases, local government is the institution that, from the citizens' point of view, requires the highest level of legitimacy and that is most directly responsible for the resolution of urban problems, which is the object of popular demand.

Since the emergence at the local level of the state of a more or less active political will for efficient urban development, municipal government has had to face a whole series of problems concerning its own institutional instruments. In the end, the quality and performance of institutional instruments is what determines the effectiveness of municipal management and its power to influence the urban crisis. In this connection, the principal problems facing municipal direction are those related to the availability of financial resources, the modernization of administration, the democratization of institutions, municipal decentralization, and citizen participation.

Financial resources are clearly a strong factor in the municipal government's capacity for action. It is important, therefore, that the state transfer to local government, in a linked way, administrative responsibilities and financial resources, whether through transfers, subsidies, or the power to tax. Up to a certain point, the municipal government can substantially increase its financial capacity by a better use of its resources, by giving priority to investment spending over and above administrative expenditure, by eliminating waste, by avoiding corruption, by creatively administering municipal assets according to entrepreneurial criteria, and by improving the methods of tax collection.

On an unencumbered economic base, the effectiveness of municipal management will still depend to a considerable degree on the modernization of administrative machinery and, in particular, on innovation in management methods and on intensive use of information technology. Cutting red tape can increase the impact of municipal government without an increase in resources. This process requires, fundamentally, a political will and technical capacity for public administration. Bureaucracy is not an incurable disease of public service.

A new municipal administration also needs to place itself in the context of a general process of democratization of the state through direct election of local representatives by the citizens—not only to realize a fundamental political principle but also for reasons of efficiency. Only an administration regularly controlled by means of free elections can decisively confront the struggle against corruption, which is the source of wasted resources and badly organized management. The probity of local government is a key element in winning the collaboration of citizens in facing any crisis. But this probity cannot be left to the honesty of individual government officials. Society's controls, through the political cost that the exposure of corruption can have that on public opinion, create an institutional climate in which campaigns for honesty among government officials can produce results. While the democratization of administration does not in itself solve corruption and inefficiency, its assistance is indispensable for any advance over this terrain and decisive for the renovation of municipal action.

Another development in city management concerns the decentralization of local government—above all in the big cities. Competence, resources, and personnel must be turned over to district, regional, and neighborhood institutions in a way that increases their effectiveness and flexibility, making possible a more direct knowledge of the specific problems of each neighborhood as well as a more intimate interrelation with the public. Decentralization should not be confused with the delegating of functions whereby the mechanisms of decision and the means of power are still concentrated at the pinnacle of the institution. Decentralization must entail a real transfer of power and resources to levels below municipal administration. Of course, a capability for administration at the central level must be maintained to coordinate different services through unified, coherent policy. But the carrying out and development of these central decisions can be done much more effectively and with a greater feeling for the problems by district councils, neighborhood groups, and other local bodies that are linked to a specific community in a particular area. These decentralized bodies are still organs of the state and therefore should be: a) democratically elected by the citizens of that area or chosen by an elected democratic municipal authority; and b) administratively subordinate to the municipal authority as a whole, so that they will not be able to use their autonomy to fragment the efforts of state management to deal with local problems. Administrative decentralization is an internal process within the state, not a fragmentation of the state.

That is why it is important to distinguish between municipal decentralization and citizen participation. They must be made into complementary mechanisms that will reinforce each other for the sake of a better management and a deepening of democracy.

Citizen participation in local government is that part of the institutional process outside the formal electoral process by which the individual relates to the administration. I am talking here about an institutional type of citizen participation—distinct from pressure groups or peoples' associations—in which citizens on their own initiative, outside state institutions, organize to defend their interests. These are called urban social movements. Even in upholding the will of the people as expressed in an election, the state develops its own dynamic based on broad administrative principles, and it cannot give ear to special interests, whether or not they are those of mobilized urban sectors. Yet a flexible democratic state must open institutional channels to popular pressure and control of its operations. This is why it is important to have institutional mechanisms of urban participation where peoples' associations and different types of interest groups can express their aspirations, suggestions, and criticisms within the scope of the administration while respecting formal rules of political decision making.

This citizen participation in urban affairs can develop at different levels. Citizens can participate in disseminating information about administrative decisions after they have been taken. They can play a consulting role in the process of decision making. And they can participate in the management of services and provide a presence in the pertinent decentralized organs of administration.

Another possible level of participation involves citizens' associations with full powers of the decision-making process. In fact, experience shows that this type of participation debases the essence of democratic administration and is the source of confusion and management disorganization. It is fundamental to the preservation of a democratic state that no social group should be able to impose its will outside legitimately established channels, for the most activist groups are not always the most legitimate. That is why participation must be kept within channels under the authority of the democratically elected administration, which must reserve to itself the power of final decision. Nevertheless, keeping citizen participation within the limits of democratic institutions does not lessen its role. Instead, the importance of social change in the dynamic of institutions must be recognized. The opening up of participation allows creative energy to be channeled from the permitted social movements, giving their demands a chance to flourish as a result of the reform of urban management. Participation is not a populist concession, but an instrument for energizing management, which, by facilitating direct contact with the citizens, airs their problems more fully, permits the formulation of more adequate policies, and makes it easier for urban policies to be put into practice.

While municipal management is the most important specific instrument for the treatment of the urban crisis, its actions are defined by the global political context. Therefore, a good administration will not accommodate policies necessary for the political transformation Latin America requires. But the whole point of my argument is that municipal management can be not only a technical instrument but also an essential lever of political change.

DEMOCRACY AND THE TRANSFORMATION OF THE STATE

Because of the priority accorded to centrally controlled power in Latin America, the importance of municipal politics has for the most part been underestimated. In terms of power and resources, local institutions have been particularly weak in contemporary Latin America. But the basic reason for this is the weakness of democratic institutions in general. In fact, the instability of the political system leads (or in its day led) to a concentration of power at the top. At the same time, the lack of democratic practice has tended to make local governments the instruments of political bosses, opening the door to corruption and allowing the bureaucratizing of inefficiency.

The political alternatives to the system dominating most of Latin America, however, have usually tended to diminish the role of political democracy, which was labeled "bourgeois" and considered a mere springboard for true "people's democracy," both in its Marxist-Leninist form and in its nationalist-populist version. Whichever the case, municipal government has received little attention, given its low capacity for influence in the strategic centers of power.

The situation changes profoundly from the moment political democracy, without labels, becomes the basic issue of the Latin American political question, an end in itself to some extent and not a means. This does not mean that the struggle for democracy is enough to achieve social change. But it is a historic objective in its own right and an element that is indispensable for a new society built for and by the people.

In the present circumstances, several of the most important Latin American countries have as their objective the consolidation of democracy. Others are planning its expansion and renewal. And others are still in the process of struggle against dictatorships. In one way or another, democracy is the main issue today in Latin America. In this issue, local government occupies a leading role. As has been pointed out, local government is the greatest point of interaction between the state and society. Democracy can only be consolidated in Latin America if it is strongly rooted in society, particularly among the lower classes, so that it may counter the oligarchic tendencies still present in the state. Local government can be the institutional melting pot in which this new political legitimacy and new popular participation can operate. But for this to happen, there must be a reform of the state that will give power and representation to local government, a fiscal reform that will distribute resources to it, and a technical buildup that will make local governments into effective instruments for solving people's problems. In the end, it is neither a paradox nor a coincidence that democracy is developing in the midst of total economic crisis. Only a collective national effort, based on legitimate political instruments, can surmount the structural problems facing Latin America today. Perhaps in the same way, out of the depths of the urban crisis a plan is emerging for the renewal of the Latin American city. Toward such a plan, democratic, decentralized, participatory local government is a possible historical vector. To change the city, it is necessary to change society and the state in a joint process where the management of daily life is united with a plan for political transformation.

TOWARD A DEMOCRACY OF TERRITORY

Liberal-oligarchic democracy has evolved through the twentieth century into a democracy of mass parties and organizations, which have been at the same time the cause and the effect of economic and social democratization as well as the means of broadening the channels of political participation. The development of administration and public services, education, health care, and so forth, the nationalization of key economic sectors, and the evolution of greater levels of cultural integration have been paralleled by a broadening of civil liberties, the extension of suffrage, and the recognition by governments of labor unions and popular organizations. The democracy of parties and masses has replaced the old exclusive liberal democracy.

But this process, which is incomplete in Latin America, has not exhausted democracy's potential, nor has it been enough to ensure for the great majority a truly pluralist political contest.

The development of political institutions and public administration tends to create a pattern of specialization and bureaucracy. When this happens, the double guarantee of concerted public action and political control by the elected and by participation of the people is lost.

In the face of this tendency, an opposing one has developed. This one promotes territorial decentralization of the state and the creation or reinforcement of autonomous representative political organizations with absolute authority in decision making, the capacity to dictate norms and to execute them, and sufficient means (in terms of finance, personnel, resources, and expertise) to do so. The institutions of the intermediate (state, regional, provincial) or local (municipal) level are those which make territorial democracy possible.

The democracy of territory tries to recognize the interior of a national community, the existence of territorially based social communities that can be the active subjects and the social support of a level of government.

This government is autonomous insofar as it has its own area of authority and the resources to carry out that authority. Territorial governments need to be able to dictate norms, establish programs of action, and make decisions that are legally valid.

The legitimacy and the effectiveness of territorial administrations and governments require that they be elective and that they be sustained by broad support and social consensus. Territorial democracy has the right to exist and the scope to develop only if it promotes ever greater levels of popular participation.

In short, political pluralism no longer expresses itself only in ideological alternatives and partisan confrontations but also by means of a diversity of governments, congresses, and territorially based administrations that facilitate the representation of interests and political participation with greater social effectiveness.

9

Law and Urban Explosion in Latin America

Rogelio Pérez Perdomo

The current development of Latin American cities poses challenges to those who practice any discipline. A universe of new relations, of problems previously unknown, confront these cities, surrounding and permeating them. In this essay, my aim is to analyze the challenges that face an old discipline, the law, and those who practice it, lawyers. Elsewhere in this volume, Abelardo Sánchez León calls the children of urban migrants—children who have been baptized in the sewers of over-expanding cities and raised in a network of violence—"the children of chaos." In contrast, lawyers might be referred to as "the fathers of order." It is lawyers who tried to make Latin American societies grow with an order that they themselves helped to create. This order was shaped by the laws that the lawyers developed, although officially these laws were presented as the result of the will of the people in judgments handed down by the authority of the republic and in the name of the law, as well as in opinions and academic works, which, more modestly, they signed with their own names.

These legal minds, however, are not the only begetter: Doctors, men of letters, architects, urban planners, and psychologists have also tried to shape actions and urban spaces, but perhaps no discipline is as conspicuous as the law in its identification with order and social conformity.

Constitutions, codes, and laws are written to organize political and social life according to a given rational plan. Cities, particularly capital cities, are the sites of the rationalization of legal power. Here, where lawyers and men with legal-political backgrounds are concentrated, legal instruments are discussed and approved. Here also are found those who interpret them, the magistrates and authors of legal opinions.

The law is, additionally, a centralizing force. Legislation is passed for the country, urban and rural, rich and poor. But just as the law that protects certain economic interests or that prohibits people from sleeping on park benches does not affect everyone in the same way, it does not affect rural areas and cities in the same way. Metaphorically, the law could be depicted as a waterfall of order that flows from the capital, occupies the main urban centers, and finally reaches the countryside.

The law is a civilizing instrument. Social relations subjected to rational rules in the most modern urban centers in the country are the model for the whole country. Santos Luzardo, in Rómulo Gallegos's novel *Doña Bárbara,* is a lawyer from Caracas who visits the plains, where he manages to impose law and defeat barbarism. Absence of law dominates the countryside, where violence, simple life, and traditional customs are found. In this lie its danger and its appeal. Rural life can also be idealized; the call of the land and the romanticizing of country life are constant themes in literature. Law is civilization, but it is also the lowliness of commerce, which is the stuff of law courts. Be that as it may, the legal profession has had the good sense to resist siren songs in praise of rural life.

Nowadays urban life has triumphed. Not only do people live increasingly in cities, but the countryside is changing. The passing of large rural estates, with all their farming enterprises, demonstrates the modernization and legal development that has come to country life. Peasant culture, weighed down under archaic legal relationships, is on the verge of extinction. Is this the triumph of the legal system?

The answer must be carefully considered. A quantitative, superficial approach would indicate such a triumph. Current writing on the law and development shows that urban development—part of a more general modernizing process—brings with it a considerable increase in the work of notaries, registrars, and in certain types of court cases called executive briefs. In lay terms, this means that there are more normal contracts and quick cases for the recovery of debts. In contrast, in a traditional and fundamentally rural society like that of nineteenth-century Venezuela, the number of cases was extremely small, and it was so important to explain why legal remedy was sought that frequently the parties and their lawyers would publish the proceedings and judgments in periodicals or in separate pamphlets. Along with this growing use of contracts and court cases came an enormous expansion in the legal profession (Pérez Perdomo 1981, 1989). There is no doubt that today in Latin America, men and women enter into litigation more frequently than in the nineteenth century. Even in relative terms, if the increase in population is taken into account, more men and women form companies and partnerships, draw up formal contracts, recover debts or have debts recovered from them, demand workers' rights from their employers, get divorced, demand child support, and so forth. But a distinction should be made between all this legal activity and the triumph of law.

In Latin American cities, alongside the increase in legal activity, there has been a rise and development of informal sectors and internal relationships. From the orthodox legal point of view, these activities are unlawful, even though one could speak of informal legal systems by analogy because they fulfill a social function similar to that of the law. But the term should not hide the fact that these activities may oppose the law, which is a "law against the law," to quote Santos (1977).

One of the sectors in which informal legal systems develop is among that part of the urban population commonly known as "the underclass." Even when this term has been criticized, as far as the law is concerned, it really is a matter of an underclass, for these people have been rejected by the law. To a very large extent, they are true noncitizens.

A distinction should be made between criminal and civil matters in regard to the underclass. In civil matters, the underclass is basically denied the opportunity to claim its rights. In some cases, this exclusion is implicit in the particular situation. An example is a conflict related to housing, which has usually been built illegally on squatters' land. To claim any legal obligation in an illegal situation is theoretically complex and very difficult. In the same way, these shantytown dwellers and others who knowingly work without a contract and on the periphery of the law compromise their ability to claim their work rights within the formal system.

But the theoretical difficulties are insignificant beside the practical difficulties that someone on a low income has to overcome to make any claim. First, there is the obstacle arising from his own ignorance of the law. Second, there is the expense; lawyers' fees and court costs tend to be beyond the means of the underclass. Third, there are less tangible costs, which are equally powerful—the expense in time and human dignity. Long lines, scant attention, rude treatment, and unexpected decisions are evils common in many societies, but they may be at their worst in Latin America.

The rejection of the formal legal system does not mean that informal relationships get out of control. Informal systems allow members of the underclass ways to make claims or voice requests. Sometimes problems are resolved in mediation centers. In other cases, there is no real solution, but at least the system allows complaints to be heard, and this is very important. Certain radio programs, for example, claim that such-and-such a district has been without water for several days or that its school is on the verge of collapse. The rejection of the formal system is not total. Frequently these people, like everyone else, need certain papers and permits that they cannot do without, and when the legal way is very complicated or inconvenient, corruption and bribery arise to take its place.

The criminal situation is far more dramatic. The absence of a proper defense and the labeling of certain groups as delinquent has the effect of making the system operate punitively without much relation to real guilt. This could be called the Kafka factor—the person feels himself overwhelmed by a machine driven by powerful individuals who use an arcane language and procedures and rules that he does not understand and whose words will be the decisive element in his life. A chance connection with a crime, perhaps passing by the scene of an offense or appearing confused or suspicious in a first meeting with the police, may subject a person to a long, incomprehensible, and distressing trial that may well result in his conviction. Informal relationships—links with the police, the corruption of government officials, previous contact with lawyers—probably benefit professional or organized criminals. The network of the formal system often allows those who should be punished most severely to get off lightest.

Lawlessness also takes place at the summit of urban society. The ecological crimes of urban developers, frauds by manufacturers of mass-market products, banking crimes, corruption by high government officials—these are crimes that are fundamentally difficult to prosecute. Usually those who commit them rely on the advice of highly competent lawyers, and their criminal responsibility is diluted and disguised.

Frequently, the public is outraged over the leniency shown in these cases. What the public does not understand is that the ministries and the courts have to act in accordance with the formal rules and the established evidence and that usually there is no real chance of a conviction. Nor does the public realize that there are many more social crimes of this sort that are never brought to law. This legally immune social group is that of the supercitizen.

In the civil sphere, many businesses operate without formal contracts. Oral agreements, reached at a party or during a business lunch, may be as effective as, or more so than, a written contract. These are the gentlemen's agreements of old that are now fulfilled not out of an exaggerated notion of honor, but from a need to continue advantageous business relationships or to maintain the prestige that smooth relations between enterprises provide. When necessary, contracts follow the informal agreement, sometimes after it has been put into effect. These contracts are the formalities regulating the registration of property sales or income tax returns.

In short, the trust of the countryside in the legal and civilizing role of the city has been destroyed not by rural obstinacy but by urban diversity. The idea of the city extending its civilizing network over the whole country pertains more to the relatively small, Europeanized capitals of the past. The development of the urban metropolises demonstrates that the law is a relatively thin fringe around the true self-regulating structure of a society. The image of a fringe may be incorrect because its boundaries are not clear and the informal system exists often in close connection with the formal. Neither can be understood independently.

My colleagues in the law have long failed to pay attention to the informal system. In the past, they were justified because these systems were part of a world that was to have been obliterated by the rationalizing order of society. This is no longer so, for the order that was to be imposed generated the informal system. An analysis of the relation between the two systems is necessary and perhaps urgent so that the order-chaos of Latin America's new urbanized society can be understood.

Having identified myself as a lawyer, I would like to make a final observation: the formal-informal mixture is not a pathological one. Perhaps it is a part of all societies; perhaps a totally legalistic world would be suffocating. If in work, love, or war, people always acted with a rule book in one hand and with a full knowledge of their rights and obligations, the world would be a much poorer place than it is. It would not be aware of compromise, friendship, and the spontaneous recognition of hierarchies. Much of the richness of Latin American society lies in the importance of this kind of relationship. But I do not intend to conclude with a defense of the informal system, much of which is ethically and socially devastating. My point is that no remedy will be successful if the links between formal and informal are disregarded. Except, that is, in the event of a miracle.

REFERENCES

Pérez Perdomo, R. 1981. *Los abogados en Venezuela.* Caracas: Monte Avila.

———. 1989. "Teoría y práctica de la legislación en la temprana República—Venezuela, 1821–1870." *Politea.*

Santos, Bonaventura de Sousa. 1977. "The Law of the Oppressed: The Construction and Reproduction of Legality in Pasagarda." *Law and Society Review.* 12:1.

10

Montevideo: Between Participation and Authoritarianism

Mariano Arana and Fernando Giordano

In the 1984 Uruguayan elections, all the political parties affirmed the need for citizen participation at the local level. It is a known fact that the authoritarian experience under the military dictatorship imposed a planned social demobilization of Uruguayan society. But slogans and mere talk about objectives apart, local participation can only be achieved by concrete public action. Shortly after the new government was installed, obvious signs of a gap appeared between what the government was doing and what it had said in its pre-election proposals.

THE ACRITICAL MODEL

In the mid-1950s a period of crisis began in Uruguay. The deepening of this crisis damaged the *batllista* model on which the foundations of Latin America's first welfare state were laid in the early decades of the century by Uruguay's president, José Batlle y Ordóñez.

Based on a significant increase in the role of the state and on the country's social makeup (an immigrant population predominantly European in origin, the absence of an indigenous population, and a high degree of urbanization), this model made possible advanced social legislation and encouraged the development and strengthening of the middle class, which was the substantial prop of its political and electoral support. Even in its physical structure, Montevideo reflected the character of a paternalistic welfare state based on this *batllista* model.

Montevideo today exhibits a continuation of tendencies that arose in the last third of the previous century. The picture at that time was one of an expanding city geared to satisfying the demand for housing, with a marked inclination toward single-family dwellings, preferably owner-occupied.

These tendencies, reaffirming the model, were to a large extent made possible by different kinds of credit and by the lavishness with which land was subdivided. Even the low-income sectors fell in with this trend and directed their aspirations into building their own homes, a custom still common throughout the country. This fact made for an urban sprawl of low population density.

Even today—despite 1947 laws allowing horizontal ownership, which encouraged high-rise construction—Montevideo has population densities of between 40 and 120 inhabitants per hectare in its urbanized area of 135 square kilometers, and in only two small areas of the city do densities rise above 400 inhabitants per hectare.

The costly infrastructure that this type of settlement demands was made viable by the allocation of sufficient resources within the framework of the income redistribution policies enacted by *batllismo*.

The public sector supported the demand unleashed by this process in an attempt to gain votes. In this way, a significant network of infrastructure was set up and reached a relatively high level of development. Although earlier figures are unavailable, some statistics from the mid-1970s are illustrative: 71 percent of all houses in Montevideo were connected to a public sewage system; 92.6 percent had municipal drinking water; and 97 percent had electricity.

It ought to be pointed out, nevertheless, that in several areas on the outskirts of the city, private water-sellers could still be found who sold and recharged storage batteries as a source of electricity. These facts are relevant when we recall the low population growth of the country in recent decades.

It is equally important to note that the city was able to develop reasonable public amenities. Montevideo's public park system, for example, was almost all laid out during the municipal administrations of the first quarter of the century. In many other spheres—road-paving, playgrounds, neighborhood centers, and the like—acceptable levels of amenities were provided, although not always equitably for all parts of the city.

In 1975, 52 percent of houses were owner-occupied. Information on the current number of dwellings, estimated at 415,000 by the 1985 census, has not yet been broken down. It may be supposed, however, that there continues to be a significant percentage of single-family dwellings compared to apartments, although in recent years the latter have certainly been the type favored by the public sector and for private investment.

Although low-quality buildings and shacks made from scrap material seem to have increased in number, the majority of new construction has been of acceptable standards.

While there have been no special policies for conserving and maintaining the existing housing stock, most buildings are made from durable materials with a reasonable possibility of a long, useful life. These features are still visible despite considerable changes experienced by the city in recent years. Such changes were not the result of demographic growth or immigration from the countryside. On the contrary, Montevideo—like the whole country—recorded a very slight population increase. The city's population increased by only 6 percent between 1975 and 1985. (The slow growth throughout the country can be explained not only by low birth rates but also by heavy emigration, the result of economic and political crisis. Despite the end of the military dictatorship, this outward flow has continued.)

Low growth does not imply population immobility; movement within the city increased densities in some urban areas and reduced populations (even in absolute terms) in others.

Not only do population shifts occur within the city, but the country itself is highly urbanized. More than 83 percent of the country lives in urban areas; nearly half—47 percent—lives in Montevideo, an extreme case of macrocephalism. Montevideo, according to the 1985 census, had 1,248,000 inhabitants. Salto, the country's next largest city, had only 80,787 inhabitants.

Montevideo's uniqueness must be set in a context of a national reality marked by stagnation and by contradictions in the productive structure.

THE CRISIS IN THE MODEL

The collapse of the model, already apparent since the mid-fifties, culminated in the breakdown of institutions and in the imposition of rigid authoritarian rule from 1973 to 1984.

The dictatorship outlined a putative "national" project to open up the country to foreign trade. This plan set aside the idea of the welfare state for its neoliberal alternative. As a result, speculation took priority over production, an exaggerated external debt was contracted, salaries dwindled in real terms, and pauperization of the population increased.

The following are a few indicators of the economic deterioration suffered by the people:

- The salary of the average worker was reduced by 40 to 50 percent from 1968 levels, in real terms.
- According to Melgar and Villalobos (1986), between 1973 and 1983, the proportion of gross national product going to wages and

salaries dropped from 36 percent to 28 percent, while the percentage of income received by the richest 5 percent rose from 17 percent to 23 percent in the same period.

• It has been estimated that the payment received in 1984 by the vast mass of pensioners and those on welfare was less than a quarter of what it had been twenty years before.

To these figures must be added the rise in malnutrition, infant mortality, and unemployment. The problem of unemployment is particularly critical. It has been estimated that at the beginning of 1984, 150,000 workers were unemployed and some 120,000 underemployed. One in four "active" persons was affected by a situation of a gravity hitherto unknown in the country. One of the most obvious signs of this phenomenon was the number of carts, sometimes pulled by horses but more often by indigent people, which daily crisscrossed the city, covering tens of kilometers to scavenge the garbage heaps of the rich. Here, people salvaged materials (food scraps, different types of metal, wood, cardboard) which they sold, fed to their domestic or farm animals, or, in extreme cases, consumed themselves.

The Deteriorating Quality of Life

The process of collapse gave rise to factors that affected the public habitat in the city as well as the quality of life of the population. In particular, the housing stock fell into unnecessary disrepair, which was damaging not only to each individual owner but to the community as a whole. Moreover, toward the end of the 1970s, Montevideo, like Punta del Este before it, underwent a speculative building spurt that had disastrous results for the city.

Decisions at the national level and opportune circumstances came together in Uruguay to shape the critical urban panorama of the capital. Rents were decontrolled; the exchange rate deflected foreign investment toward the real estate market; a vast volume of credit from public savings was offered to private developers with minimal conditions; neighboring countries (mainly Argentina) invested a significant amount of capital. All these combined to bring about a construction boom and an uncontrollable rise in land values. The consequence was mindless demolition, an increase of cleared sites used as car parks, the replacement of buildings by others of mediocre construction and impoverished design, the often compulsory demolition of poor residential areas, the dismantling of garden areas, an excessive concentration of high-rise buildings, and a disproportionate specialization of function of certain urban areas.

In little over a year, residential areas such as Pocitos irrevocably lost their character and balance. The unusual character of the port district and of the Old City next to it were seriously endangered. Residents of one of the city's most populous working-class neighborhoods, which was home to a relatively homogeneous social group supported by a cultural tradition going back to the black population that had lived in Montevideo since the early days, were forced to move to the edge of the city or into appallingly overcrowded temporary accommodations.

Public administration itself—by direct action or omission— exacerbated the growing deterioration of the community and the city environment. City squares were disfigured; trees lining streets were too severely pollarded or cut down; place names were changed. At the same time there was a growing, pathological search for monumental, ceremonial, declamatory, and in the end repressive spaces.

But the clearest evidence of official complicity with the widespread decay brought about by speculation, ignorance, and neglect was the now infamous Resolution of Executive Power of October 1979, in which hundreds of buildings were removed from the list of "Historic Monuments" and for the most part demolished.

By applying socioeconomic measures across the country, the dictatorship fed the greed of private capital over the general interest, damaging the country's heritage.

In addition to the speculative development, existing public spaces were privatized or destroyed. In keeping with the ideology of the neoliberal model that had been adopted, public space was not regarded as a useful object with a specific purpose, but as a mere exchange asset. Space set aside for public recreation cost nothing and so, according to the peculiar liberal concept, was worth nothing. It could, therefore, be exchanged for purposes other than the one for which it was intended.

That is what happened to Parque Rivera, whose dense trees were cut down to make room for a stadium. Capurro and República Española parks were practically destroyed for the mindless siting of a superhighway leading eastward out of Montevideo. The land belonging to the old Fermín Ferreira hospital was sold off to a development company. Parts of Parque Roosevelt and "El Prado" and various coastal areas were granted as concessions to the armed forces and police and, for some unknown reason, are still in the control of these organizations for their exclusive use. Such concessions usually resulted in serious ecological and landscape changes.

Access to public space has also become more difficult, a factor that is resulting in urban segregation. The extremely high cost of public transport has become a determining factor in this segregation. Many workers spend between 15 and 30 percent of their already eroded daily wages just traveling to their workplaces.

Low-income families have been—and still are—severely limited in their right to "appropriate" public space. Access to recreation areas (mostly located near the coast) has become prohibitively expensive for the mass of citizens with the lowest incomes.

The size of the public transport problem can be seen from the number of tickets sold: 511 million in 1963 and barely 270 million in 1984. During the same period the metropolitan area had increased by 156,000 residents, making the transportation problem even worse.

These factors have combined to cause a deterioration in the living conditions of large sectors of the population. The reduction in the incomes of wage earners and pensioners and the total freeing of urban rent controls have created a low-cost housing crisis.

Although the shantytowns, mostly on the outskirts of Montevideo, are nowhere near as large as the vast sprawl of those in Bogotá, Caracas, Lima, Mexico City, Rio de Janeiro, São Paulo, and other Latin American cities, their recent increase has been significant. Built on public land or vacant lots with no public services, these towns are known as *cantegriles,* the name of an elegant seaside neighborhood in Punta del Este. In addition, there is "emergency" housing on the edge of the city, which, although erected by the public sector, is still only temporary accommodation.

Around 1983 there were an estimated 3,000 homes in the Montevidean *cantegriles*—by some estimates, nearly double the number that existed just three years earlier—and about 6,000 emergency units. In all, some 50,000 persons were living in very inadequate conditions.

In the early 1970s, most of the residents of these quarters came from that sector of the population characterized as "marginal," people who worked in the "informal" sector. A survey carried out among inhabitants of the *cantegriles* in 1984 revealed that 36 percent of family heads were workers or white-collar employees in the formal sector.

But the housing problem in Montevideo is even wider. In the city proper—including upper-income residential areas and even the center—deterioration has increased. Large old houses converted into "lodging houses" are let out in appalling conditions by the room, in each of which a whole family lives, sharing with many other families the few and usually inadequate sanitary arrangements.

The most extreme cases are the squatters' dwellings. Usually derelict, these buildings are occupied by "intruders," who live there in deplorable conditions, without electricity, drinking water, or, often, even windows. Such situations have been recorded in various parts of the capital, although the phenomenon is at its worst in the Barrio Sur and in the Old City, where about 5 percent of the residents are affected by these critical conditions.

The Citizens' Responses

Despite the obviously regressive, stagnant outlook imposed by the dictatorship, there survived, or were planned in that period, various types of social, political, technical, and cultural action aimed at smoothing over the effects of the crisis and creating alternatives to authoritarianism.

There is no doubt of the effectiveness of coercive methods or of the dictatorship's intention to "atomize" society. Similarly, there is clear evidence of the capability of the people of Montevideo to overcome—albeit partially—the unjust conditions imposed on the greater part of the population.

Some impromptu action took place, or at least was initiated, in the field of emergency social services. Much of this action was initiated by locally based organizations—embryos of working-class social movements. Some of them are listed here:

• Soup kitchens and meals on wheels tried to alleviate problems of malnutrition, giving priority to children and old people.
• Shopping clubs managed, by eliminating the middleman, to reduce the cost of essential items in the family shopping basket.
• Neighborhood health clinics tried, with the support and collaboration of medical technicians and students, to offer basic treatment and to distribute free medication.

The wide extent and use of such services occurred because these services came into being when public health at the local and national level was in a critical state.

All these groups relied on neighborhood support as well as on the support of technical, religious, and union organizations. They managed, moreover, to coordinate their activities, which strengthened their operation.

Beginning as a form of reaction, little by little the movement turned into one of initiation, which led to "a change from a reformist stance to one of political change." (Filgueira et al. 1986) This is particularly evident in the context of low-cost housing.

At the end of 1982, in one area on the edge of Montevideo, a Comisión Pro Viviendas Decorosas (Commission for Decent Housing) was set up to bring together groups from seven *cantegriles* and two temporary housing sites for people evicted from farming property declared "derelict" by the municipality. The aim was to obtain mutual support and solidarity from people and institutions to reinforce the demands that these groups claimed as their right.

The changing of the commission's name to MOVIDE (Movimiento pro Vida Decorosa, or Movement for a Decent Life) clearly reflected an increased degree of consciousness.

But it was in the field of housing and mainly in the form of "Mutual Aid" where citizen cooperation was most plainly and widely expressed.

Mutual Aid's experience with housing construction proved that the users themselves were capable of making viable a collective business of some complexity (technical, organizational, economic, financial) and creating strong internal and external ties with the cooperatives, not only at the construction stage but also and principally after the permanent settlement of the cooperativists in the new dwellings.

In addition to living units, these cooperatives, by using their resources with foresight and rigor, were often able to build shops, nurseries, schools, libraries, and community centers. These community centers were turned into areas for recreation and culture as well as for meetings and making collective decisions and were open not only to the cooperativists but also to the surrounding neighborhood.

Many of these buildings enhanced the dignity of the community and the city's architecture during a period when Montevideo was being aggressively disfigured by the effect of speculative development. Paradoxically, this architecture of poverty managed to dignify and enrich the city, while the opulent, speculative building degraded and impoverished it.

The importance of the cooperative experience, nationally and in the capital, is clear from the prominence acquired by the FUCVAM (Federación Unificadora de Cooperativas de Vivienda por Ayuda Mutua, or Federation of Cooperatives for Mutual-Aid Housing) during the return to democratic government.

Also important were the activities of youth and women's organizations and especially labor and student groups which acquired increasing relevance in the country after the referendum of November 1980, when the military government's illegitimacy and lack of consensus was made abundantly clear.

All these social movements brought about—and to a great extent combined—pluralist and participatory undertakings that widened the citizens' scope for opposition and for winning increasing space for freedom.

Several research centers of a high scientific and professional level contributed technically and strategically to underpin the actions of these social movements, thereby benefiting themselves by contact and firsthand knowledge of the emerging social movement.

The Sociedad de Arquitectos del Uruguay (SAU) and the Grupo de Estudios Urbanos (GEU) deserve a separate chapter for their efforts in disseminating and denouncing the treachery suffered by the city in architectural, urban development, rural development, and environmental spheres. Unexpected public solidarity showed the degree of the citizens' sensitivity—outside the political—on the subject of the city.

Last, one must not forget the conscientiousness of those who for more than a decade, and at the risk of prison and censure, persisted in their efforts to open the way for protest and dialogue. Newspapers, humorous magazines, movie houses, and independent theaters were some of the means chosen to gather increased support for traveling the road of resistance.

In this effort, popular songs and the *murga*, a traditional carnival group that performs political satire, played an outstanding role. It was, in fact, through them that the national, democratic spirit of the people expressed itself most spontaneously and genuinely.

THE MODELS COMPARED

The present situation in Uruguay negates all attempts to restore the model of the welfare state. The economic crisis and the suffocating external debt make any idea of this impossible.

Hopes today center on a new political context that will eventually lead to an alternative style involving the commitment and active participation of the community. Once and for all, a choice must be made between a new conception in the direction of a genuine, strong, pluralist democracy and the continuation of a traditional conservative outlook with community feedback.

The first road is not free of pitfalls. But there are ways to negotiate them.

The Inertia of the Conservatives

State charity. After a little more than a year of management by democratically elected authorities, the government's decisions pointed toward continuation of a neoliberal strategy in the area of political economy. Its effect has been to hinder solution of the present critical condition of the sector of the population with the fewest resources. Social policies have aimed at mitigating extreme conditions, using public assistance plans to satisfy the primary needs of the poor.

Among these, the Winter 1985 Emergency Welfare Plan stands out, which distributed food, kerosene, and clothes to the poor. These activities, according to the statements of many recipients, were perceived as charity and were therefore humiliating.

"Client-state." During the 1984 campaign, all the political forces and social movements expressed their unanimity over the importance of pluralism and urban participation by issuing a call for "A National Program for Concerted Action." For the most part, pluralism and participation appear today to have been set aside. Clientelism, partly dismantled by the military government, began to rear its head again in the old practices of handing out government jobs and in political favoritism. This is particularly true at the local level. In the case of Montevideo—a city whose importance determines what happens nationally—the fear of losing jobs may explain the return to these practices.

The reduced percentages forecast for the financing of the Cooperatives for Mutual Aid Housing included in the Five-Year Plan point to the intention to downgrade social groups formed and strengthened by pluralist practice and self-determination. This clear rebuff of the organization that holds together these social groups can only be explained by a desire to control these nonconformist social groups.

Equally, the decisions of the city council concerned with the Plan for the Eradication of Precarious Settlements, such as those of the Unidad Asesora de Proyectos Especiales, seem to have followed a similar path.

Obstacles in the Electoral System

The obstacles to participation and the free expression of democratic will can be measured in terms other than specific political action. In addition, legal and constitutional restraints combine to make it difficult to maneuver at the municipal level, given the political problems at the national level. Because citizens must cast a single vote for both national and local government offices, they are prevented from voting for candidates of different parties at each level of government. This system also means that discussions about local government policy and city problems are given lower priority because a population with a high degree of politicization pays more attention to national matters.

By constitutional decree, the victorious party wins an absolute majority on the Junta Departamental (the city council). This lack of representation impedes initiatives by the opposition and minimizes its controlling function.

Centralization. Although the constitution sought to widen popular representation by creating local authorities, the present administration has effectively blocked this avenue of participation. Strong centralization of power in the government structure has, on the contrary, been reaffirmed. In a city with a considerable population and size, this does not allow the flexibility that would lead to participation. Not only does centralization cut out an experience of debate and analysis at the local level, but it also cuts out opportunities for decision making by those directly involved.

The limits of knowledge. The problems of cities have only recently become the object of deep consideration by experts. Contributions from the perspectives of law and urban economics continue to be almost nonexistent, while those of a sociological nature have hardly begun.

Controversy in the urban architectural field has tended toward theoretical speculation dissociated from the real city. Perhaps the absence of political demands on architects and a lack of clear direction may account for this limitation.

Bureaucracy. The heavy overstaffing in the city government and its dominant bureaucratic nature are traditional problems. The current number of city officials is estimated at some 14,000.

Technological and information manipulation. The problems do not reveal themselves with sufficient clarity to be understood by the community. This is exacerbated by unfair and undemocratic use of the media.

Individual advantage as the sole parameter. Neoliberalism has a bad effect on the quality of life. For example, discouraging subsidies for public transportation denies true democratic accessibility to the city. The loss of public space continues today, caused by the highly debatable policy of granting concessions of areas of great landscape value to private institutions, even against the wishes of official municipal bodies.

Unilateral decisions. Opportunities have not been created for public discussion about the irreversible changes imposed at the urban level.

Potential for Change

Popular organizations. The capacity for mobilization demonstrated by popular organizations is a substantial resource with which to initiate a policy of change to a participatory and pluralist basis at the city level.

The new urban consciousness. The frequent concern with urban problems in the mass media clearly reflects the latent appearance of an urban consciousness at the technical, cultural, and political levels.

The opinions of private institutions (technical, professional, and educational) are eloquent, as are the public debates.

Politically, it is important to note that in the 1984 electoral campaign all the parties for the first time submitted to the people their programs for governing the Department of Montevideo.

FINAL CONSIDERATIONS

In recent years, leaders in Montevideo, indeed the whole of Uruguay, have been traveling paths that are at best tortuous and inappropriate and at worst regressive. Some are worth reviewing.

- Economic wealth has been transferred from the poor sectors to the richer ones.
- Urban and environmental assets have been transferred from the outskirts of the city to better-off areas.
- Space has been transferred from public to private ownership.
- Administration has been transferred from the community to the state sphere. In this regard, the municipality of Montevideo lost power to the Ministry of Transportation and Public Works, which made, unilaterally, several decisions of high urban impact. Montevideo also lost power to The Mortgage Bank of Uruguay (a state entity), which became the principal organism for urbanization.

Paradoxically, in a municipality governed for more than a century by strongly centralized, even authoritarian, control, coherent plans for the city have not developed. Although building ordinances were made early at the municipal level, succeeding administrations acted at random without any overall plan for urban development.

Now that the restoration of the old model has been shown to be unworkable, current institutions are faced with a choice between:

A. The perpetuation of a neoliberal style mitigated in part by forms of national assistance that are manipulative and distinctly neoauthoritarian;

B. A new concept of city direction that will confirm the leading role of community government in defining aims and solutions made possible with the help of that kind of pluralism and participation already tried out by the people.

Faced with the failure of "developmentalism" and with the new illusion of technical and elitist modernization, the alternative now is to test the powers of thrift and restraint, of "a healthy framework of poverty." As Georges Anglade wrote, "If poverty persists and still overwhelms us, it is because we have not chosen a way out via poverty but rather have followed the methods of working and the ways of thinking appropriate to wealth."

To try this option obviously demands an accepted and shared responsibility if the whole community is to be guaranteed a true benefit.

REFERENCES

Filgueira, C., et al. 1986. *Movimientos sociales en el Uruguay de hoy.* Montevideo: CLACSO.

Melgar, A., and F. Villalobos. 1986. *La desigualdad como estrategia.* Montevideo: CLAEH/ EBO.

11

Experiments in Democratizing a City Management

Henry Pease García

Latin American cities not only adopt urban models from other latitudes but add to them from their own authoritarian tradition. As a result, cities are managed by bureaucrats and technocrats who either make decisions, without leaving their offices, based on what they assume to be the aspirations of the citizens, or else they simply leave the solution of problems to the marketplace. Thus a city's most important decisions fall into the hands of urban speculators and real estate developers. In Lima, these interests have had the backing of big money.

In Lima the traditions of communal work and citizen participation have been forgotten. Centralization by the national government left the municipalities with almost no function. City government in Lima always had a ceremonial function, but every cabinet minister thought of himself as district mayor in the section of the city where his offices were and ran the district more than the mayor did. In general, authoritarian governments placed little value on local government, but the same happened with democratically elected presidents, because the Peru of the oligarchic period was little more than a democracy on paper.

When representative democracy was established in 1980, the call for municipal elections was immediate. The open question at the time was whether the constitution contained adequate provisions for democratizing city management—a question that addressed itself as much to the possibility of counting on effective channels of citizen participation as to the real power of local governments in the general structure of the state.

The initial regulatory laws made an attempt to change the office of mayor into a copy of the central executive power and the city's aldermen into congressmen, a blueprint that did not work. This scheme, instead, kept the most conservative administrators in power, making difficult any genuine attempt at democratization. Nor was the scant provision in municipal law for opening the path to participation even explored by the municipal officers. Once reestablished, elected local government ruled by going to the people, but it did not govern from the people or with their participation in specific areas.

It is in this context that the experiments were initiated that shall be discussed here; the discussion emphasizes *what* took place rather than evaluating or interpreting those events. Since January 1984, Lima has been governed by a coalition of left-wing parties and independents collectively known as the *Izquierda Unida* (United Left), whose president, Alfonso Barrantes, was also the mayor. Appealing to the electorate with a proposal for a national democratic, anti-imperialist program that merged a socialist outlook with an explicit democratic process, this coalition had to devise realistic ways for citizens to participate in city affairs. In other words, the coalition tried to move representative democracy toward forms of direct democracy, about which so much has been said and written but on which so few meaningful experiments have been carried out.

The United Left coalition did not perceive the proposed local democracy simply as a method for electing administrators. This is what happens when acts approved by an administration or an elected administrator become mere decrees that may be discussed with powerful people or amended by a newspaper campaign but that are never imbued with the logic of grass-roots participation. Perhaps because of Peru's sporadic, frustrating experiences as a republic, representative democracy has never given the opposition much of a role. The opposition was allowed to make noise, but not much, and it did not speak with a single voice. Political consensus has only seemed necessary when the government lacked a parliamentary or a municipal majority, but, at the municipal level—to simplify the governing process—the law gives an absolute majority to the winner, whatever his percentage of the vote.

To perceive democracy in this way inevitably brings about isolation, even in a good government. To perceive democracy as a way of governing and of giving due consideration to the need for social and political consensus—at least on matters of importance—presupposes a way of treating parliamentary or local government minorities that is not merely a matter of form, but that requires an attitude very different from the one in Peru, especially toward social organizations that do not form part of the world of the powerful. To begin to achieve this more advanced form of democracy, it was clear that particular mechanisms of participation by social organizations could be tried at the local level while forms, including territorial ones, of active neighborhood participation in municipal decisions were being sought. It was not a matter of continuing to criticize representative democracy for being purely "formal" but of putting representative democracy into practice and looking for channels that would overcome its limitations. Of course, such advances do not come from either an individual imagination or from simple party ideology. In the preceding decades, urban social movements upset many of the ruling political and intellectual schemes. Participatory practices, grass-roots initiatives, and processes that roused the oligarchy from its inertia and then spurred the reform of the bureaucracy are some of the things that have happened in the course of this historical experience.

Although the coalition experiments are very recent and incomplete—the oldest has gone on for about two years—they contain the seeds of a political strategy that holds self-determination and citizen participation in government to be elements in keeping with socialism understood as full democracy. Self-determination, which is more viable at the local level, means that participation at various levels is not a fitful, but a daily, matter and is part of the strategy of response to many of the more urgent problems. Citizen participation demands that the role of "people's representatives"—in this instance, mayors and aldermen—be redefined. Matters are no longer solely their province nor the province of the party machine, if only to avoid such officials' ending up as autocrats and *caudillos* between elections. These representatives should be considered leaders and communicators who participate with the people in assemblies that allow ordinary citizens to question their mayor or alderman, who are the managers of an administration that the people can monitor. Assemblies, autonomous organizations, and civic society as a whole are the constituent elements in this concept.

What was certain from the beginning was that the local government of a metropolis has no time for theorizing about or even imagining the future. The urgency of urban problems meant that these proposals had to be tested within the reality of a sprawling city governed in a very complex way. In addition to the national government's daily interference in the city (where its headquarters are and where 30 percent of the country's electorate lives), there is a municipal organization whose apex is the Metropolitan Council, a provincial body composed of forty-one districts. Each district has a district council, which carries out several functions independently of the provincial council and where, given the electoral mechanism, the different mayoral offices are distributed among the different political parties.

To build a true metropolitan authority in this context was a major challenge for any administration. Such an authority had to get back from the national government its powers and areas of responsibility, a task weakly taken up between 1980 and 1983. This body had to present itself as an effective and nonauthoritarian option in a city where anomie and chaos had been gaining ground over the previous decade. Wherever one looked—from traffic regulations to street vendors to public transport to land use to essential services—breakdown was apparent. The challenge was to construct a democratic authority, capable of gaining citizens' respect, a challenge even military government administrations had failed in the face of the prevailing unreliability. To illustrate: A special body armed with truncheon and chain ran street vendors out of central Lima—plainly without success. To insist simply on the authoritarian solution demanded by the more conservative sectors, who were worried about image, not only obscured the causes of this vast problem, but also found the wrong way out of it, and even then only temporarily. This sort of logic applied to squatters has, in the past, cost many lives. For this and other reasons, it was not only those of us who won the elections who understood the need to make new choices.

The embryonic experiences described here have already taken root in the city. To democratize and create a municipal authority that has to be respected even by the national government is part of a continuing process, which is still incomplete.

MAKING REPRESENTATIVE DEMOCRACY EFFECTIVE: THE SITUATION AND ITS ANTECEDENTS

To speak of local democracy is to take for granted elections that are free from tampering with the voting procedure. This has been the situation in Peru since the 1980 elections. But if the concept of democracy is not limited solely to the election of personnel, one must consider the manner of governing, which raises issues of structure and management. Present legislation in Peru, as revised in May 1984, sets up a relatively democratic government structure. It provides for the election of municipal authorities in the immediate province and in each of its districts—the latter with relative autonomy vis-à-vis the provincial municipality, which has, nevertheless, considerable powers over them. An elected mayor is the principal executive and at the same time presides over the municipal council, which acts as the legislature. The council is composed of a variable number of elected aldermen, the first of whom becomes the deputy mayor, who is the second-ranking municipal authority and stands in for the mayor and acts as vice president of the council. The members of the council have comparatively more powers than members of parliament, since the former not only legislate, but can exercise supervisory and executive functions.

The mayor has a great deal of power, but so does the council when it comes to important economic and political functions. The law, nonetheless, in order to prevent procedural problems, automatically grants the winning party an absolute majority and shares out the minority seats proportionally among the losing parties, whatever the difference between the winner and the rest. It can happen then, and usually does, that the party that wins the elections is the only one that participates in government.

One of the democratic acts that the United Left and Mayor Barrantes will be recognized for is distributing the posts proportionately among all the political forces, and offering even the highest government positions (equivalent to ministers and secretaries of the city) to aldermen of other political camps. Some parties accepted and others did not. But that is the way the United Left governed. The majority of the council's agreements and ordinances also were arrived at by consensus, after long debates. The important thing, in every case, was that no political power or representative sector of the city could feel excluded from the municipal government.

While working within the confines of representative democracy, forms of local participation were envisioned. Little advance had been made on that front, however, because the municipalities have come to be governed by bureaucratic decree. Very little in the way of neighborhood organization has materialized, and the assemblies and open *cabildos,* which are important forms of communicating with people, have never achieved the continuity or depth necessary to be considered part of the way of governing nor, in what amounts to the same thing, have citizens found them to be an effective way to participate in local government.

But in the activist period of the 1970s many different kinds of social organization emerged to express the demands and constructive intent of a people plowing its own furrow despite innumerable forms of exploitation and alienation. These popular movements, through protests and paralyzing national strikes, forced the dictatorship of General Morales Bermúdez to call an election in 1977 and, although there was neither the power nor the political organization to define the content and direction of the 1980 elections, it is clear that the presence of a people who were not a disoriented, amorphous mass conditioned the various political attitudes.

After the 1980 local elections, many neighborhood leaders become mayors and aldermen. This multiplied in 1983. Then, when the change in the manner of governing at the district level between 1980 and 1983 was examined, it was discovered that there was not a single specific plan linking municipal administration to the demand for neighborhood participation. However, many assemblies and *cabildos* showed evidence of direct democracy; people did in fact challenge and criticize their immediate authorities. An absence of continuity is, nevertheless, one of the mechanisms that the bureaucracy and the *caudillismo* of mayors and aldermen use to keep citizen participation on paper while they do exactly what they want.

To overcome the limitations found at the district level, the United Left set up the Municipal Agencies of Metropolitan Lima. Some districts have been able to get support from powerful grass-roots neighborhood organizations, the best example of which is the Self-Governing Community of Villa El Salvador. But for the city as a whole, it was impossible to generalize these experiments, and the governing coalition had to seek changes in the local government's actual way of administering by encouraging new forms of organization.

It should be emphasized here that municipal experiments had been tried before in Lima, but they were little studied and even less systematized. In them, direct citizen participation was given expression, even if only briefly. In this context it is also important to point out that since the second half of the 1970s, citizen participation occurred not only through neighborhood organizations but also through organizations that people created in their struggle for survival. Health and nutritional problems began to be faced collectively. This was to be of decisive importance in another of the experiments—the program for distributing milk to children—but of even greater importance was the very ability to organize. Even tubercular patients organized themselves into associations and committees to press for medicine and help.

Thus, even before the United Left administration, the people of Lima by means of various organizations had carried out wide and significant practical action and there had also been some municipal experiments at the district level. It is perhaps because of these activities that when the municipal government came into power, one of its first acts was to legalize several organizations, which, although considered legitimate by the people, especially in working-class neighborhoods, had lacked legal recognition.

A PROGRAM OF NUTRITIONAL WELFARE BASED ON PEOPLE'S ORGANIZATIONS

To cope with the problem of child malnutrition among the poor of Lima, the coalition proposed in the electoral campaign that the municipality should make children their priority, supplying a million glasses of free milk daily, and taking action to provide basic health care. Such actions were not traditionally part of the municipal function, and the general reaction was to ask how a municipal government with few resources could meet the challenge.

What the coalition showed with this program, which was called the "emergency program for nutrition and health," was not so much that it could fulfill this most important social goal and difficult political promise but that it could create a very large popular organization. The organization consisted of 7,500 Glass of Milk Committees, which involved 100,000 mothers who organized and promoted the program. This people's organization was the nucleus of the first experiment demonstrating a democratic alternative to traditional municipal management.

The normal procedure would have been to create an enormous bureaucratic organization, which, among other things, would have absorbed a significant part of the resources. Because of the clientelistic system that characterizes Peruvian politics, probably the mayor or his wife would have formally handed out the first glasses of milk and the people would have been summoned to "receive" what others were "generously" going to "give" them. But this program involved fewer than ten municipal officials and no municipal equipment. Support consisted mainly of powdered milk and organizational backing. The organized mothers did all the distributing, storing, registration, and preparing. They also developed the embryonic organization into a strong program that today serves milk not only to children six years and under, but also to older children and pregnant and nursing women. The organization of the Glass of Milk Committees has broken its original frontiers and is now the basis of the city's primary health program, which includes health education, immunization, dental health, and preventive medicine. This has been a really impressive display of organizational ability.

The women themselves administered the program, electing coordinators and directors and holding district organizing meetings. It was these mothers who gathered in large numbers at the National Parliament to demand a law to finance the Glass of Milk program, whose first two years were funded solely by donations collected by the municipality. It was thanks to pressure by some 30,000 mothers in the Plaza del Congreso that near the end of the Belaúnde government all political parties approved the law that finances this program today and extended it to the whole country.

What Peruvian and other Latin American cities need is the option of democratic management, not by the bureaucratic apparatus, but by popular organizations. An essential condition for this is a respect for the autonomy of these popular organizations and for the cooperative nature of their programs. This strategy should be used to promote self-determination and the solving of problems by organized people themselves. There is a long tradition of this in Peru, and it was present in the genesis of "Popular Cooperation" in the 1960s. But there it was totally distorted because it reduced the role of the people to that of contributing their labor, giving them no part in decision making or management. Today in the "glass of milk" experiment, the municipality's role is that of support and coordination, and this role should be progressively reduced until management becomes the responsibility of the people.

An organization of this size and efficiency encourages hope that similar organizations might take on other municipal functions, such as price and quality control of food and various functions of urban development, that are badly and boringly performed by the bureaucracy. Were such authority given to popular organizations, these functions would be better performed and would become effective channels of participation.

Forging self-government by the people is essential to advancing the democratization of the country. The need is for decision making—but collective decision making—by taking over management responsibility and setting up services and actions to answer felt and shared demands. It is on this plane that this experiment is taking place.

LOW-COST HOUSING PROGRAMS AND NEIGHBORHOOD ORGANIZATIONS

The invasion of uncultivated land by squatters has been the main way in which Lima has grown in the last forty years. The state has been unable to plan or direct the city's growth. It has not been able to offer alternative housing to the low-income population, and even in the 1980s, when the depth of the economic crisis had swept aside all illusions about developmentalism, the government claimed to have resolved the housing problem by building apartments that cost on average $20,000. When it became clear that the central government could not solve the housing problem, it lessened the political cost by passing on part of the housing provision function to the municipality.

The only things that the municipality had done in this field until 1984 were to look into cleaning up and legalizing of squatter settlements built after the invasions, even granting property titles following a long, laborious case, which is pending in most of Lima as of 1986. Since these actions were taken after the settlements were already established, there was no opportunity to plan. After 1984 the municipality decided to take the initiative, promoting programs for low-cost housing that do not require great investment, but use the organized efforts of the population—who have acquired a great deal of experience since the first invasions in Lima. This initiative has led to better housing options that people can afford.

After an effort to rehabilitate uncultivated lands, the municipality now has five programs in operation, with plots for 30,000 families. The first and most advanced of these is in the Quebrada de Huaycán, where it is hoped that an infrastructure of public works and services can be developed to support the initiative for self-built houses by a population estimated at 135,000 people with low or very low incomes.

The municipality took the initiative by setting up the registration and vetting of families, and a system of cooperative action was immediately designed in which the organized population and both the provincial and district administrations took part. The first stage, for 12,000 families, is under construction, and about half these are now installed in the area. The program is based on the development of *Unidades Comunales de Vivienda* (UCV), residential blocs for sixty families who occupy a piece of property jointly and who function as small cooperatives.

The management committee, made up of municipality officials and organizers, is in charge of administration, publicity, public services, and the running of the UCV, including management of social infrastructure and public works. Both in the management committee and in the UCV, the population appoints and removes its representatives and works with them in the various tasks. In the year the Quebrada de Huaycán was settled, the first Settlers' Congress took place, forming an association and thus consolidating the organization of the project.

The important point here is that from the first the municipality acted neither alone by imperious action nor through individual relationships with people who in theory and in the future might benefit. It was a case of combining the particular logic of the popular organization, which had developed out of the land invasion itself, with the municipal administration. Not only did this suit the lack of resources, but it also satisfied the need to generalize from the experiment.

In the other programs, individual, rather than communal, lots were preferred, but a level of cooperative action guarantees that decisions are taken jointly.

This work has earned the respect of all the existing political parties. In Huaycán, for example, where the congress was held soon after President Alan García's victory, his party won the elections to the assembly; the victory did not affect the normal functioning of the program that had emerged under another political party. The tradition in Peru is for the ruling party to use the public sector to fund its supporters and generate clients, and that when it loses, it destroys popular organizations. The United Left has not done that. As the organization of the people advances, and consciousness is raised, it will be more difficult for parties to behave in the traditional manner.

MUNICIPAL AGENCIES AND THEIR NEIGHBORHOOD ASSEMBLIES

These two experiments have not touched the administrative structure of the municipality. These programs were carried out to make the local government act not through its own bureaucracy but through the autonomous popular organizations, drawing on their energy, creativity, and initiative. The problem that was continually posited, as it was posited in the earlier three-year period in various districts governed by the United Left, was how to democratize the organization of the municipality to allow neighborhoods to participate directly rather than through occasional assemblies and *cabildos*. This problem, moreover, pertains to the whole city and not only to its twenty most densely populated districts, where the slums are to be found. The high- and middle-income districts and the impoverished, squalid, old town have no tradition of organization. In the new squatter settlements there is such a tradition, and the municipalities must coexist with community organizations that are, to a greater or lesser degree, recognized, and whose initiatives can be accepted and, with preparation, used for support.

The third experiment combines decentralization with neighborhood participation and is being applied in a limited area, the so-called Cercado de Lima, or district capital of the province. This is the area that the Lima municipality, which is the provincial municipality, administers directly. Experience generated there can then be converted into a norm and generalized for the whole province. This experiment is taking place in a complex area composed of different populations: from the historic, monumental city center to residential and industrial zones to slums. For this, six different municipal agencies have been created; the municipality will progressively turn over to them district functions down to the neighborhood level.

Instead of beginning to transfer employees and organizing each agency according to its requirements, however, the United Left coalition set up a team of organizers who went from street to street and block to block, forming neighborhood committees. In some cases, the organizers first called together the main civic institutions, who then worked to organize neighborhood committees by blocks of buildings. Today, more than 350 neighborhood committees make up the social base of the six agencies.

As of 1986, up to two weekend meetings in each agency have been held, and in each one a "neighborhood assembly" will be formed in a few months. These neighborhood assemblies are permanent pressure groups that represent committees that respond daily to neighborhood needs. Each committee deals with a different area of need—cleaning and maintenance, consumer protection, public works, or other communal problems. A territorial structure is being defined to cover all the problems of the municipal area.

The Cercado de Lima, the city's old center, has about 600,000 inhabitants, and, as a consequence, the jurisdiction of each agency is large. But through this method of organization, each agency reaches the neighborhood directly, participating in communal decisions such as approving the 1986 public works plan or deciding where to locate trash cans.

Municipal agencies, still being formed, are thus an experiment in neighborhood participation in the very affairs of municipal administration. These agencies have had to face bureaucratic obstacles and resistance to decentralization. The experiment has not yet been consolidated, and its fate will depend on the energy with which the policy is pursued.

NEIGHBORHOOD DECENTRALIZATION AND PARTICIPATION IN THE URBAN PLAN

Another experiment does not involve a district function, but one of the typical provincial functions of the municipality of Lima, the formulation of a master plan for the city, a fundamental tool of urban development. Normally such a plan is developed exclusively by professionals and experts. Decentralization of a provincial function is more difficult because it involves several districts.

The coalition has begun to formulate the plan by setting up district planning councils consisting of councilmen, district aldermen, and specially elected neighborhood representatives. Formed in the north, south, and east wings of the city for those districts in a state of expansion, basically the slums, the councils are debating several of the functions that the metropolitan municipality has begun to delegate to them both in the formulation of the Basic Plan and in activities closely linked to urban development.

The councils and meetings have received a lot of attention, because they bring before the citizens a series of problems that concern them directly, such as which roads are to be resurfaced or paved, norms for building licenses, zoning, priorities in street cleaning, and urban transport.

The first metropolitan meeting of these planning councils has just taken place. When it covers the whole province, the meeting will constitute the best mechanism for guaranteeing that the new master plan expresses the aspirations of different parts of the city. Problems are being tackled that, because of the size of the city and the unequal levels of information, were once the exclusive province of colleges, universities, and other, similar institutions. The support of these institutions now acquires a new meaning as a result of the new approach to planning.

FINAL REFLECTIONS

The four experiments presented here touch briefly on two aspects of city administration. The first seeks direct participation by the organized population, resolving its problems with the help of the municipality but leaving the autonomous organization as the main actor in the process to follow. This is the case with the Glass of Milk Committees or the low-cost housing programs whose organizations are an alternative to the traditional way in which the state has confronted the problem.

The second aspect concerns democratization of the administration itself. This includes the municipal agencies and the district planning councils. In both of these it was a matter of opening up the municipality to the neighborhoods and creating organizations that serve as the necessary bridge to do so.

Carrying out experiments like these will ensure that municipalities will be areas of self-government rather than mere copies of the central administration. Wherever necessary, the United Left coalition fought the concept of the mayor as "a director of the city" and of the municipality as a "center of services." In this the coalition was supported by the Peruvian Constitution, which defines the municipalities as organs of local government and assigns them a wide and varied level of authority. But more than juridically, where gains have been made, the validity of the experiments will be measured in terms of power, for this power has been stolen from the municipalities time and again throughout history. Power can only come from the municipality's purpose, which is to express the organized will of local people. This is important in a big city where services now have to be run by large firms (cleaning, light, power). Even if public, such firms need to be made accountable, and only a participatory structure can make them so. This can have strategic importance in cities such as Lima, where urgent needs have swamped all capabilities to provide public services, and where enormous solidarity must be mobilized to fight the poverty of the masses and the deterioration of public services.

Thinking about whether the city of the future will be able to provide services can be depressing, even for the middle-class citizen, who now has them. His daily experience already tells him that he has no one to protest to, no way to confront the daily abuses of a bureaucracy that serves badly, deals worse, and commits notorious errors. Someone returning from a vacation, having left his house empty, finds that he has been billed for phone calls that he could not have made. To approach the company for a correction he first has to pay the bill. Someone else obtains running water after a long struggle, only to find that water is available for only a few hours a day. Such stories abound. That the municipality should have a participatory structure to deal with these problems is as important—or more so—than that it should increase its power over the management of public services, as it is in fact doing. Such a structure in the agencies and in the planning committees would revive the municipal councils as organs of management.

New forms of democratic participation are also needed to make it possible to establish the rules of the game in the city, with control by the people and without great repression. An example: When the United Left coalition took power in Lima, there was no regular transport, and the bus drivers were so powerful that even the military government could do nothing. The new municipal government imposed a ticketing system, opened bids for bus routes, and reorganized the traffic patterns in the city center. The municipality succeeded in its confrontation with the bus drivers because it had the support of the people, most of whom were fed up with the drivers.

In other words, the authority acted with democratic legitimacy, as it will have to do in many other fields if it is to manage with the support of the citizens and not appear to be something outside them. Somehow habits, usage, and customs will have to be changed. The best results have been obtained in the working-class areas, which have a greater tradition of participation and common struggle. In the case of the municipal agencies, however, the result has been similar in inner-city areas.

The United Left coalition believes this particular experiment will produce the embryo of an alternative concept of the state, whose apparatus should not do everything but should channel the abilities of organized citizens, respecting the autonomous organization of the people, supporting them in most cases, consulting in others, promoting ad hoc organizations, taking a guiding role, and using its powers to call on others instead of doing everything itself.

This is how state bureaucracy and its tendency to centralize ought to be dealt with. But state action should be based on an effective democratic concept that admits and, more, promotes the participation of all the political camps and parties. The state apparatus should not be used merely to duplicate labor unions and social organizations in general or to support one sector in a partisan way. As this is a permanent temptation, I want to point it out.

What these experiments achieved—beyond representative democracy but still rooted in it—is, on the one hand, direct participation of the organized population in local matters and, on the other, a change in the method of state management in that the administration of social programs now rests on the organized population more than on the bureaucracy.

For democracy to be complete, it cannot be restricted to local elections nor enclosed in the always tight mold of politics. But every advance in the perspective of self-government is a significant step that contributes to social and economic change, even when the change is not linear and suffers setbacks.

It is the United Left's belief that some progress was made when democracy was understood not only as a method of electing governments but also as a way of governing. There are important examples of this latter in the relationship among political parties and in the levels of consensus reached on major decisions affecting the city. But the experiments related here, regarding the transfer of the decision making and management from the municipality to popular organizations and their incorporation into direct forms of local intervention, also reflect a broadening of the concept of democracy. It is not only a matter of government by "elected representatives" but one of moving toward direct participation in decision making by popular organizations. Obviously the experiment is limited because the scope of local government is limited, but the experiments point to what is possible.

IV

Toward Recovery of Urban Community

12

Cultural Grammar and Bureaucratic Rationalization in Latin American Cities

Larissa Lomnitz and Rodrigo Díaz

Elsewhere in this volume Rogelio Pérez Perdomo argues that the political structures and formal economies of a society organize the daily life of all its members, delimiting their possible field of action and administering relationships between individuals. Rules, decrees, laws, government plans—above all, government plans—derive their special character from their objectives, which are to order and regulate community life and to establish its functional continuity. This ordering of society, however, is not homogeneous. There are instances of social action and interaction that escape from the general view, from the objectives of the formal structures, and from their aims and assertions. Put another way, the apparatus and machinery of the state and its dominant economic system, in theory all-encompassing and omnipresent, do not cover all the actions of every individual. A sphere of informal activity operates like a black box, converting "what comes from the formal structures to produce results unforeseen by the political elite and [forcing] time and again to modify its policies and to take new measures without really controlling the activities of this half-hidden, informal sphere" (Hankiss 1990, 1).

Cities can be looked at in different ways and can allow for different interpretations. This essay offers one interpretation of Latin American cities and puts forward one viewpoint. Our main interest is to call attention to those social activities that derive from cultural traditions and contexts (the informal sphere). We shall suggest that not all social activity that develops in a city is wholly a consequence of the rules of political and economic structures (the formal sphere). We want to analyze the way in which individuals use the city and its institutions given their cultural resources, which are valuable since they guarantee a historical continuity with which individuals identify personally and which they use to identify with each other.

This essay starts from the idea that the formal sphere is made up of a range of activities and community relationships derived rationally from national and local power structures, with their explicit, bureaucratized rules of conduct devised from universal postulates to make uniform and perpetuate society. Examples are rules of commerce and law, which in theory bestow on individuals equal rights and obligations and equal opportunities to lead their lives. The informal sphere, meanwhile, is made up of a range of activities and social relationships derived from cultural codes, with implicit rules of conduct aimed principally at satisfying individual interests (including those of family and close friends). These interests are sometimes peripheral and even contrary to the rationale imposed by formal structures. Within the formal institutions and interactions, community members compete with each other for the acquisition of resources in accordance with universal rules and norms; in contrast, the informal sphere weaves social networks of cooperation and solidarity around individuals. If the former responds to the need of power structures to preserve and reproduce themselves and to centralize more resources, the latter is shaped by individuals who exchange resources in order to survive and to facilitate social ascent in the formal structures themselves.

Usually, the two types of activity—the formal and the informal—are complementary and feed each other. Informal activity, however, is not always well regarded, for it breaks rules and regulations, often undermining the logic of the formal structure while at the same time modifying it. In recent years, Latin American cities have seen informal activities, hitherto hidden and discreet, grow and come out into the open.

A number of studies have tried to define this "duality" in its various guises—formal versus informal sector (Portes 1980), first versus second economy (Hankiss 1990), liberal ideology versus ideology of solidarity (Lomnitz 1974). As we understand this "duality," it does not admit of two independent, clear-cut domains. On the contrary, the two domains overlap. Nor do we think that the area of informal activity is necessarily in direct opposition to the formal. On occasion the informal can be vital for the reproduction of the formal. This "duality" is not strictly a matter of people versus institutions. Rather, it reflects the meeting ground of two ways in which society functions, each ruled by different principles and calling for different forms of interaction between the same individuals.

This twofold character is particularly important in the study of Latin American cities, where the two types of activity—the bureaucratically controlled and the culturally codified—are linked in special ways, setting up a complex and dynamic interplay that formal institutions modify and the informal sector delimits.

In recent years, in the face of the crisis Latin America is going through, interest has grown in the nature of social mobility and people's strategies for survival. Broad social sectors have resorted to strategies that, in many cases, undermine the modernization that for several decades dominant groups have tried to impose through development. Kinship, real or imaginary; neighborliness; and work relationships, which can become social relationships, have had to be readjusted and increased in scope. As a result of the ever greater centralization of political, economic, and sociocultural power, people have fallen back on a way of life that is not wholly under the sway of these powers. Instead, they are writing a different history.

The optimism of earlier decades has collapsed dramatically. The belief that industralization would solve the problems of overpopulation, poverty, and underemployment and the notion that development plans, often drawn up and justified by social scientists, would lead to economic growth, to the perfect modernization and rationalization of the state, and to the consolidation of an organized working class has shattered. Today, instead of the achievement of formal order, informality has increased and is now found everywhere in the Latin American city.

How, then, is the informal sphere to be combined with the formal? To what logic does the informal sector respond? What is its grammar, its limits? This essay offers a few answers and points out some theoretical directions that—incorporating both spheres—help explain the unique dynamic of Latin American cities. This proposal takes into account macrosocial factors and does not restrict itself to micro-conclusions. It is a theoretical reflection that helps reveal the mechanism by which the formal system dominates and also the way in which society resists and reproduces itself. We do not, therefore, wish to add to the sum of history cast in bronze—that is, history on a grand scale—but to local history, microhistory, history in which the active social unit is, as Luis González y González (1982, 37–38) points out, "usually a handful of men who know each other, whose allegiances are specific and straightforward. The collective actor is the family circle, the extended family. The soloist is the little man, not the one who is renowned nationwide or worldwide. What interests us is the inventor unknown beyond his native ground, the hero of some ambush, the generous bandit, the diamond in the rough, the martyr forgotten by the Roman Curia, the sportsman without the sporting gear . . . that is to say, the man in the street, who could be a prophet in his own land."

What is happening today in Latin American cities cannot, in our opinion, be understood if that silent world, the sphere of informal activity, is ignored. We do not want to reduce it to a mere economic category, for it is more than that. Therefore, in a first attempt to systematize it, we shall describe the cultural grammars that make up the informal sphere, the grammar of solidarity and the grammar of domination-subordination. Ultimately, we shall boil them down to their characteristics, their interrelations, and their intimate ties with the formal sphere, where the borderline is indistinguishable.

THE CULTURAL GRAMMAR OF SOLIDARITY

Like cities, with their transport systems, streets, avenues, and perfectly interconnected telephones, individuals possess their network of social relationships, through which they interact with other individuals and groups and interchange resources of various kinds—messages, moral values, aspirations, goods, services, emotions, and so forth. Each individual, then, is the starting point of a network and, at the same time, a part of other networks that at any given point include or exclude him. To be a friend of A, for example, does not mean that one is a friend of all A's friends.

At any rate, and this is particularly relevant in Latin American cities, the basis of this network of relationships is made up of two social categories of culturally defined individuals—the real and imaginary kinship network and the network of friendship. Whether inherited or acquired, each individual has an actual and a potential stock of relationships at his disposal. In practice, however, individuals construct a mental map on which they pinpoint the interchange—now close, now more distant—between family and friends on culturally based criteria such as trust, favors, and respect. In other words, in theory there exists a normative, logically structured grammar of social behavior that imposes on individuals forms of action, representations of the world, and ways of organizing their own network of relationships. But the functioning of this grammar is governed by historical circumstances of class and of individuals—the language of social life—which imperceptibly modify its rules and norms. In this way the networks of kinship and friendship must be codified by this grammar of social behavior and by its actual functioning, which creates, recreates, and also transforms it.

The nucleus of the grammar of solidarity, and the point of departure for each individual's network of relationships, is represented by the family, the kinship system. Kinship assigns and establishes positions, presents options, and indicates the area and nature of interchanges, mainly primary interchanges. Nevertheless, the category *family* means different things to different people. In the United States and Great Britain, for instance, *family* means the unit of solidarity represented by the nuclear family, and this is usually thought of as the universal model for industrial societies (Firth et al. 1970, Macfarlane 1979, Schneider 1968, Schneider and Smith 1973). In Latin America, however, the unit of solidarity is the extended family, a group of three generations—a couple, their children, and their grandchildren (Lomnitz and Pérez Lizaur, 1987).

Of course, the differences are not exclusively a matter of terms. Grandparents and grandchildren exist in all cultures. But the type of interchange and the significance attributed to it varies from culture to culture, from period to period. In Latin America the solidarity between parents and children not only does not lessen with the marriage of children, but the expectation of mutual help and support often increases. Vertical consanguinity, the group of three generations of direct descent together with lateral relationships—matrimonial alliances and the incorporation of each individual into two kinship groups—makes the kinship network the subtlest social tapestry of solidarity in Latin American societies.

If individuals wish to preserve their kinship network as a source of solidarity, they must make an effort to adapt their economic, social, and residential circumstances to the traditions and expectations of the extended family. In exchange, they receive economic support and social recognition, and they are able to take part in family rituals. These last are of particular importance to the participants, for they mean the broadest reunion of the family network—uncles and aunts, cousins, nieces and nephews—which, of course, is even greater than the network of the extended family. This, then, is the principal resource represented by the kinship network. It can take in several hundred participants, who cross over into formal power structures. If the network of the extended family is a nucleus of the grammar of solidarity, the remaining family networks add to it, one upon the other, according to cultural criteria (and with greater or lesser trust), like layers of kinship. The nucleus and these layers form the whole kinship network, which each individual depends on, contributes to, and cooperates with and where, ideally, the individual finds support. The kinship network is, in short, a cultural structure that in theory has the strength to regenerate and preserve itself in time and space. Nor is it necessarily restricted by class barriers or regional or national boundaries.

Exiles, political prisoners, ethnic minority communities, and nomadic groups have shown the power of this cultural structure.

So far, the organizing principles behind one of the networks that make up the grammar of solidarity have been broadly described. Because the use and operation of this network is tempered by historical circumstances, class, and individuals, the true dynamic of the extended family varies according to the domestic arrangements of class and family. It also varies over the course of time according to the evolution of the family group.

When rural people have to migrate to the city, their kinship networks, residential patterns, and domestic arrangements are disrupted. The extended family, or that part of it that has migrated to the city, has to adapt to ensure its survival. The same could be said for the inhabitants of the slums, who tend to reconstruct and reorganize their kinship networks in order to cope with the severe financial and social straits in which they live. In the middle and upper classes, kinship networks also make up the basic units of cooperation and solidarity, although interchanged resources are of a different kind, reflecting their assignment and position in the formal power structures (Lomnitz and Pérez Lizaur 1987). Nevertheless, in all cases blood relatives face the world as close-knit units of financial, social, and moral cooperation and reciprocity.

In its lateral character, the kinship system is not without tension. Married children belong to two competing extended families, and this competition ends only when—on the death of their respective parents—a couple can preside over its own extended family. This interplay between cooperation and competition in the bosom of each kinship network helps explain residential patterns, characteristics of the interchange of resources, family rituals, and the presence of institutions such as fictitious kinship. All this is also central to the understanding of the informal sphere, although here the other social characteristics of culturally defined individuals—the friendship network—must be considered.

Friendship, one of the great themes yet to be dealt with by anthropology, has been unjustly neglected, perhaps because its obviousness makes it seem trivial. Yet no biography or autobiography leaves out friends; many such books are in fact written as homage to the subject's friendship network. In contrast to the kinship network, the friendship network is acquired gradually and is continually being woven and sometimes unraveled. Normally, friendships are acquired at random. Nobody knows where friends come from, but suddenly people find themselves sharing experiences, responsibilities, and interests with someone else. Unwittingly, from one moment to the next, two people trust each other and exchange favors, confidences, and resources that are valuable to both. Close friendships grow continually in trust and reciprocity—and, therefore, in friendliness—or, at the other end of the scale, they are ill-starred, and some obstacle fractures them. Between these extremes Latin Americans have useful categories that seem to mean little and yet are full of meaning. They talk about "close friends," "friends," and "acquaintances," terms that are practically impossible to define, but that convey definite meaning.

Such subtle nuances and ranks help individuals evaluate friends and their circumstances and place them on mental maps of friendship. There are no rules or norms that can fully define what a close friend, a friend, or an acquaintance is or what the limits, scope, responsibilities, or duties of each are. But these categories are based on rules of behavior in terms of class, sex, age, place, ideology, and the like.

To understand the function and the tensions peculiar to each friendship network, it is necessary to reconstruct it anthropologically. The criterion of trust, a culturally determined category, can be used to explain the real social distances between individuals in a friendship network. Trust regulates the nature and type of resources that can and should be interchanged; it assigns positions and provides friendships with symbolic content. Trust is not easily stored up; it is lost and won, given and taken away. Sometimes individuals fight for more trust, at other times they try to shake off the trust they have. Trust integrates and discriminates between individuals and types of behavior; it determines privileges and induces loyalties. Trust mobilizes resources and is an active principle in the rules of solidarity. In short, trust is the basic, subtle, ineffable criterion that sets out the distinctions and boundaries between the "close friend," the "friend," and the "acquaintance." The mental map of friendship is basically a map of rankings of trust, rankings that, in the last resort, reveal the true social distances between individuals in profoundly dynamic friendship networks. A friend, for example, can go back to being an acquaintance if he fails to maintain the expectations that won him his initial position on the scale of social distances; an acquaintance can become a close friend—that is to say, can accumulate trust—by rendering a particularly worthwhile service or by being the repository of trust.

Because each friend and family member has his own kinship and friendship network, a potential network of solidarity and cooperation is created that can be mobilized according to the degree of trust and need. In this way, relatives and friends are also intermediaries in potential networks of cooperation that stay on the periphery of basic networks of solidarity—those of kinship and friendship.

This fine mesh of personal relationships spreads through cities, institutions, the application of regulations, and formal power structures. Anyone with access to any sort of resources has the chance— more, the obligation—to distribute those resources among his personal network. The distribution will be according to his map of trust, which is continually redrawn, and to his existing material and symbolic debts.

CULTURAL GRAMMAR OF DOMINATION-SUBORDINATION

In the lateral relationships just described, the participants shift about in a space where they can quite quickly change position (closeness to or distance from the subject) within the network of relationships. This is possible because the actions of the participants are continually judged and reevaluated according to whether they gain or lose trust, whether they respect or violate the unwritten laws that regulate activities in the kinship or friendship networks. In vertical relationships, on the other hand, the interchange of resources between individuals of different classes or social groups is qualitatively different, reflecting differences of power and placing individuals in well-defined positions within formal power structures. If in lateral relationships the necessarily symmetrical interchange of resources accords with an ideology of friendship or solidarity, in vertical relationships the interchange— characterized by its asymmetry—reflects an ideology of power and prestige that leads to a relationship of domination-subordination.

In vertical relationships, the participants are placed at different levels and/or control different quantities of resources within the formal power structures. These vertical relationships are intrinsically asymmetrical because the party who has greater access to scarce resources controls the needs and aspirations of the other. Not all vertical relationships, however, are directly regulated by the logic of formal power structures. There are power relationships that are sustained mainly by traditions and culture. This is why we do not rule out the possibility that these relationships, which we call *clientelistic relationships*, have their origin and rationale in the interests peculiar to formal power structures. Vertical relationships directly derived from the formal sphere of activity are relationships between impersonal hierarchies, positions, and roles, and their effectiveness lies in restraining any manifestation of strictly personal interests. Clientelistic relationships are personal hierarchical relationships that in theory respond to the special interests of the participants. They also, therefore, present informal mechanisms of interchange.

Moreover, interchange in clientelistic relationships is not that of the marketplace; cash is not its reason or instrument. In the patron-client relationship, the interchange of resources is redistributive (Polanyi 1957, Blau 1964, Sahlins 1965); the flow of resources, of course, moves almost exclusively along vertical lines. Resources that go upward accumulate at the top; when they go down they are distributed unequally according to informal criteria of social differentiation. If, in the cultural grammar of solidarity, the central criterion is trust, the central criteria in the grammar of client relationships are loyalty and prestige. The favors of the government official, for example, are exchanged for votes; the elected official then owes loyalty not only to the electors who supposedly voted for him, but also to those individuals who, being in higher positions, helped him—formally or informally—to reach his position. To keep his place and to be able to go on climbing the ladder—that is, to gain more loyalty and prestige—he has to transfer resources upward, in exchange for which he is given more support.

Clientelistic relationships often arise out of and are supported by kinship and friendship networks—for example, the father who centralizes resources and redistributes them among his family, or the friend who is in the position of intermediary between the resources and his network in the formal power structure. Relationships of cooperation and solidarity and clientelistic relationships are mobilized, then, within the culture. One stems from the criterion of trust, the other from loyalty and prestige.

The starter engine that mobilizes the kinship and friendship networks, real or potential, is the scarcity of resources. To survive or to gain access to social mobility, it is necessary to fall back on the networks of relationships to locate someone in a higher position, who can redistribute resources; in exchange, the one who is higher will expect loyalty and support. In this way, the clientelistic relationship complements the market economy and alleviates the effects of the lack of basic resources or formal power structures. It relies, in fact, on an asymmetrical reciprocity and represents an informal interchange mechanism, but, given the situation, the clientelistic relationship has the power to satisfy the needs of its individual members.

Thus, just as client relationships can be superimposed on relationships sustained by the networks of kinship and friends, so also can clientelistic relationships be superimposed on the transactions of the market, politics, and other activities, which are initially formal. For example, a relationship of loyalty and trust is possible between the owner of a business and his employees, who will protect their boss's financial interests in exchange for certain concessions in times of need. The boss-employee relationship could therefore be described as essentially paternalistic, one that creates a space in which what Gabriel Zaid (1987, 26), writing about Mexico, calls "traditional corruption" can take place. According to Zaid, "there is in [traditional] corruption a countercultural fraternity, an immersion in communal waters which resists formal channeling, a rejection of modern impersonal, ruthless culture, an affirmation of one's family, friendships, and home ground in the face of the law and meritocracy." Clientelistic relationships, then, are first an efficient mechanism for obtaining scarce resources within the bounds of the rules established by formal power structures. The efficiency and scope of these relationships vary according to the degree of loyalty, prestige, and trust. Second, clientelistic relationships represent an affirmation of the individual against the bureaucratic imposition of the formal sphere. This contrasts with market relationships, including those of illegal services, in which supply and demand are fixed without the intervention of the participants.

To repeat, the sphere of informal activity includes the whole range of social relationships, horizontal as well as vertical, regulated by cultural codes, sanctioned by implicit rules of action, and aimed basically at satisfying the participants' interests. These interests, in fact, can be anyone's, from the president, who puts his family and friends in public positions, down to the underclass, whose main interest may well be survival. Kinship and friendship networks on the one hand and clientelistic relationships on the other make up the cultural grammars of solidarity and domination-subordination that give cohesion to the social relationships and activities of the informal sphere. This sphere, however, only acquires its special character alongside its counterpart, which provides the basic mechanism of society's regeneration. This is the formal sphere of activity, the area of economic, social, and political systems. We shall not describe the formal sphere here; it has already been fully dealt with from a number of viewpoints from the Marxist to the Weberian. Instead, we shall go on to analyze the close link between formal and informal social relationships and activities, their convolutions, manifestations, and scope in Latin American cities.

CULTURAL GRAMMAR AND BUREAUCRATIC RATIONALE

Some studies have relegated the formal-informal dichotomy to the field of economics, using the terms *formal and informal sectors* or *primary and secondary economies.* Furthermore, these studies maintain that the informal sphere is a direct consequence of formal power structures (see, for example, Portes 1980).

The informal sector is made up of those workers who operate within the capitalist market but by means of extralegal mechanisms of contracting and without legal protection or access to social security benefits or job security. The informal sector provides goods and services that escape state control (regulations, taxation, fees, and so forth). In our view, the informal sector comes within the sphere of informal sanctions, and its efficiency and profitability rest on this fact. Not all of this sector, however, is informal. The secondary economy uses formal strategies, both economic and political, without which it could not exist. The formal sector of the economy, in its turn, supports informal activities that allow the value of its capital to increase. In either case, individuals who work in one or the other sector resort to activities both in the formal, officially regulated sphere and in the informal sphere, which is nourished by their cultural heritage. Resources are received and redistributed through both types of activity.

In our description we take as a starting-point the idea that a mode of production is not forged in a vacuum, but against a background of cultural legacies that are slowly changed and absorbed to make its development and reproduction viable. This cultural legacy constantly enters into the daily life of the people concerned, modifying the values, norms, rules, and principles of organization of the formal power structures and of the activities derived from them.

We should like to emphasize that the two spheres of activity interact so closely that it is not easy to tell by observation alone when an individual is acting according to the rules of the one or the other. In an ideal framework each has its function and area of action. The formal sphere is charged with providing norms for society as a whole, with making sure that universal criteria—justice, for example—predominate, that all individuals have the same rights and opportunities for survival. In other words, social reproduction is sustained by organizations that the activities of the formal sphere take for granted. The sphere of informal activity deals with individual interests and satisfies its members' need for companionship, welfare, and security. In theory more than in practice, the informal sphere has to subordinate itself to the formal and limits itself to private matters.

Yet, informal relationships and activities are not marginal, private, or incompatible with the whole social system. Moreover, while they represent opposition to the intrinsic spirit of formal power structures for administering the lives of individuals, they also permit the reproduction of these structures, since it is through kinship and friendship networks that individuals satisfy their most pressing needs. When individuals resort to these informal strategies, their activities—always spur-of-the-moment—are limited in some way by the institutional and bureaucratic frameworks in which they are inserted. In other words, individuals are responsible for seeing to it that bureaucratic regulations are adhered to, but they also use and maintain loyalties and have responsibilities to their kinship and friendship networks.

This dual position that individuals hold is particularly relevant in times of a shortage of resources, such as currently prevails in Latin American cities. Moreover, this duality provides a viable and relatively effective mechanism for obtaining access to scarce resources that enable individuals to survive. At the same time, the dual position increases the inefficiency of formal institutions, since individuals who do not have sufficiently wide networks in these institutions—normally those on the lowest rung of the ladder—are not able to benefit fully from the services formal institutions offer. As a result, making use of those cultural resources presented by the informal sphere deepens the intrinsic social differences between it and the formal power structures.

The informal sphere of activities and its cultural grammar have always been present in Latin American cities, operating to a greater or lesser degree according to the quantity and quality of resources that flow from the formal power structure. When industrialization and modernization were launched—the period of economic "miracles"—the relationships between the people and jobs and between supply and demand of resources permitted the development and consolidation of bureaucratic rationalization at the cost of cultural grammars.

Today, however, because of the demographic explosion, an unequal growth in the two sectors, and the economic, social, and political crisis, the demand for resources is greater than the supply being offered by the formal power structures. To make up for the resource deficiency and to preserve the privileges that they once possessed, individuals have had to mobilize their networks still more. This increase in informal activity is of such magnitude that it has begun to damage the universal rights and rules on which the formal power structures are founded, renewed, and legitimized. The deterioration is all the more paradoxical in that it takes place within the same limits imposed by the formal sphere of activities. But do not be deceived—the increase in the informal sector is of limited scope. It provokes changes in the operation of the formal sphere and eventually in formal institutions, but it will hardly lead to structural transformation.

At the same time that the activities of the informal sphere make formal institutions less efficient and damage universal ideologies, bureaucratic rationalization recovers lost social space by modifying itself and imposing new limits, norms, and rules. For example, it exercises greater control over the resources themselves; resources previously channeled to the rural sector may be transferred to the urban sector, and so on. The formal sphere tolerates the growth of the informal sector (it is estimated that 50 percent of the economically active population works in this sector) and seeks to broaden its political alliances. By its nature, formal-informal interaction, complex and overlapping as it is, can reflect both an apparently peaceful coexistence and a conflict between the needs and interests sustained by each one of the spheres. The domain of one or the other sphere of activity meets with continuous resistance and adaptation from its counterpart, now in the form of normative modification or repression, now in the search for solutions to counteract the new mechanisms of formal control. In reality, both spheres of activity continually set limits and find new areas of activity. Growth of the formal sphere of activities is accompanied by the increase in rigidity of formal power structures and, consequently, the inability to satisfy the individual's need for resources. Individuals, therefore, have to adapt their cultural survival strategies to the new circumstances. As a consequence, the unlimited increase in this sphere of formal activity subjects social life more than ever to regulation or to repressive mechanisms of control and domination. Thus, formal-informal interraction oscillates between violence and repression on the one hand and social anomie on the other.

In conclusion, we can reaffirm that the states and dependent capitalist economies of Latin America are further than ever from being able to offer a minimum of jobs, security, housing, or resources. This situation has mobilized the basic strategies of individuals, their kinship and friendship networks, and their cultural grammars, which almost imperceptibly damage the functioning, discourse, plans, and regulations of the formal power structure. To understand the movement and passage of Latin American cities, it is not enough to analyze the principles of their formal organization; one must also study the cultural principles that govern the sphere of informal activity—the cultural grammar of solidarity, centered on family and friendship, and the cultural grammar of domination-subordination, centered on clientelistic relationships and paternalism.

REFERENCES

Blau, Peter. 1964. *Exchange and Power in Social Life*. New York: John Wiley & Sons.

Firth, R., et al. 1970. *Families and Their Relations*. London: Routledge and Kegan Paul.

Friedmann, John, and Mauricio Salguero. 1987. *The Political Economy of Survival and Collective Self-Empowerment in Latin America: A Framework and Agenda for Research*. Unpublished manuscript, University of California, Los Angeles.

González y González, Luis. 1982. *Nueva invitación a la micro-historia*. Mexico City: Secretaría de Educación Pública (80).

Hankiss, Elemér. 1990. "The Black Box: Interaction and Conflict of Social Paradigms in Contemporary Societies." In *East European Alternatives*. Oxford: The Clarendon Press.

Lomnitz, L. 1974. *Cómo sobreviven los marginados*. Mexico City: Siglo XXI.

———— 1979. "El compadrazgo. Reciprocidad de favores en la clase media urbana de Chile." *Estudios Sociales Centroamericanos*, 7:19 (January–April).

———— 1982. "Horizontal and Vertical Relations and the Social Structure of Urban Mexico." *Latin American Research Review*, 16:2.

Lomnitz, L., and M. Pérez Lizaur. 1987. *A Mexican Elite Family, 1820–1980: Kinship, Class, and Culture*. Princeton, N.J.: Princeton University Press.

Macfarlane, Alan. 1979. *The Origins of English Individualism*. Oxford.

Polanyi, Karl, 1957. *Trade and Market in the Early Empires*. Glencoe, Ill.: The Free Press.

Portes, Alejandro. 1980. "The Informal Sector and the Capital Accumulative Process in Latin America." Paper presented at the Social Science Research Council Workshop on Latin American Urbanization, Carmel, Calif., March.

Sahlins, Marshal D. 1965. *On the Sociology of Primitive Exchange: The Relevance of Models for Social Anthropology*. Michael Banton, ed. (Monograph No. 1). London: Tavistock.

Schneider, D. 1968. *The American Kinship: A Cultural Account*. Englewood Cliffs, N.J.: Prentice-Hall.

Schneider, D., and R. Smith. 1977. "Class Differences and Sex Roles." In *American Kinships and Family Structure*. Englewood Cliffs, N.J.: Prentice-Hall.

Smith, R. T., ed. 1984. *Kinship Ideology and Practice in Latin America*. Chapel Hill and London: University of North Carolina Press.

Zaid, Gabriel. 1987. *La economía presidencial*. Mexico City: Vuelta.

13

Urban Modernity in the Context of Underdevelopment: The Brazilian Case

Jorge Wilheim

With what kind of cities are we concerned? In the case of Brazil, it is cities that were never villages. Ever since the Portuguese colonization, urban settlements have been born as full-fledged cities. These may have been small and poor, but they have always had trade, and political, and administrative functions.

The well-known rhythm of the European village—people leaving at dawn to till the land, returning at nightfall, and enjoying public events on Sunday—never existed in Brazil. Population density was too low; there were few people and enormous space. Those who worked the land did not live in villages; they dwelt in shacks that the landowner had set up for his slaves or workers.

Even the early Indian villages, known as the *taba*, were too small to sustain continuous occupancy and had to be abandoned at times. Thus, the *taba* did not lead to the development of an urban tradition.

Consequently, throughout Brazilian history, roles and linkages were developed in a dialogue sustained between inhabitants of rural and urban areas. Until the close of the nineteenth century, the rich and powerful, who lived in large, rustic houses on their own farms, would go to the cities where they maintained secondary homes for commercial and political reasons. A prosperous middle class established itself in the cities during the nineteenth century. This group grew in importance as political independence gave birth to a public bureaucracy and as commerce and banking developed alongside the growth in Brazilian agricultural exports.

No impediments existed to social or physical mobility in Brazil then. Nor are there any now. Social prejudices in the nineteenth century were selective. But information on people's background was scarce, so amid the turmoil of growth and in the absence of more qualified candidates, even the most conservative parents could not stop their daughters from marrying Portuguese or Italian immigrants of dubious origins. Moreover, life was rugged and difficult: Social and ethical values extolled the prestige of the self-made man. As for physical mobility, even now in Brazil there is always another place to go, another space to occupy. The nation still has a western agricultural frontier, a "land to discover," and many pioneers continue to populate the Brazilian far west, much to the despair of its 80,000 Indians. Many cities have been emerging along the roads that penetrate Roraima, Rondônia, and Amapá in the Amazon region, as well as in the states of Mato Grosso and Pará, which are closer to Brasília.

Brazilians move easily throughout their country. They share a common language; no dialects separate people from one another. Nor are there physical barriers such as high mountains or large lakes.

On the contrary, communication and transportation systems are efficient. Television broadcasting, throughout the entire country, offers a variety of news, entertainment, and sports. The World Cup in soccer attracts an audience of 100 million viewers out of a total population of 140 million. A good television series can easily claim the attention (and emotions) of 60 to 80 million viewers every evening for half a year. Such an event constitutes a true communion in which people throughout the country think about the same issues and copy the same life-styles.

No wonder people are attracted to the cities that appear on television. The projected image of the city is of a modern place full of opportunity in which a person can get ahead if he or she is only sufficiently aggressive and shrewd.

Individuals migrate either because they are forced to leave one place or because they are strongly attracted to another. Poverty and despair motivate individuals to leave home, whether it be a parcel of land or a small town. What motivates an individual to come to a particular place is a more subjective matter, but poverty remains a determining factor.

Thus, the saga of Brazilian urban migration is not solely an adventure in optimism. Although hope may be present, poverty and despair supply an important impetus. Poverty is generally thought of as lack of food, clothing, and shelter. However, it is also a cultural handicap in the face of the challenge of urbanization. People arrive in the big city with a limited vocabulary and are abysmally ignorant of what is taken to be common knowledge. These people may be illiterate and have few job skills. Frequently, they have been ill, weak, and undernourished, as were their parents and grandparents.

Migration tends to highlight these social differences precisely because it creates the opportunity for social intercourse and the potential for social mobility. It is important to underscore the fact that despite its modern commercial sector and urban sophistication, Brazil is still experiencing a postslavery period culturally. No country in the world displays greater inequity in its income distribution. The poorer 50 percent of the Brazilian population subsists on the same share of the national wealth that is controlled by the top 1 percent of the population—each appropriates approximately 13 percent of the country's gross national product. Such a skewed concentration of wealth has a tremendous impact on the country's urban way of life.

Privilege is important; spending spells status. Many customs derive from the culture of slavery. For example, one does not use the same elevator as one's maid. There is discrimination against blacks, although black women are tolerated for specific service functions. Brazilian machismo, often indistinguishable from male sadism, is an expression of postslavery culture.

Urbanization permits the kind of mobility embodied in the self-made man phenomenon. However, undemocratic values frequently emerge in this process. In Japan one finds what I call *telephone samurai*: those who have undergone a whole set of cultural adaptations necessary for modern urban life. In Brazil, however, one finds illiterate, undernourished migrants whose thoughts and views of reality are dominated by the fantasies of the television screen—unfulfilled dreams replace core values.

What then is the spirit of Brazilian cities? Migration to the cities is steadily falling. Most of the population growth that has taken place since 1975 in São Paulo, for example, has resulted from natural increase, not migration. And population growth is expected to fall to an annual rate of 1.4 percent by the end of this century. Nevertheless, the spirit of the cities is marked by the expectations of urban migrants and by their new modes of urban life.

To earn a living, own a home, get a job, purchase objects, send some money home, or simply send some presents to show the folks back home that "you've made it": These are common goals.

One does not need to be a law-abiding citizen to achieve these goals. People use a set of personal connections, not a set of written rules, to fulfill their objectives. Rules and laws are mere points of reference. When infringing upon them, it may be useful to know just what is at risk. But rules are tools to be used against others. Respect for the rule of law will not enhance one's social status.

To move up the social scale, one needs a set of personal connections. Urban dwellers understand perfectly well the differences among individuals whom they count among their own set of personal connections.

Differences in personal power are common knowledge. Practical values are established that contradict ethical values or any sense of fairness. When two cars collide in traffic, both drivers are likely to get out and face each other down. There will be no serious conflict so long as they both appear to be from different social backgrounds. A legal problem will arise only if both drivers appear to enjoy an equal social status. Only then will they appeal to a set of rules; that is, to the law.

I have no desire to portray social inequity in a cynical fashion. However, it is one thing to fight against such conditions in the political realm and quite another to understand the true dynamic of the local urban spirit.

For an individual to seize opportunities, he must work hard, stay alert, have access to information, be creative, and be bold. If ten million people are placed together who all subscribe to this spirit, tremendous unrest and dynamic urban creativity and production will result, but in a style similar to the *escola de samba* of the carnival, in which the participants dance individually, expressing themselves in a very personal style, but all the while singing the same tune. The zigzag of the carnival dance has a common starting point and an ultimate destination. And among so many dancers dressed (or undressed) in a similar fashion, one will always find those who look better, dance better, and perform better.

This kind of spirit leads to an insecure, ever-changing way of modern life. Struggling within this network of opportunities, the individual adopts certain pragmatic strategies. Education, symbolized by a diploma, is the best way to obtain a better job and social status. To make ends meet, however, more than one source of income is needed. A permanent position as a government clerk is a useful minimum guarantee of income, but at the same time other economic activities have to be pursued.

Personal attributes—clothing, appearance, possessions—are meaningful components used to further one's life strategy. Modernity is a value from which flows the compulsion to change, to renew, to follow fashions creating a never-ending necessity for consumption. The intense value associated with modernity leads to an easy acceptance of novelties and a relatively uncritical psychology.

If most urban people subscribe to this spirit, one may well ask whether cities can be (or even should be) planned, managed, controlled, directed, and designed. And if they can be, then to what extent and toward what end?

It would be superficial to think that Latin American cities cannot be controlled and that the apparent chaos they display should persist unchanging. People violate laws and fail to abide by written rules. They establish individual projects in their respective cities and conspire to ravish the land and overburden the ecological system. But the same people are unhappy with the general results and dissatisfied with the consequent chaos. They protest and press the government to establish some order and, perhaps, beautify the environment. They also protest against the government's inefficiency.

This so-called chaos follows a particular logic, a kind of order of its own. Henri Lefebvre once wrote that a modern city is "the site of consumption and the consumption of its site." A city of migrants obeys a logic that uses up and consumes territory. Because of the conditions of underdevelopment, such a city will grow quickly. As a result, it will spread far beyond the few paved corridors that exist, and the urban infrastructure will lag far behind the city's actual growth. Some of the concentration of income, however, leads to a wealthy, well-informed middle class that presses for the modernization of selected communication, transportation, technology, and industrial networks. In response, the city incorporates laser technology, automation, skyscrapers, slums, abandoned children, illiteracy, and up-to-date cultural programs. This is not chaos. It is an order, albeit unfair and ugly.

Individual and group interests are unequal. Within this urban logic exist islands of beauty, oases of comfort, and shining examples of "the beautiful city" that developers and builders offer every day to upscale people on the move. Thus, one finds that 18 percent of the population of São Paulo lives in old slum houses where an average of 2.6 persons occupy a room of 12 square meters and there is only 1 shower for every 15.4 persons, whereas the daily newspapers advertise single-family apartments of 400 square meters with an average of 1.2 showers per occupant.

Injustice, unfairness, and inequity are social manifestations that need to be addressed on a political level. Low salaries are to blame for the misery of the poor. Only under pressure will Brazil finally close the door on its postslavery period and change this situation.

Events in recent years reveal important changes on the political scene: The change to a democratic government in 1985 was a direct consequence of mass rallies protesting the authoritarian military regime. The initial success of the *Cruzado* Plan was made possible only by the willingness of people, en masse, to assist in enforcing price controls.

Several other examples of social changes should be noted. During the 1983 recession, with its sudden, drastic employment crisis, an association called Solidarity in Unemployment was founded. This group provided funds to groups of unemployed workers who developed new modes of production. Each month Solidarity distributed financial resources to some 150 groups, each of which included about 80 people.

What these people did with the money was entirely their own decision. Solidarity limited itself to announcing each group's activities in a bulletin it published. Some of the groups opted to make collective food purchases, others to invest in education. Some began producing crafts; others set up a bakery, a knitting enterprise, a collectively run drug store, and a collective soup kitchen. Still others began a collective farm to produce vegetables. As the unemployment crisis subsided, the Solidarity association began to assist new groups with projects to disseminate information.

The municipal program *Feito em Casa* (Home-Made) was another well-known effort in Brazil. Serving as a bridge between home-based producers and the market, the program in two years provided productive work opportunities for 15,000 people at a cost of fifty cents per individual.

During its first eight months, the Communications Network of Municipal Experiences (RECEM), a creative official program, provided assistance to 1,200 self-help endeavors in areas such as food production and distribution, free transportation, unemployment, education, care for the elderly, and collective management in housing, information systems, environmental efforts, new technologies, and neighborhood beautification.

People taking part in all of these endeavors learn that they need not wait for changes to be made for them; they themselves can bring them about. It is this political-pedagogical aspect which deserves emphasis. Having said this, still, the urban dynamic (with its migrant tradition in the context of underdevelopment) plays a role in the success of the examples given and the potential for further changes.

Something new is happening in Brazil: People still act as individuals, but political consciousness is increasing steadily; the World Cup is still a source of fascination, but people appear to agree that the future of their nation is more important. In their concern can be seen a growing sense of citizenship. People have hope, and they believe that they themselves can produce changes and collectively build a better future.

These developments underline my belief that cities can and must be planned and governed—assuming that several factors are taken into account: (a) that people act on the basis of lessons drawn from past experience; (b) that they show concern both for efficiency and beauty; (c) that planning be used only as a strategic tool; and (d) that the future be recognized for the vital, active issue it is in everyday Latin American life.

Only with a thorough understanding both of the roots of the urban spirit and of the dynamic of the present political moment can planners, technocrats, professionals, and academics correct and enrich their knowledge and rethink their own roles and objectives.

This still leaves the question of what is to be done. Following are my suggestions:

- Latin American countries should encourage stronger networks of cities in order to arrest the intense concentration of urban life in one or two megacities. This requires growth and development of middle-sized cities. Potential instruments include federal support for new economic activities in middle-sized cities, political support behind local authorities who work effectively to make cities more attractive, and an information system that promotes such cities as alternative destinations for the migrant tide that will continue for another ten or twenty years.
- A comprehensive policy for Brazil's pioneer region should be implemented that takes into account the Indian problem, strategies for construction of highway systems, land tenure, techniques of urban settlement, and social organization.
- A concerted effort toward rural modernization must be made. Small rural industries must be encouraged where they exist; where they do not, they must be established. Information, education, television, and cultural and leisure programs can all serve to diminish differences in the quality of life between urban and rural areas. Of course, no improvement could be more fundamental than a fair resolution of the struggle for land ownership in rural areas.
- There need to be specific policies for the metropolitan regions. Political and administrative issues must be confronted and programs must address megacity problems, such as sanitation, roads, mass transportation, employment, housing, political representation, and pollution. These problems must be considered in the context of reindustrialization in cities such as São Paulo and Buenos Aires.
- Brazilian legal codes must reflect the fact that Brazil is no longer a rural country, but rather a highly urbanized, modern, and industrialized one. Almost 70 percent of the population now lives in cities. Brazilian underdevelopment is no longer exemplified by precapitalist modes of production. What the country must address are its postslavery habits that help sustain its inequitable income distribution.
- It should be recognized that the urban social dynamic provides the principal energy for transformation. It supports and orients

the self-help organizations and leads them into a partnership with the government, in which the opportunity to effect urban physical changes becomes possible.

- It needs to be emphasized that participants in these transformation experiences usually start out attempting to effect a small change at the local level. Should any degree of success result, the experience is applied toward bolder objectives. A political-pedagogical aspect is linked to each concrete achievement. In this social context, urban design can play a new role as the core of political action. To fight for a new square, a traffic-free street, a public vegetable garden, or a police station is to insist on improvements in the quality of life and to impose a new way of getting things done in the city.

Many tasks will have to be considered by professionals and academics in the conception, elaboration, and implementation of these seven recommendations. Only rarely has the opening of the Brazilian western frontier been considered in comprehensive terms. While anthropologists study the Indians and ecologists examine the preservation of the rain forest, the engineers carry out feasibility studies for constructing new roads. To each his own. Only in the arts, particularly in filmmaking, has a comprehensive understanding of the issues been displayed.

Regarding the issue of middle-sized cities, there has been scant understanding of what factors tip the decision of the migrant who is on the verge of choosing a new physical destination. Just what does "a good life" mean to the poor?

Metropolitan problems present interesting challenges. I will mention only two. First, the problem of dealing with sewage and waste disposal is one that has tremendous impact on the economies of Third World megacities. Any solution will require breakthroughs in biology, technology, and decentralization. Second, city managers need to decentralize political power and allow power to flow to organized citizens. Successful attempts could serve as the basis for a socialist government of self-management in Latin America in the coming years.

The lesson is that ideas can indeed have great significance. When ideas are effective, their dissemination can stir emotions and provoke action as well as thought. Therefore, greater attention must be paid to ideas that best serve the public and to their dissemination through the most appropriate forum—television, radio, exhibits, lectures, daily newspapers, leaflets, books, cinema, street theater, or other artistic expressions.

14

Lima and the Children of Chaos

Abelardo Sánchez León

Since 1950 the people of the Peruvian countryside have been slipping into the city of Lima through the back door, uninvited and without manners. They have been making the city their own, seizing, invading, and carving out a territory for themselves, modifying the city, making it into what it is today, all in a span of thirty-five years. Spurred on by economic necessity, these migrants not only break the laws, especially those regarding private property, they ignore them. The laws of survival come first as they remake the city.

The new Lima that became apparent in the 1960s changed the map of the country. It concentrated even more political and economic power and changed population ratios. Lima is thirteen times larger than the country's second city; its San Martín de Porres district, site of a land invasion in 1954, is today more heavily populated than any city in Peru except Arequipa; from Carbayllo to the new town of Mariano Melgar, Lima is a total of sixty-two kilometers long and includes more than 25 percent of Peru's population and more than 50 percent of its urban population. The Lima of today, with its population of five million, has changed Peru and these changes are also its problems—because Lima is a problem difficult to unravel.

A large part of the population, particularly the children and young people, lives in poverty. These are the children of chaos, of poverty, and of urban violence. This vast population exists in a city that does not offer them any chance of personal and social growth, though it has allowed, and even encouraged, a number of creative, organized initiatives.

Using rough concepts, it can be argued that capitalism in underdeveloped countries functions on a basis of an unlimited supply of labor, which leads to low wages and job insecurity. This reality favors the development of informal activities, often associated with the incredible inventiveness of Latin American working classes in their struggle to stay alive and find a way out of unemployment. These activities function as a corrective force on the system and should not be seen in social and economic isolation nor as part of a different or parallel society. The informal sector is peculiar to the working classes of Latin America, with their cycle of insecurity, instability, and low wages. It is the true expression of the way in which capitalism works in Latin American societies.

Thus, a city like Lima produces an immense population with distinctive traits: people who know only despair; young people who live alongside criminals, and drug addicts, who may at any moment fall into prostitution; people who carry in their lungs a concentration of smog.

The city's economic function does not rest mainly on an urban proletariat, which is the vanguard of political thought, conscious of its rights, and grouped in labor unions. A labor movement certainly exists; a political vanguard exists with specific claims, demands, and grievances. But there is also a generalized poverty, an enormous section of the city whose residents squabble and fight for a foothold, who do not accept poverty but demand their share.

Population growth in Latin America has no counterpart in the development of a productive structure and in the satisfaction of needs. Meanwhile, it generates still more chaos and poverty. Another way of seeing things, however, is to understand the growth in Latin American societies of what is called the informal economy. What is certain is that the formal, stable, salaried type of relations, typical of urban economies, is on the decline. Projections show that 49 percent of Latin America's active population works informally. There is work but the type of work generated is not salaried or formalized. Latin American cities are not heading for chaos but they are steering toward social fragmentation, a world much more similar to European cities at the end of the Middle Ages, according to Manuel Castells (1976).

This phenomenon, baptized "informal," can be linked to time-honored survival techniques of the working classes. But in its present-day incarnation, it leaves Lima with a population deprived of security and stability, with repercussions in the cultural sphere and in social relations.

This informal sector, without laws for social security, with little hope of employment, and with material poverty is all the more dramatic when the age of the Peruvian population is considered. About 40 percent is under the age of fifteen and another 20 percent is between fifteen and twenty-four, which means that adults make up only 40 percent of the population of Peru. Nearly three-fourths, 72 percent, of these young people live in urban areas. One third of the country's population aged fifteen to twenty-four—1.2 million—lives in Lima.

These young people, who are the children of migrants from the countryside, were born and grew up in slums that have existed for over thirty years. Their population does not know the drama, which so fascinated the anthropologists of past times, of integrating and adapting culturally to the city; they are city dwellers. If in the past a country person arrived in fear and was cowed by the buildings, the traffic lights, and the racism of Lima, today it is the opposite. The young people have grown up in the crowded streets of the slums, they know the rocky slopes of El Agustino, the stagnant waters of El Pino, the open sewers, the puddles, the potholed roads, the thatched huts, the sand pits, the barrels of contaminated drinking water, nights without electric light, the rubbish dumps, and the murky waters of the Rímac.

A sign of the disintegration that afflicts Lima is the presence of lunatics, who wander the city streets in total abandon. Their number does not matter; what is of interest is the process by which built-in unemployment can turn a person, of whatever age, into an urban lunatic.

Imagine an impoverished young person from the middle class, a migrant from the country, struggling to find work. First, he must keep up his physical appearance if he is to get an interview; a stain on his shirt might prove fatal. If it becomes harder and harder for him to afford to eat lunch in a restaurant, he will eat from a street stall. Restaurants of this kind, with their shaky tables and chairs, are plentiful along all of Lima's busy streets. If weeks and months go by without his finding work, the young man will be tempted to pick through garbage piles, rummaging for scraps of food, but to do this without arousing suspicion he will have to pretend he is slightly mad. He will by now have the necessary clothes, a dirty, worn suit, and he will show every sign of dereliction.

The young man is a step away from taking the crucial decision. He is almost a tramp. He has probably had to leave his home, and he will have decided to live in the streets. But to do this he has to carry on like an urban lunatic—to accept his dirty appearance, filthy hair, and lack of clothes. Gradually, he will be seen by everyone else as just another of the madmen produced by the city.

In this subculture, which is different from that of the Parisian *clochard,* he will be an outcast who wanders the city on foot, strengthened by fear and the possibility of acting within a range of far greater possibilities than those available to him as someone unemployed trying to live within the formal canons imposed on anyone looking for work. Asylums do not accept him because there are not enough of them and they are full and expensive. The police may pick him up in their patrol cars and drop him outside the city in the sand pits of the south, from where he will set out for the city, practically naked, guided simply by an instinct to survive.

The different mechanisms of survival that multiply in Lima have created a network that guarantees their continuance. Housing in the center is not only subdivided or rented so as to take in families with low incomes, but is redivided into an endless number of rooms and beds, like strange hotels that provide mattresses or bedding on the floor so that the population of the new towns can sleep after working as street peddlers in these areas of the city. These are the so-called warm beds, which ensure that the informal population can, with ad hoc logistical support, do its work. Many areas in the central city or nearby commercial zones have become parking lots for the street vendors' carts. At the same time, slum houses are subdivided into workshops, tailor shops, and hairdressers' shops, which guarantee a supplementary, or perhaps the sole, income for many families.

Something very important is happening in Lima, something which has led to the formation of a new urban culture with radically different guidelines and values from those of years before. It is impossible to understand Lima only by viewing the well-to-do classes or those people formally integrated into the economy. The slum is by definition an appropriation of space without order or planning, but at the same time it is an institution and an organization. The slum works organically. It has an identity apart from its problems and common interests. Lima is a city that defines itself by its popular sectors, with their own rules of the game, which, if necessary, are imposed on the social system. For more than forty years the slums have been struggling, and their achievements are by no means negligible. Today they are run as cities within cities.

What will the young people who are going to be living in Lima over the next decades make of their city? What will become of them? What are their expectations and what will have died out forever if present conditions continue? Several psychologists have warned about the dangers of the syndrome of "the child-adult," characterizing the condition as a personality defect. They believe that the "child-adult" skips key stages in his psychic evolution. He goes to work before he is ten years old, socializes in the streets, and walks many kilometers every day, using all his energy to survive without keeping back anything just for living.

According to some Peruvian psychologists, many children daily suffer material deprivation in their homes as well as the tension and violence that permeate their family relationships. Such deprivation and abuse undermine the psychological development of the child's intellectual capacity, sense of security, emotional stability, and creative potential. These young people are marked by frustration. They are the children of the economic crisis, and now they are looking for work and housing in a country where they can only get educational certificates of dubious value and unstable, badly paid jobs.

These working-class young are regarded by the official culture as lumpens, drug addicts, delinquents, and subversives. The Peruvian Communist Party, the *Sendero Luminoso* or Shining Path, choosing the path of violence to change the social order, recruits these young people from the slums into its most important social base in the city. These youngsters are the most likely to assume radical positions, even risking their lives. When members are arrested they form a special society within the prisons, following strict rules. In a war situation these young are seen by the Shining Path as the first line of fighters, those who most need food and care. In the prisons the young *Senderistas* are the first to get nourishment in the collective distribution of food.

Behind this privilege, which the young enjoy, there is another aim on the part of the Sendero Luminoso leadership. In prison, these young people learn about collective social behavior, about new values, which arise from the idea that the young are the least contaminated and the most ready to learn new teachings. From this point of view prison is not only the natural prolongation of the battlefield but the ideal place for indoctrination and socialization, a school that imparts knowledge, experience, and values.

This is all the more interesting when one realizes that in Peru there is a tradition of prison literature and even an interpretation of the city as a prison. Many recent events show this prison world in all its crudity, which links different actors in today's reality—political subversives, kidnappers, drug traffickers, and common criminals, risen in rebellion against the prison organization and the social system.

It would not be unreasonable to claim that among other forms of socialization taking place in the city we could mention that which takes place behind bars and say that together with the new activism of the slums (neighborhood organizations, soup kitchens, mothers' groups, cultural and recreational clubs for teenagers) they both, with their obvious differences, make up living classrooms for the young of today as opposed to traditional schools, the mass media, and advertising, which only lead to short-term frustrations.

Besides the destructive urge of a radical political option that implies rebellion against the whole social system, based on capturing the mind of the young as part of a strategy of armed confrontation, another alternative for building popular power exists. This second option rests basically on the organization and participation of the people as one of the most effective ways of democratizing civil society. In the city, the neighborhood organizations are a prerequisite for taking initiatives and defending their interests. This widely internalized prerequisite has allowed a considerable advance for those social groups that have not "received a city" in the way that developed countries have done, but have "made a city" beyond a collection of housing and services to create an urban organization different from the rest of the city.

This is a new development. It is the response to a new mentality based not only on the demand for rights, but on the people's ability to initiate, to organize, to work out financial techniques and networks. The district municipalities fulfill a decisive role. They allow (or should promote) communication among the different slum organizations so that alternative solutions to common problems can be proposed and discussed.

Today in Lima organizations exist that escape state regulation. In the slums the older neighborhood organizations, mainly concerned with obtaining services such as water and electricity and negotiating with the state, exist side by side with newer organizations that have influence on social practices—recreational, youth, and cultural clubs, nurseries, soup kitchens. These organizations do not exhaust themselves in demands and claims on the state but manage a new kind of relationship among themselves, promoting solidarity and creating the means for carrying out reforms in a relatively independent way.

These organizations are not confined to the slums but include other social actors, many of them living in the slums but working elsewhere. These include street vendors, cooperative markets, municipalities, and associations of small businessmen and factory owners.

This process, expanding over the 1970s, does not mean, however, that the dominant sectors have receded or are on the defensive in urban places. Their power has not been undermined economically or politically. In fact, it has been helped by the massive presence of the enormous working-class sector, which constitutes a growing market and at the same time allows property speculation and investments in already urbanized areas.

This organizing movement, which has an intense participation at the grass-roots level and which is not necessarily controlled by specific political parties nor guided by the state, constitutes the new face of the Peruvian city. It does not constitute the social base of a political movement. It is a movement in search of its own form, voice, and presence, providing a popular and collective response to such needs as employment and housing. This mass movement is, in my view, the main actor in the new city, which by articulating answers and initiatives is displacing the state and private capital from social reproduction.

It is therefore at this moment that the most important questions concerning the new social actors are being asked. They are young from the working-class world, from the working-class movement, but they are not workers. Diversity, fragmentation, and destructuring are phenomena that should not be set aside. The absence of political parties functioning in relation to this mass movement gives it two faces. On the one hand, it can be seen as an amorphous movement without discipline or guidelines, similar to the working class; and on the other, as an urban movement making up its rules, relationships, and objectives, and advancing without making these things explicit.

The Lima slums have by now an organized tradition based on participation that is supported to some extent by the local governments, but from these slums also arise angry groups in armed subversion. The first invaders and migrants built their houses on these slopes and struggled for their space. Their descendants were educated and fed in Lima, and they know the city. A cheap source of labor without skills, they stand up for themselves. However they act, their discomfort will be disorderly. Their anguish is violent and their poverty rebellious.

At the risk of seeming simplistic, it could be said that the young urban working class has two options. It can destroy in anger the city in which it grew up, the city that denied the young any of its benefits and that offers them nothing but unstable, badly paid informal work. Or the young can join that great movement, which includes organizations based on new social practices that administer their own land and participate democratically from below and whose influence should and does stretch far beyond the slums.

REFERENCE

Castells, Manuel. 1976. *Movimientos sociales urbanos en América Latina: tendencias históricas y problemas teóricos.* Lima: Pontífica Universidad Católica.

15

Urban Alternatives for Dealing with the Crisis

Guillermo Geisse

The invitation extended to a group of scholars by Professor Richard Morse to rethink the Latin American city would not have made much sense in the 1970s. Today it does, because Latin America finds itself in the midst of a crisis marking the end of one historic stage and the beginning of another. The economic crisis, reflected in an external indebtedness of enormous proportions, is merely one manifestation of a greater crisis of a cultural, ethical, and political nature from which no Latin American country has been able to free itself. And, as in any global crisis, the sense of exhaustion of the conceptual schemes belonging to stages that have come and gone opens the way to a mental search for alternatives for change, which in "normal" times go unnoticed. One escapes from crisis situations by means of deliberate changes, and it thus becomes imperative to rethink those concepts, values, and ideologies that inspired the development of the stages already gone by. I hope to contribute to a rethinking of change in the Latin American city, in the new economic and political context that will determine the growth of the cities for the remainder of this twentieth century.

THE NEW POLITICAL-ECONOMIC CONTEXT

One might expect a high degree of consensus with regard to the hypothesis that the development of large cities will take place in a historical context that might be characterized by the following five ingredients:

The first ingredient is the historical persistence of the tendency for both the population as well as economic activity to become concentrated in a small number of large cities in each country, and in some cases in a single city.

It is true that over the past ten years, decentralizing forces have emerged that in some countries have tended to provide a greater equilibrium in the spatial distribution of the urban population. In some cases, the large cities have decreased their rate of growth compared to the medium-sized and even small cities in the same country. Their growth in absolute terms, however, continues to be overwhelmingly greater than that of any other city, given the enormous difference in size between the large city and the rest of the cities, at the beginning of the trend toward decentralization.

For example, a population increase of an average of three percent per annum in one medium-sized city of 100,000 inhabitants, which in previous decades had remained at a standstill, represents an absolute growth of 35,000 inhabitants over the course of ten years, whereas the decrease of an equal percentage in a city of 5 million inhabitants, whose prior growth was on the order of 7 percent, represents an absolute increase of 2.5 million new inhabitants during the same period. It is important, then, to remember the difference between relative and absolute growth when drawing conclusions from the current trends toward the decentralization of the population.

In the 1980s it became increasingly clear in several countries that the "core" was no longer restricted to the capital city, or major city, of each country, but rather extended to the borders of the core region, with a radius of 150 to 200 kilometers from the major city. With the core thus redefined, even though the annual rate of population growth tended to decrease slightly in the large cities (both capital and major cities), the population and its corresponding economic activity are much more concentrated than they were previously. This is because the concentration will not be fed solely by natural increase and migration from the big city, but also by the annexation of small and medium-sized cities located on the periphery of the core region. The latter tend to grow at an accelerated rate, as the economics of crowding, previously the exclusive domain of the metropolitan areas, extends to the entire core region. Obviously, the process of spatial enlargement of the core is facilitated by the traditional tendency for decisions regarding investments in interurban infrastructure to favor the core region.

A second ingredient of the political-economic context that will most likely shape the changes to take place in the city is the impoverishment of the urban majority and the deepening of the internal social inequalities that mark the beginning of the postcrisis stage.

One of the effects of the economic crisis is precisely the impoverishment of the population and deepening of the internal inequalities in the city occurring over the past five years. In reality, according to Alejandro Portes (1976), Latin America has always been characterized by great internal inequalities even compared with countries of other regions having similar income levels. According to Portes, the inequalities in income have become greater during periods in which the rates of economic growth have been relatively high. From this it appears that the inequalities cannot be attributed entirely to the current crisis.

The drama of the crisis consists in the fact that increasing poverty and the deepening of the social differences occurred simultaneously with a concomitant absolute decrease in the purchasing power of the poorest 60 percent of the population. For the majority of the population, the possibilities of obtaining access to urban land, housing, and services through the market are nonexistent. For the remainder of this century, the large majority of the population of the large cities will belong to the so-called marginal sector, whose access to urban land, as well as the ways these populations construct their urban habitat, will depend on their own strategies. As of 1986, their housing slips completely through the official system of procedures and standards. There can no longer be any doubt that the "abnormal" will become the rule for the majority. Accordingly, it is time to reexamine the total concept of the city in light of the experience of the urban masses in building their habitat and in the ways in which they integrate themselves into the city.

Third, the new context emerging as of the early 1980s is shaped by a decrease in capital resources allocated to infrastructure and urban services.

This reduction is a direct manifestation of the economic crisis affecting all countries in Latin America. As is well known, the common pressure in this crisis is the enormous external indebtedness created over the past ten years—exacerbated by an increase in the interest rates on international capital. It is not appropriate for this seminar, and even less so for this essay, to analyze this debt crisis. But it should be remembered that during the next ten to twenty years, between 5 and 6 percent of the gross product of the region will have to be earmarked exclusively for the payment of interest on the debt unless agreements are reached that are radically different from those existing to date between the various parties, including those agreements considered to be most successful.

The indebtedness will, for a long time hence, affect the capital investments required for social infrastructure projects, which are concentrated principally in the large cities. The scarce capital available for investment is likely to be directed toward economic infrastructure, and particularly toward infrastructure to support export activities, which determines the ability to meet the obligations created by the debt and to fulfill the goals of economic growth. The emphasis on investment in economic infrastructure, rather than in social infrastructure, is particularly dramatic because it occurs at a historic moment in which the large majority of the population has witnessed a reduction in absolute terms in their levels of individual consumption. In addition, the situation is made more serious because the indirect forms of redistribution of income, normally embodied in government programs for housing and services, are not cut off.

The fourth ingredient of the political-economic context of the city is a process of redemocratization spreading throughout the region.

During the past decade, Latin America has been witness to a veritable wave of democratization, with the removal of a series of military regimes, which lasted for more than a decade in several countries.

As a direct result of this trend, political channels have reopened through which the demands of the urban masses for infrastructure and services reach the highest levels of government.

Understandably, the pressure created by social demands is and will continue to be greater in those countries that suffered through regimes of political authoritarianism and economic monetarism, which imposed the cost of economic growth on the popular sectors via low salaries and a process of "marginalization." The demands heard now were repressed for more than a decade and have been nourished by new contingents of urban population.

Unless they move substantially away from the centralization that characterized the democracies that preceded the military regimes, the new democracies will find themselves trapped, on the one hand, by the historical tendency toward the centralization of the political-administrative structure and, on the other hand, by social demands that, failing to find answers at the intermediate levels, will exercise pressure at the very pinnacle of the state, which will have less capacity to respond than it did in earlier periods.

The fifth ingredient is the process of rebuilding the civil societies produced during the past decade.

The recomposition of civil society is manifested in the resurgence of a wide variety of independent organizations. These organizations respond to situations of impoverishment and marginalization with strategies based on individual and collective efforts as well as on informal integration into the economy of the city. In some countries, the appearance of such organizations has been accompanied by the adaptations of traditional organizations as required by the macropolitical circumstances. Such is the case with the Catholic Church and the research institutions in Chile. The church has now taken over certain social welfare functions traditionally carried out by the state, and the independent academic institutions have assumed responsibility for a large portion of research activities, which in preceding periods were carried out entirely by the universities.

PROBLEMS AND CHALLENGES OF URBAN PLANNING IN A NEW CONTEXT

It is now time to ask in what way this new political–economic context can affect rethinking the city in the next fifteen years. A distinction must be made between two levels: the national urban system and the internal structure of the city.

With respect to the national urban system, the dominant thinking in the urban studies literature has been influenced by the process of urban concentration and by the relationship observed between this process and underdevelopment. This relationship is expressed in terms such as *overconcentration, hyperurbanization,* and *decapitalized urbanization.* Slow economic growth, social marginality, and the inequality of income between regions were seen as abnormalities created by excessive urban concentration. Urban planners and researchers have been responsible for the dissemination of this veritable "anti–big-city" prejudice and as a result have been the driving force behind the dominant thinking in the politics of regional decentralization.

Regional decentralization proposals were quite popular during the 1960s, and several different varieties were incorporated in official planning in all countries. It was assumed that social inequalities and income differentials coincided with regional inequalities and that regional decentralization was the most appropriate instrument for implementing a policy of redistribution. Later evaluations show that the policies of regional decentralization had little effect in slowing the rate of concentration of the population and contributing to the redistribution of income.

Not all researchers and planners shared the view that urban concentration was a problem per se, which is so common in the literature today. I personally am more comfortable among those who emphasize the urban processes by which the benefits and costs of urban concentration are distributed among the various regions and social groups of the country. Very good arguments have been put forth to support the thesis that the benefits of concentration are appropriated by a social minority, whereas the costs are unloaded on the rest of society, particularly on the poorest.

The corollary of this thesis is that the best policy of regional decentralization, with an eye toward redistributive objectives in economic and social matters, seeks to assign the costs of urban concentration to those who receive the benefits, thus lifting this burden from the poorest members of society. I am certain that such a policy would lure economic agents toward regional locations having a lower social cost per unit of investment to a degree not achieved by policies providing incentives for decentralization. This way of looking at the "regional question" leads to the second level: that of the internal structure of the city, analyzed in the political-economic context whose five ingredients were summarized at the outset.

Of the distributive process operating within the city, the development of land through the real-estate market is perhaps the most important. The strategies followed by the social agents with regard to urban land use is the factor that most influences the growth, internal organization, and special composition of cities, as well as the distribution of the benefits and costs of urban activity among the various social sectors forming part of it.

POVERTY OF AND POVERTY IN THE CITY: A NECESSARY DIFFERENTIATION

In previous writings, I have found it useful to distinguish between poverty *in* the city and poverty *of* the city. The first of these two forms of poverty is manifested in high levels of unemployment, low income, precarious health conditions, lack of social security, extremely low levels of education, and the like. All of these characteristics are useful in estimating poverty *in* the city just as they would likewise be useful in estimating poverty *in* the rural areas. In contrast, the expression "poverty *of* the city" is manifested in the lack of access, or reduced access, to resources that are characteristically urban: urban land, services, and employment centers. Both types of poverty are obviously interrelated; however, they are best analyzed separately.

The studies that indicate most clearly the need to make this distinction are those referring to the informal sector. *Informal sector* is a term originally coined by economists, whose principal preoccupation is the problem of employment, its effect on income, and the noncontractual and, accordingly, precarious way in which the popular sectors participate in the labor market. On the basis of this strictly economic definition, the population of the informal sector and its impact on low income has been estimated by the UN's Programa Regional de Empleo para América Latina y el Caribe to be approximately 20 percent, and up to 30 percent in certain countries.

For purposes of rethinking the current impoverishment in the city, the economic definition of the informal sector does not suffice. The informal sector must be examined from a broader perspective that includes not only labor activities, but also activities involving the development of the popular habitat outside the bounds of official norms and standards, collectively organized artisan-type production, illegal access to urban services, exchange of services not included in economic statistics, and distribution of goods and services based on face-to-face contact.

Not all individuals or families are "informals" in all activities carried out all the time; nor do all members of the family carry out informal activities. There exists a wide variety of combinations in a given family and in a given neighborhood or community. However, one characteristic is common to all combinations, and that is the low level of productivity, which translates into an unequal integration into the formal city. This is basically an unequal integration of the "sell cheap and buy dear" variety. Using this definition, the informal sector includes considerably more than 50 percent of the population of the city, and some sources indicate that for some cities this figure could reach 70 percent.

No matter which definition is used, the informal sector is not "marginal," or, at least, is not marginal in absolute terms. To speak of the informal sector is to speak of the poverty *in* the city produced by unequal integration (and not by marginalization). It is an unequal integration that is functional to the accumulation of productive capital, and for this reason the informal sector must be located *in* the city and near the modern urban sector.

In contrast, the poverty *of* the city is not the result of unequal integration, but rather of the absolute exclusion or marginalization of the informal sector from the resources that are characteristic of the city. And the reason for this absolute marginalization is very simple: The other source of capital accumulation in the modern sector is income from land, which derives from the permanent appreciation of this resource. The principal factor behind appreciation is residential segregation, which is in part a consequence of differences in income, a segregation that occurs everywhere in the world where the land market operates, and is in part the result of land speculation. Land speculators use many different instruments, including those that interfere with the free play of the market, such as the establishment of "private land banks" and political influence on decisions regarding the location of public investments in infrastructure and services. Although the poor have to be located physically nearby, as a necessary condition for contributing to the rate of return on productive and commercial capital, the maximization of the income from land demands that they be separated. Close, but separated.

During the 1970s and early 1980s, this type of dialectic between unequal integration and spatial exclusion had reached extreme proportions, particularly in those countries that imposed models combining political authoritarianism with economic neoliberalism (the latter, naturally, for those operating within the market). The price of land increased as real estate speculation took place at unsurpassed rates, allowing some speculators to amass large fortunes. The hegemonic agent for the amassing of wealth was the financial sector of the economy. Unlimited access to credit, which in turn had its source in external credits, made it possible for real estate developers to control the whole process of urban land development from the purchase of land to the marketing of the houses. The entire supply of land was cornered by blocking the access of the masses to this basic commodity.

From my vantage point, the poverty *of* the city has been growing since the 1970s and at a much faster rate than the poverty *in* the city. The best indicator of this differential growth is the considerable increase in the number of families in the formal sector that have been forced to live in marginal areas of the city that are crowded and lacking in one or more of the basic services and where living conditions are precarious. The considerable increase in the rental submarket in the popular peripheral neighborhoods of the city and the emergence of the category of the *allegados* (informal renters) are also indicators of the growth and diversification that the marginal urban sector has undergone during the past decade.

In short, the unequal economic integration and spatial marginalization of the popular sectors of the large city is a functional combination of the two forms of accumulation of urban capital to which the poverty *in* the city and *of* the city must adjust.

THE ADAPTABILITY OF THE SURVIVAL MECHANISMS

The marginal urban sectors are endowed with two survival mechanisms. The first is the mechanism by which the urban poor participate in the urban markets (labor markets and markets for the production of goods and services) on the basis of informal relationships. The other mechanism is predicated on solidarity, and its base of operations is the local territory or neighborhood.

Local solidarity can be both explicit and implicit. Explicit solidarity consists of exchanges within the local area that are not included in economic statistics. Implicit solidarity consists of the redistribution, also within the neighborhood or local area, of the income of the residents (who have managed to obtain work in the city) by means of a process of purchasing in local stores at prices higher than the average prices in the city taken as a whole. In this regard, there is no difference between the poor of the developing countries and those of the developed countries.

The relative weight of these survival mechanisms—informal integration into the modern sector and local solidarity—varies in accordance with the economic cycles within a given model. Hence the importance attached to the effort at the beginning of this paper to configure the political-economic context in which the growth and reorganization of the cities will take place from now through the year 2000. The city of Santiago is an excellent case study for demonstrating the relationship between the degree of internal integration of the city and the global political-economic context.

During the 1960s and the early part of the 1970s, the democratic administrations of Chile were quite active in developing infrastructure and housing programs aimed at solving the problem of the poverty of the city. These programs were consistent with macroeconomic models adopted at the national level, which made economic development dependent on the expansion of internal demand. For that very reason, the redistribution of income and political participation were explicit objectives of the process of national economic development. In no other period in the history of the city of Santiago have the poor sectors of the city enjoyed a greater degree of urban, economic, social, and political integration.

Unemployment rates never increased beyond 6 percent and, more important, there were never any differences in this respect between the low-income communities and high-income communities of the city, the differences in income between the two notwithstanding. The social matrix of local solidarity was weak, as a result of which the low-income neighborhoods were veritable "dormitory suburbs." In this regard as well, there were no significant differences between those neighborhoods and the high-income neighborhoods. All of the peripheral neighborhoods depended on the center of the city, on the industrial districts and, generally speaking, on the rest of the city for the provision of services and employment.

In contrast, during the mid- to late 1970s and early 1980s, the city lost its social, political, and economic integrity. The model adopted was more interested in integrating the national economy into external markets than in its own internal integration, as though the two concepts were mutually incompatible. The opening to the external markets was carried out under the principle of the privatization of the economy and the reduction of the role of the state in the management and regulation of development, which was entrusted to the discretionary will of private agents.

Under this model, it was hoped that the opening to the external market would allow full use of the comparative advantages of the country's natural resources as well as external savings (external indebtedness). The latter compensated for the low internal rate of savings, which decreased together with the stimulus given to consumerism, which was reflected especially with regard to imported products, aimed primarily at the high-income sectors but which, in some areas, included other sectors as well. The comparative advantages were not limited to raw materials. By means of political repression and the breaking up of the labor organizations, the administration ensured a low cost of labor.

Toward the end of the 1970s, before the crisis that began in 1982, the income level of the poor sectors of Santiago was even lower in real terms than it had been ten years earlier, and unemployment reached 25 percent, compared to 6 and 7 percent during the 1960s. Even worse, under the neoliberal authoritarian regime, unemployment in the poor areas reached 40 to 60 percent. Finally, according to figures available in 1983, public housing programs were reduced by half, while the prices for land increased at rates never before seen, a result of massive speculation, in which the financial sector, entirely out of control and resorting largely to external indebtedness, played a dominant role.

The integration of the lower-income sector into the markets of the city decreased notably as reflected in the unemployment rates, with the exception of the informal sector. Explicit solidarity, that is, the exchange networks between families, became the most important factor in the survival of poor families, thus intensifying the matrix of intraneighborhood relationships. At the same time, implicit solidarity increased and intensified with the appearance and multiplication of nonresidential, low-productivity activities in what used to be low-income dormitory suburbs. The spatial marginalization and the accentuation of the inequality with respect to integration into the city left no alternative as regards access to land and housing to an increase in density, resulting in unprecedented levels of crowding.

The city faced a crisis of internal integration. On the one hand, the differences between the modern city and the marginal city (that is, the internal dualization of the city) emerged as evidence that no observer could fail to see. On the other hand, the marginal areas grew. Entire communities, which previously were linked to the rest of the city through economic, political, social, cultural, and physical flows, became isolated like so many islands.

As is well known, the authoritarian model in the political sphere and the neoliberal model in the economic sphere did not produce the results that its backers announced in Brazil, Argentina, Uruguay, and Chile—although there were, to be sure, differences between the individual countries. For the three first-named countries, the political-economic postcrisis context is now in full swing.

In this context, what paradigms of urban development would be both viable and creative in the face of the need to compensate for economic limitations by mobilizing the populace previously relegated to the fringes and whose participation constitutes the basis of support for democratic development?

ELEMENTS OF AN ALTERNATIVE URBAN DEVELOPMENT

In the first place, economic policies aimed at the decentralization of the industrial sector toward the more remote regions must be abandoned; the enormous capital cost that such policies imply cannot be justified in light of the poor results obtained in the recent past. However, decentralization is not thereby entirely eliminated as an option, and the demographic pressure on the big cities may be reoriented toward small or medium-sized cities located on the periphery of the incipient core regions. In other words, it is now time to accept the fact that most of the population of Latin America is going to live in large cities and that the phenomenon of urban concentration will be even more accelerated than in the past with the addition of a new factor: the annexation of cities on the regional periphery.

It is time to test hypotheses that attribute the causes of urban problems not so much to the size of the cities as to the insufficiency of their structures and inefficiencies of their administration.

Second, the austerity demanded by historical circumstances could act as an incentive and as support for a renewed planning effort, freed from the exclusively discursive character of the past. The principal planning instruments available for managing the growth of the city are investments in urban infrastructure and, to keep the city functioning, expenditures on urban services. With investment funds and expenditures decreasing year after year, there can be no more excuses for the usual lack of coordination among sectoral investments (housing, transportation, network services, and so forth) and for the continued neglect of modern administrative and financial techniques that can help correct the habitually neglected maintenance of the city.

The preference given to expenditures for initiating monumental and costly technological projects, which are frequently abandoned along the way, should give way to solutions based on the organizational creativity and efficient administration of existing projects.

Third, there is a need, now imperative, to combine private-sector capital and labor with the meager fiscal resources earmarked for the cities. The intersectoral programs for infrastructure investment and the efficient administration of services (such as those suggested in the preceding point) are not sufficient to ensure the effectiveness of urban planning. That is even less so when one realizes that the very stability of the political systems cannot be guaranteed in situations in which urban supply and demand grow dangerously apart.

The incorporation of the private sector into urban policies must distinguish between the formal and informal private sector and the corresponding modes of public-private interaction.

With respect to formal-sector coordination, there exists a vast and varied experience in the cities of the capitalist countries of Europe and Asia, whose absence in Latin America has no explanation other than one of a historical-cultural nature: the deep chasm between the state and society, the origins of which date back to colonial times. There can be no escape from the urban manifestation of the crisis without crossing over this chasm. Urban structures, such as those proposed in the first point, are not viable under a system that allows speculators unrestricted control over the land.

The power of the state to control, pressure, and negotiate with the urban investor lies in a general plan for consensus, in a program of "support" for infrastructure and services and, above all, in such mechanisms as zoning, expropriation, the rights of priority, the reconditioning of lands, and the use of mixed enterprises that have been applied so successfully in various European countries, as well as in Japan, South Korea, and Taiwan. The basic principle of coordination between the public sector and the formal private sector for the development of the city lies in a recognition by both parties of their mutual advantages. For the municipality, the integration of efficiently managed private capital investments into a plan of collective interest that responds politically to the whole of society is an obvious advantage.

For the private investor, the municipal plan regulates the prices of land, facilitates the approval of credit, and allows support services and infrastructure to be made available in a timely fashion, thus internalizing a portion of the positive external economies of a harmonious urban development. The crisis can also contribute to the configuration of a new scenario for the real estate market. In some countries, the slow rate of economic growth decreases the aggregate demand for land by softening price increases, making it more attractive for the landowner to negotiate with the state than with the real estate developer.

In contrast, integration of the informal sector into urban policies is practically impossible, given the current systems and behaviors of planners and the planning process. In this case, it is not a question of modernizing either planning or administration, but rather of radically and creatively readapting them, for there are no models to borrow from industrialized countries.

In the formal sector, the public infrastructure and urban service programs are financed through taxes of several kinds and tariffs. The marginal neighborhoods are in no condition to make monetary payments to those programs and are accordingly excluded from them. Moreover, such exclusion is justified in some countries on the basis of the unconventional and "illegal" nature of marginal neighborhoods.

Perhaps under current circumstances, it would be possible to convince the planning bureaucracy that the marginal neighborhoods can pay for their "taxes and tariffs" with work and organization—not with work dedicated to the construction of houses for individual residents, but rather with collective labor, locally organized, for the improvement of the neighborhood and of its support base.

The models for planning community self-help efforts directed at local development must be constructed creatively on the basis of examples existing in all Latin American cities. Their enormous potential as an urban development force notwithstanding, most of these examples face the indifference and, at times, intolerance of political authorities and the administrative bureaucracy. Often the only form of action the authorities are willing to attempt in their pilot projects are substitutes for, rather than supports or complements to, the self-help efforts generated at the local levels. As a result, local efforts end up being completely overshadowed.

The principal challenge in this mode of coordination is to restructure planning systems so that models of urban administration and financing include self-help efforts in support of collective improvement as a counterpart for the public funds spent on infrastructure and services, which have so far been directed almost exclusively toward the formal sector.

Finally, the integration of the general public, whether from the formal or informal sectors, into the process of urban development cannot be carried out without the effective decentralization of political-administrative power to the municipalities and from the cities to local organizations. Decentralization is necessary for a more efficient administration of the public resources earmarked for cities, which governments insist on handling at the central level. It is also necessary for political reasons. At the current juncture in history, in which the gap between capital resources and urban demands will increase year after year, the decentralization of the decision-making process is tantamount to the decentralization of the conflict from the office of the "president" himself. In addition, neither the formal private sector nor, to an even lesser extent, the informal private sector will be willing to integrate its respective capital and labor into public policies that have been formulated and implemented without its participation.

REFERENCE

Portes, Alejandro, and Harley Browning, eds. 1976. *Current Perspectives in Latin American Urban Research*. Austin, Texas: Institute of Latin American Studies.

CONTRIBUTORS

The Editors

Jorge E. Hardoy is president of the Instituto Internacional de Medio Ambiente y Desarrollo, ITED-América Latina, Buenos Aires.

Richard M. Morse retired as secretary of the Latin America Program of The Woodrow Wilson Center and is former William H. Bonsall Professor of History at Stanford University.

Other Contributors

Mariano Arana is professor of history and architecture at the University of the Republic, Montevideo, and member of the Uruguayan Congress.

Jordi Borja is assistant mayor of Barcelona and professor of sociology at the University of Barcelona.

Enrique Browne is a practicing architect in Santiago.

Matthew Edel, deceased in 1990, was professor of urban studies at Queens College, New York.

John Friedmann is professor of urban planning and program head at the Graduate School of Architecture and Urban Planning, University of California, Los Angeles.

Guillermo Geisse is president of the Center for Environmental Research and Planning (CIPMA) and professor of urban and regional development at Catholic University, Santiago de Chile.

Fernando Giordano is professor of architecture at the University of the Republic, Montevideo, and adviser to the Ministry of Tourism, Uruguay.

Larissa Lomnitz is professor of anthropology at Universidad Nacional Autónoma de México, Mexico City.

Manfred A. Max-Neef is executive director of the Development Alternative Center (CEPAUR) in Santiago de Chile and rector of the Universidad Bolivariana, Santiago.

Henry Pease García is former assistant mayor of Lima, Peru.

Rogelio Pérez Perdomo is researcher at the IESA-Instituto de Estudios Superiores de Administratión, Caracas.

Bryan Roberts is professor of anthropology at the University of Texas, Austin.

Abelardo Sánchez León is researcher at the DESCO-Centro de Retudios y Promoción del Desarrollo, Lima, and a novelist.

Jorge Wilheim is a practicing architect and urban planner in São Paulo and former director of planning, São Paulo.

INDEX